# HEADS UP

## THE CHALLENGES FACING ENGLAND'S

## LEADING HEAD TEACHERS

# HEADS UP

THE CHALLENGES FACING ENGLAND'S

LEADING HEAD TEACHERS

## DOMINIC CARMAN

LUME BOOKS

LUME BOOKS

First published in 2021 by Lume Books
30 Great Guildford Street,
Borough, SE1 0HS

ISBN 978-1-83901-354-6

Typeset using Atomik ePublisher from Easypress Technologies

www.lumebooks.co.uk

*To Charlie, Tristan and Isobel*

# Table of Contents

| School | Head |
| --- | --- |
| Abingdon School | Miss Felicity Lusk |
| Alleyn's School | Dr Gary Savage |
| Benenden School | Mrs Claire Oulton |
| City of London School for Boys | David Levin |
| City of London School for Girls | Miss Diana Vernon |
| Dulwich College | Dr Joe Spence |
| Eton College | Tony Little |
| Haberdashers' Aske's Boys' School | Peter Hamilton |
| Hampton School | Barry Martin |
| Harrow School | Jim Hawkins |
| James Allen's Girls' School | Mrs Marion Gibbs |
| King's College School Wimbledon | Andrew Halls |
| King Edward VI School Birmingham | John Claughton |
| King Edward VI High School for Girls Birmingham | Miss Sarah Evans |
| Lady Eleanor Holles School | Mrs Gillian Low |
| Magdalen College School Oxford | Dr Tim Hands |

| | |
|---|---|
| Manchester Grammar School | Dr Chris Ray |
| Manchester High School | Mrs Claire Hewitt |
| Merchant Taylors' School | Stephen Wright |
| North London Collegiate School | Mrs Bernice McCabe |
| The Perse School Cambridge | Edward Elliott |
| Radley College | Angus McPhail |
| Royal Grammar School Guildford | Dr Jon Cox |
| Royal Grammar School Newcastle | Bernard Trafford |
| St Mary's School Calne | Dr Helen Wright |
| St Paul's Boys' School | Professor Mark Bailey |
| St Swithun's School Winchester | Miss Jane Gandee |
| Tonbridge School | Tim Haynes |
| Westminster School | Dr Stephen Spurr |
| Winchester College | Dr Ralph Townsend |
| Withington Girls' School | Mrs Sue Marks |
| Wycombe Abbey School | Lady Cynthia Hall |

# CHAPTER ONE

# EDUCATION EDUCATION EDUCATION

It's a story of ambition, anger, inspiration and pride; a saga of jealousy, joy, struggle and sweat; a chronicle of humour, pain, tears and triumph. Welcome to the world of headship.

Every school is unique, as distinctive a community as the men and women in charge with all their foibles and idiosyncrasies. In telling the tale of headmasters and headmistresses at thirty-two of England's leading independent schools - who they are, how they got there, what they do and the problems they face - much lies beneath the untainted narrative of outstanding achievement, brilliant teaching and world class, all-round education. Relentlessly punctuated by stress, demands and pressure, the challenges of headship are bravely met with fortitude, stamina, and a resolute strength of purpose. As the imprint of each personality is revealed, narcissists rarely seem to thrive. But when heads openly use words like 'evil,' 'treachery,' 'betrayal,' 'poisonous' and 'malevolent' to describe their staff, then all's not well in the state of some leading schools. In response, heads do not sit complacently in their studies taking endless tea and biscuits. Confronted in turn by children, parents, staff and governors, they sometimes fight battles on several fronts behind closed doors.

Before opening them, it is important to examine first the external world in which they operate, where for the moment, antagonism from those praying for their demise is more noisy than deadly. Independent schools succeed by delivering the very best teaching for those fortunate enough to benefit. Mapping the landscape carved out by developments

1

in secondary education over recent decades shows that a much-improved maintained sector has significantly affected its independent counterpart, mostly for the better. In detailing these systemic changes and their history, this chapter also charts a course for the future as independent schools become more international, preserving their raison d'être and preeminence while forging stronger domestic links with academies and the wider school community.

Education is wasted on the young - only as adults do we fully appreciate the truth behind Shaw's witticism. However well or badly, and to whatever degree, we have all been educated; so were our parents and grandparents. For those who have children or plan to have children, schooling is as important as their health and happiness, while the success and welfare of students are equally paramount for those who teach. To Benjamin Franklin's two certainties - death and taxes - a third must surely be added: education. Providing an essential start in life, a good education is the birthright of every citizen and the idea of improving education is universally accepted. Such truths may be self-evident, yet few topics provoke stronger opinions or produce greater emotion than how we teach our children.

When Churchill wrote of his Harrow schooldays, that "Headmasters have powers at their disposal with which prime ministers have never yet been invested," there appears to be more than a touch of Winstonian hyperbole. Until, that is, you talk to the current Harrow head, Jim Hawkins, who says of his role, 'It is a bit like public life, it's like being prime minister of a small country.' In formulating policy and allocating resources, it is the power of prime ministers and their governments, not headmasters, which sets the parameters for state-funded education. "Ask me my three main priorities for government and I tell you education, education, and education," promised Tony Blair, before becoming prime minister.

The intervening years witnessed major financial investment in infrastructure - the biggest capital investment project since Victoria ruled - as hundreds of schools were built or upgraded to become new crucibles of learning. Inside the new classrooms, there can be little doubt that most pupils have fared better since Blair's proclamation. An unspoken political consensus now exists that parental choice and competition are generally beneficial: teaching and results have improved, even after grade inflation. Put simply, more children achieve better grades and considerably more go on to university than ever before. And university entry is the key endgame for secondary education, enhancing the prospects of a good job on graduation.

A good degree certainly affords most graduates better career opportunities and higher earnings than non-graduates. The latest Higher Education Initial Participation Rate is 49.3% (source: Department for Business). Spawning a mass intelligentsia, this expansion of tertiary education is unparalleled in history. But a note of caution must be sounded: it may not be as much a cause for celebration as some suggest. Across the spectrum of degree-awarding institutions, quality and value are highly variable because different classes of degree indicate divergent levels of academic ability, and ultimately, employability, much dependent upon the subject and where it was awarded.

Take one step back and the same applies to A levels: E grades and A* grades both count as passes, although with manifestly contrasting levels of performance. When cumulative pass grades from A* to E total 98%, virtually no-one fails. The brutal truth is that good grades do matter to compete for university places, and in the labour market. And yet we are burdened by a perverse obsession with no-one failing, which deludes teenagers about the realities of life, where success in anything requires others not to succeed - getting a job or playing in a team, life is competitive. Sometimes it is not enough just to succeed, others must fail.

Furthermore, do half of all jobs require a degree? In a word, no. Rapidly increasing undergraduate numbers have not been matched by sufficient graduate employment opportunities with only one in four new jobs requiring a degree (source: Institute of Education). Alongside those who enjoy career success brought by academic achievement sit many for whom a degree creates frustration and misplaced optimism, particularly when there are no graduate vacancies for which they are qualified or suitable. No-one signs up for a three year degree, carrying hefty tuition fees, in the hope of stacking shelves or packing boxes. NUS research shows that a quarter of graduates who take non-graduate jobs - in retail, construction or catering - are still doing the same job three years later, creating an army of underemployed.

There were 787,205 graduates in 2012, up 51% in a decade (source: Higher Education Stats Agency). That number may slide, or at best, plateau - thanks to overseas students taking up the slack. Domestic university applications have fallen since tuition fees increased: compared to official forecasts, English student numbers shrank by 9% in 2012/13 as once-aspiring students have decided that lower-tier degrees cannot provide sufficient competitive advantage in the labour market. Enjoying a flight to quality, most Russell Group university courses are much sought-after; conversely, several lower-tier universities are suffering steep declines. There is also a mismatch in skill requirements for employers faced with inadequate numbers of applicants who have done apprenticeships or vocational qualifications and countless graduates whose degrees offer little value.

The poverty of expectation strikes earlier still for many who discard their degree ambitions, simply never have them, or lose interest in education and opt instead for social immobility. Universities were recently told by the universities minister, David Willetts, to recruit more white, working-class boys from state secondary schools because their application numbers were so low, and falling further, compared to girls from the same background. Willetts wants these boys to be treated like ethnic minorities, and specifically targeted for recruitment. Their aggregate performance has deteriorated since Ofsted adopted the conclusion from *Failing Boys* (edited by London's Institute of Education): "White, heterosexual, working-class boys" are more motivated by the culture of the three Fs - "fighting, fucking and football' - than the three Rs.

Girls comfortably surpass boys at every level. This does not reflect superior intelligence so much as superior industry: teachers know that most girls work harder. As one wag commented, 'Girls achieve more at school because they are watching the future while the boys are watching the girls.' Forty years ago, the feminist mantra was equality; today, the practical reality is superiority - in educational performance. And not just in the UK. Women surpass men at every level of education in every developed country from the United States to Sweden. Of the 559,000 applicants to British universities by the January 2013 deadline, 57.2% were girls (source: UCAS). Visit universities and a gender imbalance is often visible: women now account for 62% of all undergraduates in the UK's 31 medical schools, for example. If girls are the future, the real challenge for today's heads is how to get boys back on equal terms, performing like the girls sitting next to them.

Against a background of improving results and increased university entrance, what part do independent schools play? In essence, they make an outstanding contribution, most notably in England, as disproportionate providers of an educated elite - an epithet that may cause some hackles to rise. There are around 2,400 independent schools in Britain, attended by 620,000 children. More than 7% of British children attend them; above the age of sixteen, that figure increases to 18%. They are routinely scorned as children of the rich. Some are, particularly in schools where you can smell the money the moment you enter the driveway. It's an inconvenient truth, but most are not: like the best independent schools, the politics of envy can be highly selective.

Take someone unquestionably rich who receives universal praise: Lionel Messi. Endorsement income and his FC Barcelona salary combine to reward this sublimely gifted Argentinian footballer with £100,000 a day for his talent. No-one complains; they just admire. Then consider a working couple whose joint earnings total £100,000 a year. After deductions, that reduces to £71,000 net. They have two children, educated privately in local day schools. Annual cost including extras: £32,000 (£16,000 each) - 45% of their combined net income. This leaves them with £39,000 a year to live, or £3250 a month for everything: much better off than lots of families, but certainly not rich. Just middle income, middle Britain. Many couples or single parents of children at independent schools have annual incomes well below £100,000. They are not rich, except in aspiration: wanting to give their children a better start than they had. Do these children deserve contempt when mum and dad make sacrifices, sometimes big sacrifices, because they think it's worth it?

Although rarely publicised, nearly one third of pupils in independent secondary schools receive scholarships or bursaries. Some places are free, although most heads would like to offer many more - if funds were available. Aspiration is high, international demand has never been stronger, yet domestic demand is flat, and in some areas, falling. Austerity, a weak economy, and above inflation fee increases have put independent education out of reach for many among Britain's squeezed middle. There is much beyond academic achievement that adds to the appeal of independent education, or as Eton head, Tony Little, puts it: 'There are plenty of cheaper ways of getting a good set of A levels than coming to Eton.' The quality and spread of music, art, drama and sports in independent schools is supplemented, not just by first class teaching, but by first class facilities.

There is also confidence: a key aim of independent schools is to produce confident pupils who are self-assured, and able to fight their corner.

To see where independent schools fit in the ever more complex jigsaw of secondary education, it helps to scrutinise the impact and history of the biggest pieces in the puzzle, the maintained sector, better known as state schools. Grammars, leading faith comprehensives and academies are most in demand. Super-comprehensives, often led by super-heads, get great results. Selection is key, whether by geography, aptitude, faith, or sometimes, a combination of all three. According to LSE research, "overt and covert selection" is greatest in London, where more than 25% of schools discriminate by faith, while more than half of oversubscribed academies commonly select by interview.

Mass academisation is the centrepiece of the present government's education strategy. To bolster the state sector, successive governments have employed the academies programme using private sponsors - originally the brainchild of Labour's Lord Adonis. The mission is to improve standards and performance by breaking down the educational apartheid and social segregation embodied by the historic separation of the independent and state sectors. Power is decentralised. Funded directly from Whitehall, academies become independent of local authorities, affording them complete control over admissions and the curriculum. Starting under Labour, 203 academies opened between 2000 and 2010; today, more than 3000 schools have academy status.

Most deliver excellent teaching and provide unprecedented opportunity, but the state sector still faces many problems. After forty-one school visits in 2013, Ofsted chief, Sir Michael Wilshaw, said, 'The consequences of underachievement in state schools are a grave moral and political danger, as well as an economic failure.' He argues that independent schools should do more to help, 'They are part of a whole system that needs to do well. I'm sure they want this country to be a cohesive society. I'm sure they don't want such big gaps in performance between the poorest children and the most prosperous children to be so apparent. It's up to them to try and narrow those gaps, along with teachers in the maintained system.'

In a dismantling of the Berlin Wall between the state and private sectors, top name independent schools already sponsor academies: roughly a third make a significant contribution through full or co-sponsorship - in part thanks to Adonis, who has done an excellent job in proselytising unbelievers. Trafford, head of Royal Grammar Newcastle, cautions, 'If independent schools wish to be "acceptable", to bask in the favour of politicians, they would do well to sponsor an academy.' Independent boys' and co-ed schools predominate in sponsorship because they have much deeper pockets through longer established foundations. Representing 200 schools, the Girls' School Association has rejected sponsorship calls, leaving it to up to individual schools. Their primary concern is risk: how future governments may change the status quo, leaving independent schools with lame duck academies, effecting more radical alternatives which prove very costly in financial or reputational terms. So far, fifteen independent schools have converted - or plan to convert - to academy status. Forced by financial pressure, many more will follow.

During his 2012 party conference speech, David Cameron described academies as 'state schools given all the freedoms, and carrying all the high expectations, of private schools. That's my plan - millions of children sent to independent schools, in the state sector. I went to a great school and I want every child to have a great education. I'm not here to defend privilege, I'm here to spread it.' Parents speak proudly of their children attending an academy and they are highly sought after. The nearest to my south London home, the Harris Academy in Crystal Palace, has neither academic selection nor any religious ethos. Yet in 2013, there were 2,212 applications for 180 places. That level of demand - over twelve pupils per place - exceeds the most sought after of independent schools. Meanwhile, the more controversial free schools programme, which allows parents and teachers to open and run their own state schools, has seen nearly 200 approvals since the first 24 free schools opened in September 2011. Progress has not entirely matched the rhetoric: free schools currently educate 0.4% of pupils, a figure projected to increase to 0.8% in 2015. Labour has pledged not to allow the opening of any further free schools.

For a full appreciation of how the independent and state sectors compete and co-exist, it helps to focus through the long-range lens of several decades. Back to the year 1965. A twelve year old schoolboy, Anthony Charles Lynton Blair, better known as Tony, was preparing for his entrance exam to Fettes, a leading Scottish boarding school, often labelled 'The Eton of the North.' Via Fettes, Tony's educational path to Oxford and beyond was set. For his contemporaries and for the next generation, 1965 was arguably the most important year in modern British education, heralding the birth of comprehensive schools. Their conception was ideological: comprehensives would erode the class barriers perpetuated by a system more dependent on background than on merit - they would encourage social mobility.

Before their arrival, education was arranged under the Tripartite System. State secondary schools were grammar, secondary modern or technical. Designed to teach engineering, mechanical and scientific skills, the technical schools were regrettably marginal, educating roughly 2% of pupils. The choice, between grammars and secondary moderns, was never a choice at all. Instead, a divisive, flawed eleven plus exam - still used by a few education authorities - was sat by all children to determine if they were bright enough for grammar school. For the 25% who passed, and secured a place, the opportunity of O levels, A levels and university entrance was on offer. For the remaining 75% who failed, there was little chance of academic progress: most children left school at fifteen with no qualifications. In allocating people's futures, this was an appalling waste of talent and denial of opportunity. One in eight grammar school pupils went to university compared to only one in 22,000 educated at secondary moderns.

Independent schools was an infrequently used term in 1965. Fee-paying schools were mostly public schools: often boarding, relatively few in number, and at the top end, outstanding in performance. Oxbridge entry in 1965 was comprised: 54% public school and 46% direct grant/grammar schools. Only 4% of all teenagers went on to university. There were only thirty five universities, ten of which had opened between 1961 and 1965, serving 160,000 students compared to 2.5 million today - 435,000 of whom are from overseas.

Labour's victory in October 1964 was secured by their radical blueprint for a dirigiste Britain, notably in education, with the aim of dismantling the Tripartite System. In advocating universal comprehensive education, Harold Wilson promised - with rhetorical flourish - to end the tyranny of selection by ability. It was part of a wider reaction to an English governing class regarded as over-privileged and out of touch, best exemplified by Harold Macmillan's coterie. As prime minister from 1957 until 1963, the patrician Macmillan had thirteen Old Etonians in government; fifty years on, Cameron has twelve. The defeated Conservative prime minister in 1964, Alec Douglas-Home, was an Old Etonian, as were his two predecessors,

McMillan and Anthony Eden, who had in turn succeeded Churchill. During thirteen years in government (1951-1964), under four different leaders, the Tories failed to expand grammar schools as the Germans had done, nor did they improve the secondary moderns, by enabling their pupils to take more exams. Unwillingness to reform created understandable resentment.

Unlike his two public school predecessors as Labour leader, Clement Attlee (Haileybury) and Hugh Gaitskell (Winchester), Wilson was a Yorkshire grammar school boy and former Oxford don. In selecting their new leader in 1965, the Tories chose another grammar school and Oxford product, Edward Heath. Men of equally modest background, Wilson and Heath personified the new philosophy of the age: meritocracy. But just as grammar school meritocracy arrived in power, proving its worth as an instrument of change and social progress, it was immediately attacked by another former public schoolboy.

Awarded separate Oxford degrees in Classics and PPE, Charles Anthony Raven Crosland, also better known as Tony, was appointed as education secretary on 22nd January 1965, two days before Churchill died. These were not 48 hours that changed the world of education, but symbolic perhaps of a revolutionary turning point in a decade of unprecedented reform that followed. Capturing the spirit of the sixties, Crosland's ambition was not simple reform of the type employed by his predecessors, it was revolution - of the champagne socialist variety. The Croslands listed their address in *Who's Who 1965* as 19 The Boltons, Kensington. The house next door to their former residence changed hands for £55m in March 2012 - from Land Registry figures, the highest value UK property sold last year. According to critics, Crosland was 'concerned more about the distribution of wealth than its creation.' His concern about education was less subtly expressed. As later recalled by his widow, Susan, in her much-acclaimed biography of her late husband, Tony said, "If it's the last thing I do, I'm going to destroy every fucking grammar school in England."

What Beeching did for the railways, forcing people off trains and onto the roads by closing lines and stations, Crosland set out to do for education: forcing kids out of grammars and into comprehensives. He labelled it 'an experiment.' If Beeching's realignment was inevitable, so arguably was Crosland's educational reform. As large new comprehensives were built, the physically smaller grammars declined in number and influence. Kick-started in the sixteenth century, grammar schools had been given real impetus by those passionate advocates of self-improvement, the Victorians, who saw them as an engine of social mobility, providing a ladder of opportunity for poor, bright children to progress to university. Crosland aimed to kick that ladder away from millions of working class boys and girls without providing a fully effective replacement or giving little thought to other alternatives: adapting the grammars' selection process, increasing the number of grammars or developing secondary moderns to mirror the grammars. In the firing line were 1300 fully state-funded grammar schools and 175 direct grant grammar schools, where up to 50% of pupils were funded by the state; the remainder from fee-paying parents.

Crosland made substantial progress as many grammars folded or became comprehensives. Back in office, between 1970 and 1974, the Tories accelerated the process. It is often forgotten that the education secretary responsible - a Somerville College Oxford graduate and former Grantham Grammar girl - was the late Margaret Thatcher. Her twins had been deftly dispatched: Mark to Harrow and Carol to St Paul's Girls'. Although Thatcher axed more grammars than any education secretary before or since, they never died out, and the 160 or so that remain are selective state schools, heavily oversubscribed by mainly middle class parents. In 1976, when Labour finally abolished the direct grant grammars, 119 opted for independence. As Richard Crossman, Labour diarist and Old Wykehamist, had noted when the policy was first mooted, 'We've got ourselves in the strange position where we are going to abolish Manchester Grammar School and keep Eton.' MGS survived by becoming independent; Eton still flourishes.

Jim Callaghan, Wilson's successor in 1976, had sent his daughter, Margaret, to the independent Blackheath High before her journey to Somerville. Callaghan's education secretary, responsible for finally scrapping the direct grants, was Shirley Williams - like Carol Thatcher, another Old Paulina, and predictably, a Somerville graduate. She lived in Kensington only a stone's throw from Crosland. When her daughter's direct grant, Godolphin and Latymer, opted for independent status in 1977, Williams moved sixteen-year-old Rebecca to the sixth form at Camden High, a girls' grammar which was turning comprehensive, year by year, below the sixth form. It became fully comprehensive two years after she left.

An anecdote from David Levin, City of London Boys' head: 'I recall a Polish surgeon, who said, "Can I just get this right. You're going to take £13,500 a year off me and there's going to be an upward only review, every year for seven years. Not only are you going to take the money off me, but my son has to put himself through three gruelling tests and an interview for the privilege of me paying you £13,500?" I said, "Yes." We then talked about why parents were prepared to make such sacrifices to come to independent schools. I told him about my prior career as a grammar school head, selection and the abolition of grammar schools. His final statement was, "Mmm, in Poland we had communism and that was bad, but clearly in England you had Shirley Williams, and that was much, much worse!"

Comprehensivisation produced even sharper divisions between the state and private sectors. Under the impact of grammar and direct grant schools that chose independence, and the more academic public schools, like Winchester, there was a radical improvement in standards: the independent sector raised its academic game. It was going to win a meritocracy war, to produce outstanding education and compete on that basis. With an anti-standards agenda in parts of state system, they had an open field. This extended to the old socially-elite private schools, like Eton and Radley, which hadn't been uniformly high on academics. The bottom third in these schools was never university material - academic achievement was considered déclassé. 'Eton was a comprehensive school for the very rich, but it became a grammar school for the very rich,' says Adonis. Where Eton lead, others followed.

The thirty-two heads interviewed for *Heads Up* run schools with some of the highest academic attainment in England, owing their success to rigorous selection, superb teaching and supportive parents. There are fifteen boys' schools, eleven girls' schools and six schools which are fully co-educational, or with co-ed sixth forms. All are in the top 100 and the vast majority in the top 40 of any results-based league table. A tribute to their lasting impact, twelve interviewees run former direct grant schools. The others are a mix of the most distinguished boarding schools, such as Eton, Winchester, Wycombe Abbey and Benenden, and preeminent day schools, such as City of London, KCS Wimbledon, St Paul's, Withington and Westminster, which combines day and boarding.

These men and women - 80% of them educated at grammar or direct grant schools - operate in an environment where being independently-educated provokes hostility and prejudice. In a nation strangely discomforted by educational success, anything that smacks remotely of elitism carries a stigma. Too clever, too successful, too privileged. For politicians, the high level academic achievement of independent schoolchildren is an embarrassment. They rarely speak about it nor the attendant benefits for our society. Why? Because they are terrified of the opprobrium that would follow, not simply from other politicians, but from the media where self-appointed polemicists label independent schools 'the unjustifiable existence of social segregation in education.'

Teenage sports stars and tabloid celebrities are tirelessly championed by the media, yet comparatively few column inches and little air time are given over to high level academic achievement by our schoolchildren, especially if they are independently-educated. When was the last time BBC cameras visited the highest performing schools, such as Westminster or Wycombe, on A level results day? Just imagine the outcry if they did. Their star pupils remain unacknowledged, except for teenagers like Nick D'Aloisio, featured on BBC News after he was paid £20m by Yahoo! for Summly - a mobile news app he designed at home while revising for his GCSEs at KCS Wimbledon. His success provoked comment from Dr Tony Sewell, founder of Generating Genius, a charity focussed upon 'getting children from disadvantaged backgrounds into universities to study the Stem subjects of Science, Technology, Engineering and Maths.' Sewell told the BBC, "Public schoolboys dominate sports, arts and the technology section. Private schools have a culture of independent thinking, they give students a sense that they are knowledgeable and confident. In comprehensives it is the reverse - to be ignorant is to be the star."

Elsewhere, the independently-educated dominate our screens: from Jeremy Paxman, David Dimbleby and Bill Turnbull to George Alagiah, Nick Robinson and Andrew Marr. They speak little of their schooling. Nor do those exemplars of BBC English, Susannah Reid, Sophie Raworth and Stephanie Flanders - three Old Paulinas of the same vintage. This eloquent triumfeminate deliver their vowels perfectly modulated, a modified version of Received Pronunciation that first hit the airwaves under Lord Reith. BBC RP has changed, just as the Queen's accent has evolved since she acceded to the throne, but it's still posh to most ears. 'It is impossible for an Englishman to open his mouth without making some other Englishman hate or despise him,' wrote Shaw in *Pygmalion*. His observation holds true today. Being educated at an independent school, less acutely typified by accent than in Shaw's day, is more subtly characterised by shared mores and vocabulary. In a divided society, many would see the fault line as independent education, rendering John Prescott's 1997 declaration - "We're all middle class now" - transparently false.

So what is the evidence? Notwithstanding the enhanced performance of our burgeoning academies in teaching standards and academic results, the independent sector delivers academic excellence of the very highest order, disproportionate to its size. Of course, there are indifferent independent schools and some genuinely bad ones. But first and foremost, the very best independent schools remain elite academic institutions, and most of the very best schools in the country are still in the independent sector. Many will recoil from such statements: in Nigel Farndale's words, England is 'a public-school-excellence-hating country.' To recognise the fact that elitism, particularly academic elitism, has a productive place in delivering a high proportion of the best and brightest undergraduates is not just deeply unfashionable, it invites hatred of the type Shaw identified. Yet it is a fact, not an opinion. Between 2009 and 2011, four independent schools - Eton, Westminster, St Paul's and St Paul's Girls' - and one selective state school, Hills Road Sixth Form College, Cambridge (with nearly 2000 students in Years 12 and 13) - produced 946 Oxford and Cambridge entrants between them. In the same three year period, the 2000 worst-performing state schools, two thirds of the English total, collectively produced 927 Oxbridge students (source: Sutton Trust).

This disparity is further reflected in a north-south divide. You are thirty-two times more likely to go to Oxbridge if you live in Kensington and Chelsea rather than Blackpool. In 2012, there was one successful Oxbridge applicant from Hartlepool (population 92,000) while 130 came from the London Borough of Barnet (population 332,000). Thirty-five times more likely to get in than their Hartlepool counterparts, Barnet kids are mostly middle class from selective state grammar schools. A similar picture emerges if you take a broader perspective from the twenty-four strong Russell Group of universities. DfE figures show that among all secondary schools and colleges in England, with A-level results in core disciplines considered good enough by the Russell Group, 150 out of the top 200 - 75% - were independent schools. State school pupils frequently choose the wrong A level subjects, according to Dr Wendy Piatt, Director General of the Russell Group.

That figure of 75% is achieved by independent school pupils who constitute only 18% of the national total above the age of sixteen. Half of all Oxbridge places go to pupils from these 200 schools, and nearly half the pupils at schools represented in this book go on to just five universities: Oxford, Cambridge, UCL, Bristol and Durham. In 1965, there were more working class Oxbridge undergraduates than today. The politicians promised that progress would be achieved through access to education at the highest level, but over the last fifty years social mobility has regressed - a further waste of talent, rightly deemed disastrous and immoral.

The anger may be misplaced, but it is no wonder that the attacks are relentless: 'Let's face it, independent schools and independent school heads are basically fair game. We're right up there with the Master of the Foxhounds for them to have a go at, and there is a long way to fall,' says Elliott, head of the Perse in Cambridge. The 'them' he refers to are politicians across the spectrum, champions of elusive social mobility, yet too embarrassed to praise the excellence of independent schools, and often hypocritical journalists, many of whom were themselves privately-educated. Similar views sometimes prevail among privately-educated publishers. As one wrote in response to the proposal for this book: 'No thank you! I have very Bolshevik views on independent schools!' It's a view not shared by a majority of the public. ISC research shows that 57% of parents would choose independent schools if they could afford to, up from 48% a decade earlier, making them more desirable than ever.

Adele is among them, having announced that she wants her son to go to Eton. Another south London comprehensive girl, the late Jade Goody, died of cancer in 2009 at the age of twenty-seven. Her drug addict father disappeared when she was two. Leaving school without qualifications, she found fame and fortune through ignorance on Big Brother - cruelly derided, she became an unlikely celebrity. Although she had received a bad education, Jade was bright enough to realise the value of a good one. Ambitious for her two young sons, she wanted them to have the education she did not, leaving her money in trust to cover the cost of their independent school fees.

If the target of comprehensivisation was based on a simple principle - children of all backgrounds and abilities should be educated successfully in a single school - then the outcome was rather different. 'Why half the comprehensives failed,' the second chapter in Adonis's excellent book, *Education. Education Education*, says it all. As chief education adviser and the minister of state for education under both Tony Blair and Gordon Brown, he accepts that Crosland's experiment failed. Or at least half of it did. Adonis wrote: 'For all the idealism of their pioneers, a large proportion of the comprehensives were little better than the secondary moderns they replaced and very few were highly successful.' In a broad stigmatisation, the reasons he cites include weak leadership, poor teaching, low morale and social deprivation.

While Adonis concedes that successive governments got it wrong on education between 1965 and 1997, Ed Miliband, the first comprehensive-educated Labour leader, loudly admits that his party also got it wrong on immigration between 1997 and 2010. But he retains a discreet silence on the subject of independent schools, although his brother David called for the removal of their charitable status during the 2010 party leadership race. Under Labour, no new grammars were opened between 1997 and 2010, but the addition of new buildings allowed the number of pupils educated in the existing state grammars to increase by 23% from 128,712 to 158,610 (source: Hansard). It remains to be seen what Labour might advocate in their 2015 manifesto, fifty years on from Crosland. According to a recent YouGov poll, 56% of voters share David Miliband's desire for independent schools to lose their charitable status. Since 2006, the Charity Commission has had a public benefit test of charitable status for independent schools to meet, requiring them to offer educational benefits to those who cannot afford to pay fees. The test has to be passed before they can receive breaks on VAT and Corporation Tax.

Removing charitable status would inevitably mean fewer bursaries and higher fees, forcing more parents to choose state schools, adding to every taxpayer's bill. Many independents would close, leading to job losses. As Elliott (the Perse) says, 'Every time an independent school goes under and turns itself into a free school, and is therefore being paid for by the public purse, everyone says, "That's wonderful." This country's nearly bankrupt and they're cheering taking on a liability from the private sector to the public sector.' Nevertheless, charitable status seems a likely candidate for future attack - as part of a slow death strategy - given the persistent strand of Labour thinking that seeks to eliminate independent education altogether. At an Oxford Union debate in October 2011, the current shadow minister of education, Kevin Brennan, proposed the motion, "This House would abolish private schools." Total abolition was last proposed in Labour's 1983 election manifesto, later referred to as the "longest suicide note in history" by their then shadow home secretary, Gerald Kaufman.

The coalition government has left independent schools alone. David Cameron went to Eton, as he is frequently reminded, and Nick Clegg to Westminster. Stephen Spurr, head of Westminster, recalls: 'I remember when the coalition government came into power and an Old Etonian and an Old Westminster were, respectively, prime minister and deputy prime minister. People were calling out: meritocracy is dead. Well meritocracy is the best-prepared person getting to the top, supposedly. It is not social engineering.' In part for political expediency, although they would vehemently deny it, Cameron and Clegg are choosing state secondary schools for their children. Clegg recently selected the London Oratory for his son, as did Blair, although Tony's offspring also received additional private tuition from Westminster schoolmasters. A comprehensive turned academy - all boys (up to 16), Catholic, and highly-selective - the Oratory is no ordinary state school. Family houses in the immediate catchment area fetch between £2m and £4m.

Meanwhile, our best-known black British politician, Diane Abbott MP, who ran a left-wing campaign for the Labour leadership against the Milibands, sent her son, James, to the independent City of London Boys, one of the capital's finest schools. Abbott had previously attacked Blair for choosing the Oratory because it was selective. Calling her own decision 'indefensible' and 'intellectually incoherent,' she insisted that in a London state school her son would have been 'lost to the world of gangs.' Educated at Harrow County Girls, a selective grammar before turning comprehensive after she left, Abbott epitomises a largely unreported phenomenon. The 'posh white boys' label, first used by her to describe Cameron and Clegg, is employed by some commentators to characterise independent school kids in general. Again, the reality is different: they are more ethnically diverse than their state counterparts. In independent secondary schools, 25.5% of pupils nationally are from ethnic minorities. Exclude boarding schools, and this rises to 28.5% (source: ISC), compared to 24.5% in England's state secondary schools (source: DfE).

Unconcerned by white middle class hang-ups about privilege and status, many ethnic minority parents unashamedly focus on success and achievement when deciding their children's education. In the Asian educational powerhouses - Hong Kong, Singapore, Japan and South Korea - elitism is not a dirty word. Nor is it in British Asian households. Over half of all NHS doctors under forty are Asian. Nationally, the highest performing ethnic group in exams is Chinese, with an impressive 90% achieving five GCSEs of grade C or above. Yet head teachers in England's state schools are still disproportionately white - 95% in 2011, compared to the overall white population of 86% recorded in the 2011 census. Only 1% of state school heads come from a black Caribbean or African background. In charge of leading independent schools, there is not one Asian, black or Chinese head. This will change, and change fast within the next generation. When 52% of all secondary school pupils in Birmingham, and 67% of those in Inner London are ethnic minority (source: DfE), the ethnic profile of heads will inevitably shift as a consequence - just like the current position with doctors, it's only a question of time.

Some past changes in independent schools were slow in coming. Only fifty years ago, Sir Michael Burton, a King's Scholar, became the first Jewish head boy of Eton. In 1945, the school Fellows (governors) passed a statute making scholarship entry conditional upon the fathers of candidates being British by birth: its purpose was to limit the number of Jewish applicants. Jews were, in the words of Eton's Provost, Claude Elliott, 'too clever' or 'clever in the wrong way.' The statute was not removed until the 1960s following personal intervention from Harold McMillan. Today, Burton is himself a Fellow.

And not all changes in independent schools have been successful. According to Adonis, they have made a serious error of judgment in recent decades: allowing their cost base to get of control. 'From the 1980s onward,' said Adonis in a recent speech, 'there was fierce competition for theatres, swimming pools. Independent schools wanted to gold plate all their assets. There was a big reduction in class sizes - ten or not much more - became an article of faith, half the level of the state system. And they pay their teachers more. Put all of that together and you have had private school fee inflation of two, three, four, five times the level of inflation at large. As Tony Crosland said to local government in the 1970s, "The party's over." Well the party's over now for many independent schools. If you're running a private school outside the south east, and it's not one of the big selective grammar schools, you are in either a reasonably serious or critical financial situation. Lots of them are thinking of becoming academies. I don't understand why there isn't more debate about cutting their cost base, getting much better value, enlarging class sizes, reducing head counts. There is a big crisis on the bottom line; they are very slow to adapt to economic whirlwind. Quite a lot will go out of business in quite a short period of time.' His gloomy forecast, echoed by some heads in subsequent chapters, is their greatest collective challenge.

In looking back half a century, it also helps to look forwards to the world in which independent schools will operate. Demographic forecasters predict that ethnic minority and mixed-race Britons will be in the majority before 2065 - an ageing and declining white population may eventually become part of history, studied by children in future centuries. As Britain becomes truly international, the visible face of independent school headship will soon reflect that too. Most leading independent schools, increasingly co-ed rather than single-sex, think internationally, not nationally, reflecting the aspirations of parents and students who see education through global eyes: a world of multinational companies and international finance, linked by borderless technology. Nick D'Aloisio was born in Australia; work took his parents to London; they chose KCS Wimbledon as his school. An embryonic Bill Gates, this young computer entrepreneur - a Mandarin and Russian speaker, hoping to read PPE at Oxford - is already part of tomorrow's global elite. And an ambassador for his school.

Increasingly, his future contemporaries may move from another continent to an English independent school, before ending up at an American university. Commercially, a substantial further increase in overseas pupil numbers is essential to the survival of many independents. Significant numbers already come from overseas, particularly from Hong Kong and China, and more are going overseas, routinely considering Ivy League frontrunners - Harvard, Yale or Princeton - in addition to Oxbridge or London. Last year, fifteen KCS sixth-formers gained places at US universities; nearly three thousand English independent school pupils elsewhere took the same path. A typical independent school in twenty years might have between a quarter and a third of pupils from overseas, possibly more. As the government tirelessly tinkers with GCSEs (broadly with opposition support), AS Levels and A levels, while devising a new National Curriculum, some independent schools are purposefully less parochial, having opted instead for IGCSEs, pre-U and IB (International Baccalaureate) exams.

'Heads need to think beyond these shores,' says Spurr (Westminster). 'We are seeing an increasing number of pupils going to American universities, and one has to ask: why? Some 20% of Westminster's pupils will now be going to Ivy League universities and other colleges in the United States each year. Vice-Chancellors of top universities in the UK are going to have to wake up. At the moment, they're not that interested in noting why top pupils from this sort of school are going to top universities in the States. It's reaching a tipping point. They've always believed these are pupils who can't quite get into Oxford, and so they go to Yale. Actually, it's more difficult to get into Yale or Harvard, percentage wise, than Oxford or Cambridge. Again, you have to ask yourself: why? One of the reasons is because, looking to the future, we feel the world is going to be dominated by the United States and China, and our own country might serve as the Athens of the fourth century BC, in being a kind of intellectual university city state of London, able to provide the learning which the Roman statesmen who are ruling the world will be very happy to have, to give the icing on the cake.'

Our man of the moment, the much-criticised Michael Gove, is the most controversial education secretary since Crosland, although Williams and Thatcher are strong title contenders. 'The fact that I think Gove is quite a good education secretary probably damns me in the eyes of 90% of the population,' says Andrew Halls, head of KCS Wimbledon. Chairman of the Headmasters' and Headmistresses' Conference (HMC) in 2013-14 is Tim Hands, also head of Magdalen College School Oxford. He condemns Gove's 'growing political interference' and 'politically-driven reforms' in the curriculum, exams and university admissions, adding that with Nick Clegg, "it is one rule for him and another rule for everyone else." Expect more fireworks.

In targeting simultaneous curriculum and exam reform, Gove also thinks internationally, influenced by the teaching methods and academic performance of the Asian powerhouses, dominant players in the triennial Programme for International Student Assessment (PISA). British schools fare badly in these rankings. Comparing competencies of nearly half a million fifteen year olds in 69 countries, the latest PISA ranked British children 16th (4th) for science, 25th (7th) for reading and 28th (8th) for Maths (2000 PISA rankings in brackets). Despite improving national results, and an extra £30bn spent on education, Britain fell significantly behind because other countries' PISA rankings improved faster, particularly in Asia. Pursuing a combative mission to catch up - through rigour and reform - Gove is not yet taking a critical mass of the domestic education establishment with him, not even in the independent sector.

'We are blessed by comparison with our colleagues in the state-maintained sector,' says Little. 'Most of these things (new legislation and regulation) don't really affect us. You've got to be aware, but you can filter it out. An interesting statistic: between 1944, the Butler Education Act, and 1984, there was surprisingly little primary legislation, other than the introduction of comprehensive schools. Since 1984, there's been one a year. It's really quite bewildering. At the moment, Michael Gove, it's as though he's on speed.' In saying this, Little is speaking of a privately-educated politician who calls the dominance of public schoolboys in all aspects of British public life "morally indefensible." Elliott (the Perse) adds, 'Gove has many good ideas but perhaps he's the classic journalist: he keeps coming up with good ideas, but hasn't got a track record of implementing them. He's gone way beyond the highest common denominator for educational change and is now in the territory where there are so many ideas out there that we've got basic anarchy and things will just not happen.'

Whatever the merits of his ambition, Gove is confronted by the politics of our educators, generally conservative with a small 'c'. Change is resisted. Comforting it may be for teachers cynically to regard politicians as knowing the price of everything a pupil is taught and the value of nothing which is learnt, but on one change the vast majority agrees: they would prefer political intrusion be removed from the classroom, leaving them free to teach.

Since our headmasters and headmistresses were at school, and since they started teaching, much has changed. The purpose of education, the character of schools, the nature of exams, the expectations of pupils and parents, the role of teachers, are all changed, and changed to an extent, and at such a pace, few would have believed possible in so short a space, without any breakdown in the system. Managing change, being catalysts for change and delivering excellence through change are immensely demanding tasks - far more intricate in their difficulties, challenges and opportunities than most of us outside teaching can hope to understand. From behind their study desks, in classrooms, and out and about in their schools, these busy, dynamic, talented people are shaping young lives, using every power at their disposal.

# CHAPTER TWO

# MAKING OF A HEAD

'Where did you school?' Uncle Monty enquires of Marwood in the cult film, *Withnail and I*. Before he can answer, Withnail mendaciously interrupts: 'He went to the other place, Monty.' 'Oh, you went to Eton!' responds Monty with ostentatious satisfaction. Old Etonians and Old Harrovians commonly used to refer to pupils of 'the other place' in this fashion; members of the House of Commons and House of Lords still do. Of the twenty headmasters interviewed for *Heads Up*, only one, the current Eton head, Tony Little, schooled at Monty's 'other place'. But of the other nineteen, no less than five built the foundations of their headship by becoming Eton beaks, as teaching staff are known, for between five and seventeen years each: Savage (Alleyn's); Claughton (KES Birmingham); Spence (Dulwich); Spurr (Westminster) and Townsend (Winchester). Paying homage to Withnail, Spurr quips, 'I went to Eton by mistake.'

Former Eton head, Eric Anderson, kingmaker of more than a dozen heads during his fourteen year tenure, used to scour the pages of *Who's Who*, looking at existing headmasters' dates of birth, before pointing his beaks towards headships of their new schools, as retirement loomed for present incumbents. 'Eric was essentially my mentor: he pretty well made me,' says Spence (Dulwich). To become headmaster of a leading independent school, you don't have to have gone to Eton, but it doesn't do any harm to have taught there.

There is, however, much more to headship than having been an Eton beak. Wycombe Abbey is the closest thing to an Eton for girls: a high sibling overlap exists between the two schools, they do regular socials together, and their term dates are timed to coincide. But it is much smaller

(560 girls vs 1100 boys) newer (1896 vs 1440) and most staff do not live on site, although plans are underway to increase their number via a long term building programme. At Eton, all 160 beaks live on the premises, the same as at Winchester and Radley. Nor is it a training ground for heads in the same way: Wycombe girls move on in greater numbers to the City, the Arts and the Law rather than the teaching profession; most good staff tend to stay put. An exception is Dr Felicia Kirk, former Wycombe Director of Higher Education, appointed in 2013 as head of St Mary's Calne. Retiring Wycombe head, Cynthia Hall learned her craft at St Paul's Girls', where she was head of English. 'It's quite difficult to leave St Paul's,' she says. The only school to feature more than once, in the list of twelve headmistresses interviewed, is North London Collegiate, attended by Low (LEH) and Hall.

So where do our leading headmasters and headmistresses come from, what is their background, where did they school, and what gave them the necessary qualities for headship? Their stories are as varied as their personalities. Beyond intellectual depth, a love of teaching and innate management skills - all uniformly shared - their paths to headship are refreshingly diverse; their individual stories absorbing. Among the most striking is Ed Elliott, head of the Perse in Cambridge.

'I was born into an agricultural family,' says Elliott. 'My father began life as a bus driver. I have a twin brother who's still a farm labourer. My entire family have probably moved about six miles in a thousand years. Suddenly, I was a very black sheep who emerged from the system: the first one in my family to get past sixteen in education, let alone go to university, end up in an independent school, and run one. I went to a grammar school in Worcester, when they still existed. I was a product of late 1970s social mobility and benefited accordingly.' Elliott always wanted to be a teacher. 'One thing that links a number of heads together, is they often had some problems in their childhood and, if not rescued or reformed, they were clearly supported by teachers,' he says. 'Mum died when I was eleven. The family had a complete meltdown. It was only because I was at a grammar school, with people who taught me very well, who believed in me, that I got where I am today. Those teachers were inspirational. I took a lot from them.' Elliott has come a long way since getting a first from Oxford, in Geography. In his early forties, he still has far to go.

A man who has gone far is Dr Christopher Ray, the recently departed

High Master of Manchester Grammar: he is now head of The British School Al Khubairat in Abu Dhabi. Ray was born in a poor part of Rochdale, today home to the most deprived estate in the country, with 75% unemployment. 'The only ambition I had was to get out of Rochdale,' he says. 'Before applying to university, I hadn't been further south than Chester Zoo.' Ray went to Rochdale Grammar, despite winning a place at the better Bury Grammar, seven miles away. 'My mother took me to see Cyril Smith (then a councillor, later Liberal MP for Rochdale), who was chairman of governors at Rochdale Grammar. He said I would enjoy myself more at Rochdale because they played rugby rather than at Bury, where they played soccer. The truth is he knew that my mother was exceptionally poor and she would not be able to afford the bus fares to Bury. I could walk to school in Rochdale.' Ray didn't apply to Oxford because of the stories he had heard about it being incredibly expensive: he chose UCL, later moving to study further at both Oxford and Cambridge in his twenties.

Marion Gibbs went to many schools. As head of James Allen's Girls', she tells her girls she was a rebel. 'By the time I got to Cheltenham Pates, the grammar school, I was a house captain. I wasn't a prefect because I was too naughty, but house captains were voted for by the girls. I was seen as quite a leader in probably positive and negative senses.' Before developing ambitions to teach, Gibbs had thought of becoming a hairdresser when she was very young. 'This is deeply psychological, which shows I have control freak tendencies,' she explains. 'When you're very small, the person holding the scissors near your ears is clearly the kingpin.' She read Classics at Bristol. 'I'm the only person in my family to have an O level, let alone an A level, or a degree. The fact that I did not get married and have children at eighteen is quite remarkable.'

For Joe Spence, former Master in College (housemaster to the King's Scholars) at Eton and now Master of Dulwich, 'school was not brilliant.' He recalls: 'We lived in Bristol, Bath, Coventry, Stow-on-the-Wold, and London. I moved around a lot of schools, so I had the benefit of always having to start again and make myself part of a community that was ready-formed. I had the disadvantage of hitting those moments of "Whoa, I'm not sure I understand this." Schools were a lot less forgiving then about catching up than they would be today. I can name the couple of people who made a difference at school, as so often, English teachers. I was at St

Philip's Grammar School, Edgbaston. That wasn't a great time. Then we moved in my O level year down to the Salesian (in Battersea); I had three years with them. School didn't quite work for me. I always liked doing things for myself, learning for myself, quite autodidactic by character. That was probably exacerbated by never being in one school for very long.'

As an Eton schoolboy, who read English at Cambridge, Tony Little, the current Eton head, had no ambitions to teach. 'I'm very suspicious of eighteen year olds who have already decided they want to be teachers. It doesn't seem to be a natural progression,' he says. 'It's something that tends to come a little later. It runs the risk of shutting off other opportunities, other experiences, simply by not thinking it through, or experimenting.' Not from an academic family, nor a privileged one - his father was a baggage handler at Heathrow airport - Little was the first male in his family to have been educated beyond the age of fourteen. Were his parents ambitious for him when he won a full academic bursary to Eton? 'My mother was in a rather unarticulated way. She was the one who encouraged application to the choir school through the local church. My father was more sceptical, more worried about it. He didn't quite know what he was getting into. Looking back, he was a very good case of a man who had been disadvantaged by circumstance. He was a bright guy, never had any opportunity.' Independent education is frequently seen as being synonymous with privilege, but the stories of Elliott, Ray, Gibbs, Spence and Little show that many heads did not have privileged backgrounds. Quite the contrary. Through adversity, they made their way entirely on merit.

At Odgers Berndtson, Diana Ellis is the leading headhunter in England for independent school heads, who agrees that adversity can help to give would-be heads an inner steel and external compassion. She points to 'a most unusual and amazing man,' Patrick Derham, head of Rugby, 'He's quite open about this: his mother died when he was very young and his father sent him out to sea. The most he got was CSEs, but he still managed to get to Cambridge. He is so driven, absolutely fantastic. He wants as many students as possible to have the opportunity that he had, who wouldn't otherwise (via the Arnold Foundation). He's built relationships with primary schools all over the place, who will then say: look, we've got a person here. He finds them all. He told me of a youngster whom he's given this opportunity - the boy had written to him himself, very unusual, and said: 'I want to come to your school.' He was so surprised and interested, he asked the boy to come along with his mother. Apparently, he lived on the most dreadful estate, was being abused at home and life was just hell. Patrick thought that there was some talent there, that he'd like to give him a go. I said: "Is that fair when he's just going to go back from Rugby and that cross-section of society?" He said: "I was worried about that and I asked his mother and the answer was: every day that he can be away from that home the better." ' In September 2014, Derham will succeed Spurr as head of Westminster.

Some heads enjoyed a more comfortable upbringing. But apart from Little, only three heads - Vernon (CLGS), Haynes (Tonbridge) and McPhail (Radley) - went to boarding school, attending respectively: St Michael's School, Petworth (closed 1994), Shrewsbury and Abingdon. The majority attended grammar and direct-grant schools, the latter category being abolished in 1976, at which time many of the more prominent brands, like North London Collegiate and Manchester Grammar, became independent.

Three interviewees were raised overseas, attending local schools and universities: Lusk (Abingdon) Spurr (Westminster) and Townsend (Winchester). Lusk studied Music at Victoria University in Wellington, NZ; Spurr read Classics at Sydney, while Townsend read English at the University of Western Australia. Felicity Lusk is a feisty, fast-talking Kiwi. Spurr and Townsend, a formidable pair of intellectual fast bowlers, are distinctly more Lord's Pavilion than the old Sydney Hill: their immaculate RP delivers no linguistic hint of their Aussie origins, in cadence or pitch. Both men schooled, at different times, in the shadow of the Hill at Sydney Grammar: Spurr as a schoolboy, Townsend as headmaster. After leaving his native Natal, Levin (CLBS) brought his deep, well-modulated South African tones with him to read Economics at Sussex. Of the remaining twenty-eight native Brits, the universities and choice of subject make for interesting reading. Seventeen (61%) went to Oxford (eleven) or Cambridge (six). Two apiece went to Durham, Bristol and Reading. One representative each went to: UCL, KCL, Sussex, Sheffield, and 'an unusual one for a public school headmaster', Southampton, according to Cox (RGS Guildford), where he studied Biochemistry.

Equally significant is that five of the non-Oxbridge contingent went on to study or teach at Oxford: Spurr, Townsend, Bailey (St Paul's), Ray, and Hands (MCS Oxford). Ray even managed a stint at Cambridge for good measure. In summary, 50% of the twelve headmistresses attended, and a striking 80% of the twenty headmasters, either attended or taught, at Oxbridge. Sixteen of the heads interviewed went to, or taught at, just one university: Oxford. Of course, this sample size is far too small to be scientific for serious statistical analysis, and the message is therefore clear: if you want to maximise your chances of getting ahead in leading independent schools, there isn't only one place to go, there are two. Oxford and Cambridge graduates also traditionally referred to their counterparts as having gone to 'the other place.'

When it comes to their academic specialism, arts and languages dominate. Comprising 81% of the total, the top seven subjects read at university were: English (eight), History (six), Languages (six - Modern Languages three; Classics three), Music (two) PPE (two) and Chemistry/Biochemistry (two). Only one mathematician features - Hawkins at Harrow - while there are two female scientists: Hewitt (Manchester High), who read Chemistry at Sheffield, and Vernon (CLGS), who read Biology at Durham.

Diversity is keenly monitored throughout the public and private sectors. So are there any gay heads of independent schools? Definitely, yes. Are there any who are open and 'out'. Definitely, no. Although much information is gathered by the DfE in the School Census, no questions are asked about sexuality. In terms of ethnicity, every interviewee is white. Look at heads in all the leading independent schools and it is the same picture: all white. Haberdashers' head, Peter Hamilton, says his pupil profile of 1400 boys is '33% Jewish, 33% Asian and the rest everything under the sun: we are an absolute pure reflection of north London.' Britain is set to become more ethnically diverse than the current 14% non-white population revealed by the 2011 census. Nationally, 28.5% of independent day schools pupils and 26% in boarding schools are ethnic minority (source: DfE). Hamilton believes 'it will not be too long' before an ethnic minority head is appointed in a top independent. 'It may well just reflect the fact that ethnic minorities haven't gone in enough quantity in to independent teaching.'

Of ethnic minority candidates Ellis has recently put forward to governors, she has 'two that immediately spring to mind, two deputies we've interviewed, and one in particular, we've really pushed for headship - sadly, hasn't got there. He's bright, so I think he will in time. He'll be our first. But he won't leap into one of the top schools.' Does she envisage, in twenty years, that we will see more ethnic or mixed-race heads? 'I wouldn't think we'd rush to do that,' she says pointedly, 'because what people are buying is British education, and therefore, they want to see a British leader.' Seven of the thirty-two heads interviewed have since moved on: two to headships overseas, three to other jobs, and two have retired. Of their replacements, all are white.

'I like talking to journalists on the whole; it probably comes from being married to one,' says Hall at Wycombe. Her husband, Lord Hall, is BBC director general, described on appointment by BBC Trust chairman, Lord Patten, as 'the right person to lead the BBC out of its current crisis.' One of Hall's predecessors, Greg Dyke, on assuming the DG role in 2001, declared the BBC to be 'hideously white,' after finding the organisation's senior management was more than 98% white. The glass ceiling has since been lifted, if not altogether removed. Progress of ethnic minorities in tertiary education appears conspicuous from browsing website photographs of prominent academics at our leading universities: Oxford, Cambridge, UCL, Imperial and LSE. Among the 650 MPs elected at the 2010 general election, twenty-seven were from an ethnic minority. To be truly reflective of their collective constituencies, that number should be more like eighty-five. In serving their collective constituency, where more than a quarter of pupils are ethnic minority, there is a clear need for the glass ceiling in the independent sector to be dismantled: some heads need to be appointed from ethnic minorities. There will undoubtedly be many in future. The question for governors is: when?

Enough data. Why did they become teachers in the first place? 'So many heads fall into headship or fall into teaching - I'm an exception: it's something I always wanted to do,' says Lusk. She is not alone. Oulton (Benenden) wanted to be a teacher at the age of four. 'All my early life, I wanted to be a music teacher,' says Trafford (RGS Newcastle). Some did other jobs before teaching: McPhail (Radley), Ray (MGS) and Martin (Hampton) worked for the Bank of England; Haynes (Tonbridge) was a stockbroker; Claughton (KES Birmingham) worked at Rothschild; Marks (Withington) became a senior corporate financier in her thirteen years at Bank of America; Low (LEHS) was at Courtaulds; Vernon (CLGS) spent twelve years in industry. Ray and Spurr taught for several years in universities before teaching in schools.

For most, it was more evolutionary, although background played a part. 'I used to tell my family all the time that the very last thing I would do was become a teacher. Many of them were teachers already. I knew how hard they worked and it seemed to me that they weren't terribly well rewarded for that,' says Marks (Withington). At Radley, McPhail says, 'All my family had taught.' Ten interviewees had a parent or parents who were teachers; four had parents who were heads: Halls, Hands, Hawkins and Wright. Perhaps not surprising. More remarkable is that four of the heads returned to the schools where they had been pupils as headmaster: Little, Claughton, Martin and Hamilton, who was a boy and later head at King Edward VI, Southampton before moving to Haberdashers. From September 2013, the new High Master of Manchester Grammar, Martin Boulton, continues the trend: he is an Old Mancunian.

Hands (MCS Oxford) was one of those brought up in a teaching household, 'My father was a head. I went to a grammar school in London, where the headmaster was, unfortunately, an alcoholic before the time of his appointment. Quite frequently the worse for wear in the day, he was very sad, but also very good, very caring. A friend of mine said this chap was brilliant to him personally when his father died. My parents chose the school, in quite large measure because of the headmaster, ironically because he'd been in the navy in the war. He had what were known as "bugger's grips" which you have on your upper cheeks. My father had a big series of heart attacks through running together four schools in Chiswick. He worked very hard: he did the timetable himself. But school was fairly carefully hidden from me at home. I suspect that I took on board by osmosis a lot of his thinking about things, and the decisions I make are genetically influenced.'

Teaching careers can provide a quick route to the top for the talented few. Vernon got her first headship at Downe House after only six years in the classroom; Marks had a similar fast track before getting the top job at Tormead in Guildford. Both came to the profession after successful careers outside, believing it gave them added perspective and experience. The youngest headship appointee, when teaching from day one, is Helen Wright, who became head of Heathfield at the age of thirty, after only seven years as a teacher. No independent headmaster can match that achievement.

'My background was really important,' says Wright. 'The strong moral grounding I had. You take it for granted as a child growing up. My father was a priest in the Church of England, he's retired now, and he went through many different changes. He was very driven by his faith. We moved a lot. When I was born my parents were congregationalists, but then he became ordained into the Episcopal Church. His faith has had a powerful impact on me, although as a child I didn't realise it. You always go through a period of rejecting what your parents think and feel, and then you come to a position of admiring and recognising it for what it is. He would never let the grass grow green, he'd never sit back and become complacent, so that's had a big impact on who I am.' Wright has always been 'driven' in everything she has done - from the girl guides, sunday school teaching, schoolwork, Oxford and her teaching career. 'Human beings: our natural state of contentment is through change,' she says. 'That's why we have pioneers, that's why we have explorers, that's why we have people who you need to keep pushing the boundaries, we need to keep pushing the boundaries.' At forty-two, and after two headships in England, she recently moved to Australia, becoming head of Ascham School in Sydney.

Gibbs applied for more than one headship before becoming head of JAGS in 1994, describing it as: 'A privilege. A huge privilege. Best job in the world.' Awarded a CBE for her numerous services to education in 2012, she recalls one of her first applications: 'It was one of those where you have trial by lunch or dinner, you rotate through the governors, sitting next to them. There was a wonderful old lady, who sat next to me, and said, "My dear, you look like a bright young thing. I wouldn't waste your time on this school: it's going bankrupt faster than you can say."'

On getting their first headship, one head recalls: 'Somebody put an advertisement in front of me. I looked at it and thought: absolutely no way. Then I thought: well, don't be a coward. If you want to make change, you've got to put your head above the parapet, and go for it. I thought: Well, if I at least apply, there's no way they'll appoint me. I haven't been in senior management, I'm only a head of department. Just apply and then I'll think: well, if I don't get it, at least I've given it a shot. To my absolute shock, and I'm not being modest - it was one of the greatest shocks I've ever had - I got it. I remember the Chairman of Governors phoning me. I had to suppress a scream because I simply couldn't believe I'd got it. But I did. I felt absolute terror, because I hadn't intended to get it at all.'

Mark Bailey, High Master of St Paul's, combined his teaching career with professional rugby: he played for many years as a winger at London

Wasps and won seven caps playing for England. He believes this has enabled him to develop the qualities needed for headship: 'In rugby, you are only as strong as your weakest link, and therefore, knowing your strengths and weaknesses, being honest about them, and being very comfortable about being honest and open about strengths and weaknesses, and working collaboratively to minimise weakness or to emphasise strengths - you can apply all of that to headship. The other way it helps is if you have made a complete prat of yourself in front of 80,000 people, and taken the criticism - entirely just - afterwards. I think that has helped too.'

Independent school heads are better paid than they used to be. The salary range of those interviewed for this book - between £150,000 and £250,000 a year - averages at a little over £200,000, typically with pension and housing benefits on top. On discovering that I had interviewed the head of the school where his son is a sixth former, one parent made the following observation, 'I've read in the newspaper that he earns more than I do. Unbelievable. Is he worth it?' 'Every penny,' I responded, a little surprised that someone should question a head's value in that way. As chief executives of their business, heads work very long hours and carry significant responsibility. 'The great problem of being a head is that you need to have sensitive antennae, but also to have a leathery protection. That's what makes the job most difficult,' says Bailey (St Paul's).

So what do schools look for when appointing a head? Ellis explains: 'The public face of the school that is the head, has become increasingly important. That's not just for better known schools, the Etons and Winchesters of the world, who then might make a statement on education nationally, but for the middle size schools, particularly, I'm afraid a lot of the girls' schools, the whole business of numbers and winning parents and pupils to come to the school of the right quality, it is a really important aspect of the role. I find that the personality, someone who's got a little bit of... they use the word 'charisma' all the time for which I think the dictionary definition is: a God given gift, but I know what they mean. It's very difficult if the person doesn't make a pretty quick impact.'

To make that quick impact upon their staff and pupils, new heads may consider Aristotle's three rhetorical techniques of persuasion: stating their purpose (ethos), selling their vision (logos), and appealing to the emotions (pathos). They may already possess a compelling self-belief in the power of their abilities. But from his reading and experience, Hands

(MCS Oxford) advises caution, comparing headship to assuming the captaincy of a ship: 'You'll never step on board after you've gone, and you never step on board before you start. Don't ever try. It's only your ship on the basis of your office.'

# CHAPTER THREE

# ADOPTING THE PERSONA

'It is quite extraordinary, even in a large school, the personality of the head, even the mood of the head for the day, it seeps through the school in the most extraordinary way, much more than it would with a chief executive,' says Ellis, who has been placing independent school heads for more than two decades, including several in this book. 'The ubiquitous Diana Ellis of Odgers with her silken voice,' enthuses Ralph Townsend, whom she placed as head of Winchester. She knows them all. And their personas. But what is a persona, and how does it seep through a school?

'A schoolmaster should have an atmosphere of awe, and walk wonderingly, as if he was amazed at being himself,' wrote the great Victorian, Walter Bagehot. More recently, Sir Michael Wilshaw, Ofsted chief inspector, observed: 'The best head teachers are often quite odd people.' It made headlines. But is it true? Are they odd? And by odd, did he mean eccentric, unusual or weird? The answer is largely subjective. A head who may seem eccentric and endearing to one person might appear weird and unappealing to another. The collective responses of parents and pupils are habitually polarised by generational attitudes: they see things through a different prism. What parents like, children commonly do not, and vice versa.

When professional headship developed during the nineteenth century, as the number and size of public schools grew substantially to serve the needs of the British Empire, the persona of an eccentric headmaster emerged. This generally humorous stereotype combined peculiar habits, distinctive quirks, and a sometimes avuncular manner. Before the Education Act 1902, proper supervision of schools did not exist in the way that we now take for granted. Heads often did their own thing. At their worst, they were far from eccentric, they were truly appalling. Authoritarian headmasters - the feared embodiment of ferocious cruelty - loom large in the novels of Charles Dickens. Wackford Squeers at Dotheboys Hall, in *Nicholas Nickleby*, and Mr Creakle at Salem House School, in *David Copperfield*, were monstrous creations, drawn from what Dickens had seen and heard: 'poor discipline punctuated by the headmaster's sadistic brutality.' Compelling Victorian caricatures, malign and benign, live on in children's literature: from the merciless Miss Trunchbull, in Roald Dahl's *Matilda*, to the delightful Albus Dumbledore, headmaster of Hogwarts. More sinister fictional wickedness - the Squeers and Creakle personas - also stretches to the present day, where real life examples of violent, abusive heads, now retired or dead, still make occasional headlines.

Anthony Chenevix-Trench (C-T), Eton head from 1964 to 1970, rejoiced in flogging boys. The College's vice-provost, Tim Card, later recorded his behaviour in *Eton Renewed, an authorised history*. Viewed by victims as a flagellomaniac, C-T abolished the traditional public birching of boys by the head on their bare buttocks, replacing it instead with private caning, which he administered personally in his study. Boys had to lower their trousers and underpants and bend over before he 'gleefully' beat them. *The New York Times* reported: 'When he was drunk, which was quite often, Chenevix-Trench had an unpleasant habit of beating the students with a savagery unusual even by Eton standards, and then sobbing penitentially afterward.' After Card's book was published in 1994, *the London Times* received numerous letters from Old Etonians, including one which said: 'He once flogged the living daylights out of me with a strap on my bare backside and went on to beat all twenty-one students in a divinity class in a single afternoon.'

I interviewed Tony Little, Eton's current head, in the same study where beatings took place - Little was himself an Eton pupil in C-T's time - and asked him about his former head's persona: 'It's a very difficult question to respond to, even with the benefit of hindsight,' says Little. 'I was a young boy, and in a place like this, by definition, the headmaster is particularly remote. Chevenix-Trench, in the times I came across him, personally, was warm and genial. But, I would have had no reason to know anything about him, other than there were one or two celebrated cases, when things went pretty dramatically wrong.' C-T was moved on by Eton, becoming Head of Fettes, where his boys included a rebellious teenager named Tony Blair.

'There were stories of the wrong (Fettes) boys receiving corporal punishment,' according to Lorn MacIntyre, 'from a man who didn't seem to know what day of the week it was.' Another former Fettes pupil confides, 'I always found Chenevix-Trench kind and inspirational. After he beat me he gave me a glass of sherry, saying he imagined he had enjoyed the experience more than I had.' C-T died in 1979, while still Fettes head. Corporal punishment in state schools was outlawed in 1986 - by just a single vote in the House of Commons - before Blair's government finally banned it, in 1999, in the independent sector.

The cornerstones of effective modern headship, combined with the seeds of pastoral care, were laid by Victorian pioneers: Thomas Arnold, Dorothea Beale and Frances Mary Buss, whose achievements were underpinned by enormous charisma, energy and passion. The impact of their powerful, compassionate personas finds a much more obvious parallel in today's heads, although few would openly declare themselves to possess the full range of Arnold's impressive attributes, as described by Isabel Quigley, 'He ruled Rugby with a grand, commanding air…an impressive figure, controversial, handsome, committed, much criticised, he was anyone's social equal and raised the schoolmaster's position among other educated people.'

While modern heads bear no resemblance to their fictional counterparts, the imprint of a head's personality is just as integral to their school as Dumbledore at Hogwarts. 'When you take over a school, the psychological commitment needed is very demanding, even when things are in a good state,' says Winchester head, Townsend. Essential to the persona of any head is the ability to demonstrate that they are in control: if they are not, then somebody else is. Bailey (St Paul's) summarises the impact of the different persona types: 'Through some mysterious process, whatever the head is, or stands for, usually permeates the corridors.' Their common purpose may be to demonstrate persistence, intelligence and reasonableness as trademarks of their public persona, yet the spectrum of personalities is remarkable. The heads interviewed range from the quiet, cerebral and reflective to gregarious, amusing and loquacious. Occasionally, the great volume of words offered by some heads can appear like a meringue: much bulk but no substance.

From research done by RSAcademics, Russell Speirs points to charisma as being key, 'There is a noticeable difference between the importance that governors ascribe to charisma and the importance that heads themselves do, and indeed their staff. Those that think that charisma is more important are the governors and parents; the people already within the school seem to think it's less important. Certainly, heads themselves don't really regard it as important.' Hard to define, charisma is unmistakable once seen. 'The combination of personal warmth, flair and individuality, of doing things in a slightly different way, a noticeable way, even a memorable way. It's having a personality that attracts people, that engages them, that appeals,' says Spiers, 'that makes other people want to be with that person. And having a presence, which doesn't need to be big or loud, but there's something about them that you notice, the cliché, when they walk into a room, but certainly when you spend a few minutes with them. Charisma is innate, but over time one can learn to be more confident in oneself because you can't be charismatic without having an inner core of self-confidence. It is one of the magic ingredients that makes for a superb head because if they are to lead the school in a particular direction, if they're going to take the people with them, then there's got to be something about them and not just their ideas, but something about them as a person that people want to follow.'

Heads themselves identify different qualities. Charming and purposeful, Oulton (Benenden) believes that the most important attribute for headship is to be a good listener. She listens with unusual intensity. Some put on a show. 'The best heads are always good actors,' argues McPhail, the jovial Radley Warden, confirming the dictionary definition of persona: a social role or a character played by an actor. 'Most heads enjoy being a bit showman-like, deep down,' agrees Hamilton at Haberdashers. A head whose engaging laughter runs through any room like a peal of bells, Vernon (CLGS), takes a different stance: 'When girls see me cycling around with a bicycle helmet, one immediately loses one's dignity. There's no point in pretending: children see through pretence very quickly. Pupils, parents and staff will see through any mask.' The lesson: be yourself.

At Dulwich, the reflective Spence develops the argument, 'Nothing the head says is ever missed. The longer you're head, the more you realise that nothing you say goes missing. That little comment you made, that you thought nobody heard, will be brought back five years later. You will be told: but you said. I do believe, and try to live by: be yourself. It's a performance for which I don't have to do much prep. I don't have to try too hard to act because I live it. In my presentation, I call it *My Ten Personal Commandments*. It starts with: be yourself. Its second note is: be brave. Those two in contrast are quite interesting.' Heads uniformly recognise that they are on show all of the time, in school and outside, and that their actions are carefully monitored. 'What we say, and what we are, carries enormously amplified consequences,' says Haynes (Tonbridge). Savage (Alleyn's) confides, 'You need to have a persona. It's difficult, because there are moments when you want to say, "That's such bollocks, isn't it". But I don't; I moderate my language.'

Being self-aware is critical. 'If you the head are cold and barking and difficult,' says Hamilton (HABS), whose machine gun delivery conveys a quick mind, 'Well then it's hardly surprising that the school reflects that. If you are open and warm, but firm and friendly, then it's not surprising that you hear both those attitudes and that language being echoed back at you.' At City of London Boys', Levin says, 'I would like to think that I was associated with a clear vision, and that everyone was in no doubt as to what the school stood for and where it was heading, and that all efforts were designed to go in that particular direction; therefore, certain things would automatically be appropriate, and others wouldn't. So the mantra here is: "We don't care who you are, where you come from; it's what you have done and what sort of person you are that matters." That's the main driver.'

Levin's persona - naturally warm and approachable - is similar to that of the equally thoughtful and measured Elliott, at the Perse, who believes the question of persona management is worse in some ways as a day school head 'because the boarding school head, 175 days of the year, you're in school. The rest of the year, you've either got a house somewhere else, or most of your children have disbursed to the four corners of wherever. As a day school head, and particularly in a place the size of Cambridge, which is a large goldfish bowl, 365 days of the year, whether it's in school, in term, or just shopping in Waitrose, you are the Perse head. You are very well-known, you are very visible, you are always on show, you're always representing the organisation, even on your days off.

'I've taken a walk on Christmas Day across Grantchester Meadows, only to be stopped by Perse parents talking about Oxbridge results. You never escape it. The dinner party circuit. You get invited out but it's an extension of your work. You're sat there with parents in an informal setting, but they are your customers. It's a glass of wine, maximum. You have to know how to divert on to innocent small talk and you know the sort of amusing anecdotes which will get a laugh, but will not be too risqué, or reflect badly on the organisation. But it is 365, 24/7, even more so now because we live in the world where everyone's got a mobile phone and can take an image. I recently went to someone's birthday party, a Perse parent, also a friend. The karaoke machine was coming out. That's time for the head to exit stage left, very quickly. I rest assured that the rest of them are thinking, rather like they do at the common room party, "The head's gone, phew. Sigh of relief. We can let our hair down." But, I'm doing them a favour by going.'

JAGS head, Gibbs, is equally forthright: 'Interestingly, most people would say what you see is what you get. I am a bit of a whizzywig person in some ways. As I sit talking to you, I'm talking to you as headmistress. I have slipped that role on. Although I don't have a veneer, I have a half-second guard on saying something really stupid because you are always representing your school. I say to people: when you're a head, you cannot go out on a Saturday night and get drunk.' Trafford (RGS Newcastle) has an opposing view, 'I think I am always me. I don't think there are different personas. At home, I wasn't very different as a dad when my kids were growing up. So over the years I've probably been given brownie points for that by people, that I'm consistently me. And I'm mischievous. I like a beer, so yes I do get drunk, and I may well say much more than I should do if I'm in the pub or whatever. But that's true to me.' In common with heads everywhere, Gibbs still teaches, utilising a good sense of humour, integral to her persona. 'I think a sense of humour is absolutely essential,' agrees Vernon (CLGS). 'I don't think you can get through life without humour. Obviously, it is a serious job, but at the same time like most things in life, there are going to be humorous moments. The girls and their humour keep you totally grounded and totally sane.'

For Wright (St Mary's Calne), her persona is indistinguishable from her other life: 'When I'm with my family, I don't see that as separate from school and when I'm at school I don't see that as separate from my family. I don't separate them out. I am who I am. In this role, you have to always take a deep breath and shed yourself of that sense of being completely distinct because if I go out into town, people will see me as the headmistress, so don't make that a bad thing. Just think: that's who I am. I'm a headmistress with a wonderful family. All those aspects of me at home, you would see at school. The girls would see that as well. I invite girls into my home, but inevitably, there are things which I do at school which I don't do at home. I don't normally stand up in front of people and give a formal speech, but I do find myself using similar sorts of negotiating techniques as my children grow older. Some people like the fact that they get in a car, go away at the end of the day, and transfer into their own self. Yes, there are moments where you've got to be terribly formal about things, moments which are really difficult and full of conflict, but that doesn't mean that the essence of the school isn't there. How you portray yourself on precise occasions, to precise cohorts of people, is going to be slightly different, but it's no good if you're not authentic.'

The persona in the classroom is different from outside, as Hall (Wycombe), explains, 'I just try to be as friendly as possible. I teach all the eleven year olds when they come into the school. I tell them that the reason I'm doing that is so that they're not afraid of me, that they always feel they can come up and speak to me. Children need to understand, and do understand very easily, that there are different roles for a head to play. So the headmistress who's standing at the door of chapel, making sure that they stop talking when they go in, is one face of the head, and the head who is concerned because a girl's upset, or fallen out with her friend, or wanting to make sure that she's happy about something else, is another face. You expect that the head has these different roles. In the classroom, the head who's just dotty about children's literature and wants to share enthusiasm, that's because I'm a head who has always loved teaching, and I want to impart that to them as well.'

Beyond the classroom, the impact of a head's persona can be immediate, as Hands (MCS Oxford), reveals: 'I'm ashamed to say that the first time I worked as an assessor for a governing body, it was at the Perse; I went two rounds of interviews, watching the governors. I was shocked at myself, that I had made up my mind about the candidates within the first fifteen seconds. They walked through the door, they sat down. I looked at what they wore and my mind was made up. I have to acknowledge that the persona, the manner is terribly important, which is a dreadful thing to say. It isn't something you can affect.'

Superficial they may be, but clothes are part of everyone's persona. In a blue or grey suit, a headmaster's appearance, unless he wears distinctively unusual shirts or ties, or is notably scruffy, does not normally attract much comment. Attention paid to headmistresses can be greater. North London Collegiate girls covet McCabe's impressive gold-heeled stilettos and St Swithun's girls firmly approve of Gandee's elegant style. Gandee also shows a crucial ability to laugh at herself, as evident from a YouTube spoof interview posted by a sixth former, titled *Dance Dare*: unknown to the headmistress, the upper sixth are seen dancing behind her as she speaks.

In 2010, Felicity Lusk became the first female head of an all boys' boarding school, Abingdon. Shortly afterwards, she did a fashion shoot for *the Telegraph*, together with a lengthy interview. 'The last thing I would want to look like is what people call a typical headmistress', she told journalist, Alison Taylor, who reported her views on the relative merits of dresses, leggings, boots, cardigans, evening gowns, coats, handbags and scarves. 'I often have to change my clothes several times a day,' said Lusk. 'I bought this green velvet suit for my 50th birthday. It has an interesting hourglass cut that really plays to my strengths without showing off acres of cleavage. Discreet but still quite sexy. I think that my dress style says, 'Here's somebody who means business.' I don't tend to buy labels but I have got some pieces in the wardrobe that are really special by Thierry Mugler, Versace and Armani. The other thing I believe is really important is what you wear underneath. I absolutely swear by Rigby & Peller. My pupils seem to like the way I dress.' Three years on from *the Telegraph* interview, Lusk told me that the article and similar media interviews 'were ridiculous, but the spin-off was that it raised the profile. The number of applications for places has gone through the roof, particularly from Hong Kong. It's really worked for us. I don't think it did any harm at all.'

A clear distinction exists between the everyday persona adopted - masks worn to fit the occasion at the expense of personal identity - and the head's true personality, when tested by traumatic events. To paraphrase TS Eliot, they are supremely adept at preparing faces to meet the faces that they meet. But when the going gets tough, adversity provides the real test of substance over style: what a head is made of, rather than the carefully-manicured or coiffured image they present for external consumption. Some find this hard to articulate, while others have thought deeply on the subject, especially when confronted by tragedy - either personal, or in the wider school community.

Marks, the wise head of Withington, has spent many years fundraising for a charity she helped to establish to increase awareness of diabetes. Her daughter, Stephanie, who was Type 1 insulin dependent, died in June 2002, as a result of complications, on the day she finished her AS exams. In May 2010, Sir Ian Botham, an active patron of her charity, officially opened The Stephanie Marks Diabetes Resource Centre at St Peter's Hospital, Chertsey, financed partly through Sue Marks's efforts, saying: 'Stephanie Marks was only seventeen when she died. My daughter also shares her life with diabetes.'

Marks recognises the profound impact Stephanie's death had upon her, 'My leadership style changed immensely after my daughter died. Personal circumstances do change everything: she died just before the end of my first year as a head. It is fundamental to the way I've done the job because it made me realise that you can't ever put yourself in somebody else's shoes, unless you have experienced the same thing. There are various aspects of life that I have experienced, which I now feel I can empathise with, that tragically, being one of them, losing a child, but also being divorced and a single parent. It's made me a bit more humble about the idea that if I hadn't experienced something, I can't possibly imagine how it feels. I'm much less quick to react to parents, whose style might be rather confrontational or aggressive, because I'm much more aware that I don't really understand what their motivation is, how they're feeling. Nietzsche said, 'What doesn't break you makes you stronger'. Well I would say, in my case, that it probably made me softer. I was very black and white about things. I recognise that. It was one of the criticisms of me in appraisals. After Stephanie died, after my marriage broke up, and after being ill with a serious post-operative condition, in 2008, it's made me realise that nothing's ever black and white. So I'm probably, I hope, a much less black and white person than I was. I'm much more inclined to listen than I might have done at the beginning of my headship.'

Lady Eleanor Holles head, Low, says it is 'a very emotional job, running a school,' evidenced by the personal tragedies she has had within her school community. 'Tragically, in my first headship at Francis Holland, in the October half term, I'd only been there for a few weeks, one of the Upper Sixth contracted meningitis, and died. Some years later, a member of staff committed suicide; we were told on Saturday night. On the Monday, I had the first round interview for this job (headship at LEH), which obviously Francis Holland did not know. But I had to go into school that

Monday morning - we got round all the staff at the weekend and told them - and tell the girls.

'What happens to me in those situations? I go on to automatic pilot. That's just personal, to do with the way different people react, isn't it. But in a situation like that - we also had a death of a member of staff in a car crash one day - I just don't get emotional. Now that doesn't mean I don't get emotional later, or that I don't care. But I am able to take a, right now, what do we do, approach. I'm now going to do x, y and z. This is what I'm going to say. I'm going to do a press release or whatever, or an email to parents which says as follows. I suspect a lot of heads are like that. You just say, "Right, this terrible thing has happened." You've got the public thing; you can't afford publicly to fall apart. But you can't afford to privately either, because you don't have time for that.

'You've got to be strong; you just think: I've got to do the following things. I need to phone the Chair of Governors. I need to do this, this and that. You go through it, and you have to be able to just shove the emotion or fear about your own position, or fear for the school or, depending on the situation, the tragedy of the family. You have to think incredibly pragmatically and be very calm. Because if you're not calm, if you've got something really terrible happening, then if you've got any little bit of terror inside you, people are going to pick that up, and other people will go into a tailspin. So you've got to hold the community together at those times.'

McCabe found personal grief hard to manage while being North London Collegiate head, 'By far the most difficult time in my headship was when I lost my father,' she says. 'I found that incredibly difficult to deal with whilst running a school. I found it really difficult to talk in assembly. A colleague of mine, James Sabben-Clare, who used to run Winchester, is on my team in the Teaching Institute. James and I work very closely on all the programmes. I remember him saying to me: he found it incredibly difficult when his parents died, both of them at different times, when he was at Winchester.

'I found that quite consoling because I couldn't understand why it was that I really couldn't speak in assembly. I couldn't even read a notice. It's something to do with that kind of emotional drain. When my father died, I just took myself off and spent time with my brother, sister and mother. I wrote the eulogy and found every photograph of him and…it's emotional resilience isn't it? Just coping when things get thrown at you all the time, because you've got all those communities coming at you: girls, old girls, former staff, staff, parents, former parents, governors, former governors.'

In recalling tough experiences, some heads reflect Low's phlegmatic approach. At Eton, Little recalls his baptism of fire as head of Chigwell: 'My first experience of headship, the first three things I had to deal with, and I remember when the third one came up, I thought this is a candid-camera. This is a joke. This is one of these spoof exercises in starting life as a head. The first thing I had to deal with was the suicide of a fourteen year-old, two days before the beginning of the term. I never met the boy. Nonetheless, my very first day, I had to re-order everything so boys could go to a funeral in the morning, before they came back in the afternoon to hear the new headmaster doing his 'up and at 'em, new tomorrow.' That was not easy.

'It was then followed by picking up a copy of a letter from my prede-cessor to a senior head of department, saying: If I was still here, at Chigwell, I'd sack you. But I'm leaving this letter for my successor, so that he can do it. That led to quite a fun interview. The third thing was a married woman on the staff coming to see me to complain bitterly about another married woman on the staff, who was having an affair with the married chaplain, and how appalling this was. In my sweet naivety, as a young head - I've learned since - I was twenty minutes into this conversation before it dawned on me that the reason she was so exercised was that she was having an affair with the chaplain as well. She'd just found out about the other woman. We parted company with the chaplain. In some ways, when I look back, I'm quite glad I had that experience. It's the short sharp shock: this is kinda what you have to do.' The lesson: stay calm under pressure.

# CHAPTER FOUR

# LEADERSHIP

Leaders want to lead and for others to follow. They have visions, objectives, targets, strategies and plans. In their quest for success, they lead by example, argument, diktat, consensus, thought, and by sound management. According to theorists, leadership has challenges, laws, personalities, secrets, styles, and a host of other epithets and additions. Since Plato first approached the subject in the fourth century BC, leadership has developed over the last fifty years into an obsession for every company and organisation. In search of more capable leaders, schools are no exception. Several heads referred enthusiastically during interview to current works they were reading on the subject - in the hope that the studied wisdom of others would help them to do a better job. For school leaders, objectives may include: providing a clear sense of direction; attracting customers into the school; communicating clearly; being flexible; taking measured risks and building the right team. To which you can add management-speak such as: 'listening with humility, acting with courage' or 'earning rewards through building trust.'

In his *Republic*, Plato observed, "The object of education is to teach us to love what is beautiful" - not a mantra to be found in any Harvard management textbook. Today, business triumphs over aesthetics: profit not poetry matters. 'Headship is much more of a chief executive role than it used to be,' says Smellie. 'Heads divide, there are very different models. You get the type of head, a cult of personality, who thinks 'I'm going to make this school great because I'm going to make my own reputation' To be fair to them, they may also be thinking about the school. Then you get the other type of head, much more understated, more of a teacher, who actually looks to bask in the reflected glory of their pupils and other members of staff. Increasingly schools have to decide: what do we want.'

Sir Michael Wilshaw has proclaimed that he wants "less tolerance of poor leadership, everything flows from poor leadership." His comments were underpinned by Ofsted figures revealing leadership in 24% of state schools – more than 5000 institutions - was rated less than good. Only rarely does a man or woman become head of a great school without being a great leader. At the risk of sounding unctuous, all the men and women interviewed are great leaders of their schools. Most striking is how they contrast as individuals. Beyond the orthodox traits of intelligence, dedication to the task and genuine enthusiasm for what their school does, they are surprisingly disparate in personality and approach. They may share a common purpose of well-being and happiness, they may articulate a uniform vocabulary of learning and achievement, but as human beings, they are much more varied than you might find in the boardroom of a major company or the partnership of a professional organisation. It is their distinct individuality that makes them good leaders: each does things in his or her own way. There is no right or wrong, they are as different as their schools. For this reason, rather than cherry-pick opposing views on leadership, the following quotes - one from every head - provide a window into their personalities. Some are short, a few are longer: the substance matters, not the volume of words.

Abingdon - Felicity Lusk

'The art of leadership is to sow the seeds of ideas and often things come back much improved. I'm very happy for other people to take all the credit, even if I know perfectly well I've sown the idea somewhere. I don't have a problem with my senior team taking all the credit, or groups of governors, I just want to get the direction. I do move at a pretty fast pace, so change comes very quickly in an organization: I find I can move a culture on. If I sit around waiting I'd probably get bored.'

Alleyn's - Gary Savage

'Making the school more comfortably, more self-consciously intellectual without losing the roundedness, the richness of the co-curriculum, the excellent pastoral care - that's the trick, to have it all. But it's got to be gradual. You take the temperature, you absorb by osmosis, you understand where the school's coming from. Because, as a student of the French Revolution, I'm well aware of the dangers of thinking that you can rip the garden up and start again from scratch. And then contribute in a way which is resonant with your values and your preferences; in this case, my intellectual academic preferences. Then try to embody that in what you say, how you say it, what you do. Because people are looking to see whether what you do resonates with what you say, and the values you profess to hold. They'll think you're a fraud if you don't. So, to be a leader of a school community, you've got to be sure what you believe in; what is just, in terms of discipline, and what is right, in terms of education.'

Benenden - Claire Oulton

'I've got a business brain, I like numbers, and although my passion is education, I do like business. I like running a business, making it a successful one. I can understand and make business decisions. I do a lot of listening and looking. But I'm a worrier and if you are a worrier, this is not an ideal job. It may make you a better head that you worry about everything, but it's not very good for your health. I mind very much about people and my staff, as well as my girls, being happy and fulfilled. Having to make really tough decisions about people's lives, I hate it. I wasn't suited to it, I'm not tough enough, even now I'm not really tough enough.'

City of London Girls' - Diana Vernon

'Whilst I certainly wouldn't suggest that all of the girls would want to emulate me in their own professional lives, up to a point, I've got to be some sort of role model to them. It won't be as a head, but as an individual, as a person. Girls will come to me and say they want to do this or that. Members of staff want to do things and I'll say fine, let's go, go, go. Because that's where the energy and the buzz will come from. Give them that 'can do', and off they go. Having a 'can do' attitude is something that will really set them off in future. They will get that in huge measure from me. I will always say yes, get it, do it.'

## City of London Boys' - David Levin

'I have grave misgivings about micro managing, being centralised, having to be involved with everything, see everything and indeed, okay everything - what I call 'small school syndrome.' I prefer delegation, very clear responsibility so the person delegated to has a very clear and distinct remit. He's told to get on with it, he has every support of the head even if it goes wrong. A decision goes wrong, you back him up. However, the caveat is: no surprises. So delegation does not mean abdication.'

## Dulwich - Joe Spence

'My leadership tends to be redemptive. I'm always likely to be someone who wants to give another chance. In the schools I've led, the compliments I accept would be ones, such as in the first school I led, Oakham, and hearing from my deputy: 'Do you know that what I most remember is when you demanded that X or Y be given a second chance, and it proved to be the right decision." That's good and the fighting, as a housemaster, on behalf of one's boys, or as a head, fighting those who say: "It's outrageous! It's got to be treated seriously and don't you realise this! The impact on others if we don't make an example will be…" The apology, without ever creating a culture of over-apologising, is very important. And realising when one has got that wrong.'

## Eton - Tony Little

'Undoubtedly, there will be those who will say, on certain occasions, I've been too soft or been rather roundabout in my approach to particular situations. I've always strongly taken the view that you work with what is there (in terms of staff). And you make the best of what is there. I almost hesitate in what I'm about to say because I don't speak in this kind of way normally. Aware that it's a hostage to fortune, I may sound completely ridiculous. I do think a key part of (leadership) is living the life, and being an example. In other words, I try to be open and decent with people, whatever age they are, whether it's a member of the support staff or a young boy. I give them time and treat them equally in that way. It's a conscious effort to do that, in the hope that,

that in itself becomes a point of reference. Whether it does or doesn't, I couldn't begin to judge.'

Haberdashers' Boys' - Peter Hamilton

'I like to think of myself as a very benign dictator. I listen very carefully and have my own views. We operate as a fairly democratic group, but I won't stand any nonsense from anybody - adults as well as boys. Everybody likes to know exactly where they are. That doesn't mean to say that we're not very sympathetic and understanding, and yes, there are disagreements and differences of opinion, but I won't have anyone throwing tantrums and banging on the table - that applies to boys, staff, parents - that's just not the way to do business. If you can get that instilled very early on, in a funny way it's a release for the boys because they know what they can and can't do. I certainly don't see myself as the sole holder of all wisdom. I see myself in the role of encouraging and supporting, freeing – provided it's done within parameters I like. It's the wrong image, but I see myself as the master puppeteer, placing people in the right place in order to achieve the aims that we've got and being there to support them – rather than: that shalt do that.'

Hampton - Barry Martin

'It's walking the talk, getting out there. I sometimes say, "I'm off, I'm going round the school, see you in twenty minutes." I walk about, into a classroom when there's a Latin lesson or a Chemistry experiment. They don't find this remarkable. They say, "Oh hello, come to see what we're doing, fine." I'm not spying; they're used to it. It's a part of the fabric. It's showing an interest, making them believe and understand that you do care at the micro level, even though you've got a macro job.'

Harrow - Jim Hawkins

'The analogy is being the head of a family where, in crisis, people look to you - in good times, they look to you for what's important. What's the direction, why are we here is absolutely critical. In terms of a well run institution, if there are established values, the head could be away for weeks at a time, and it would keep going, as long as in people's minds, there is still good leadership there. I'm very wary of the vanity side. I find it difficult when I hear heads say "my school this and my school that". They're not our schools, they just aren't. We are stewards of something and there's a real problem if one gets to a stage where it is about the cult of the individual. One has to be, one should be humbled by the nature of the job. You have your few years of hopefully maintaining what's important, and adding something new to the process. But it's never "my school." '

James Allen's Girls' - Marion Gibbs

'If you don't know the name of every girl in the school and something about her, you're not a very good head. You have to model, that's the way all good leadership works. So you are positive, encouraging and you praise. A preferred model of leadership would be someone who's prepared to roll up their sleeves and get involved. I am very happy to get involved. I don't micro-manage, but I am seen around the school: accessibility is important. Modelling the role that you want, the type of headship that you want, your senior leaders have the same under-standing: very good, clear communication, verbally and in writing; being encouraging, never writing a child off, but always being prepared to look for someone's potential, and being prepared to be surprised, and give a second chance.'

KCS Wimbledon - Andrew Halls

'A head should lead and you should be able to predict the things he's likely to believe in because they should be open and shared with his community. You want a head that's got his views and has a track record of decisions. It would be very depressing for staff if they thought they couldn't have an argument with me. That's where strong leadership is not autocratic, because it's open to questioning. In my case, it's open to doubt because I'm always worrying about what I've just done. It can make headship a bit painful to worry constantly, but I probably worry more than people think, partly because I tend to feel a moral imperative, if I see a nettle out in the middle of a field, to go and grasp it. I don't like leaving stuff undone; I sometimes wish I could leave a bit more undone.'

KES Birmingham - John Claughton

'If I were a member of staff, with John Claughton as their headmaster, I'd think: bloody hell, this is a shambles, and my planning, organisation, consultation and methods were all over the shop. In a fireside chat, Eric Anderson told me, "You know what Wellington said when asked in old age whether he had any regrets - I wish I'd praised people more". I was a very demanding, very critical, much too fiery, aggressive teacher and cricket coach. But in thirty seconds, Eric taught me that I should tell kids they played well, as well as tearing strips off them. I changed from being a wild, savage, aggressive coach and teacher, into being much more generous spirited. Staff here may feel I'm whimsical, unclear, not well prepared, not organised enough. I hope they'll forgive me in the end because they know my heart's in the right place.'

KEHS Birmingham - Sarah Evans

'Women fall into two categories: those who lead in a traditional male style, adopt male characteristics, and use the role models of successful men. The other is women (like me) who have a much more challenging job, who want to change our ideas about leadership, by not being prepared to accept the way in which men have led for centuries. Trying to challenge that by showing it's possible to run successful organisations without being all the things that men have traditionally been, and that other qualities are more sustainable, and in the long term, more deep-rooted. Gender is a very black and white thing. I'm not saying no men have those qualities. But it's not ego driven, not driven by competition. It's not about people winning and losing, it's about moving everybody forward together. The idea of status is much less important; communication and people focused work is more important. It's not about me being the wonderful person: everyone's got to recognise that. It's not about me needing to be told how wonderful I am, and surrounding myself with people who tell me that, and me beating everybody else down. It's accepting that people are never all winners or all losers; it's much more of a nuanced world.'

Lady Eleanor Holles - Gillian Low

'The iron fist in the velvet glove, that inner steel every head has got to have. It matters that you're seen, that you exude warmth, and that you have a great deal of resilience. You have to have a seed of it, then you've got to make yourself have it. Because it's a tough job when you're at the top, there is no-one else in the school that does the job. You are alone, even if you're not alone: in the end, the buck stops with you. You've got to be reflective. You can't just bulldoze your way through. People respect you when you say: 'I am going to think again about that'. Having the strength to do that is very important. The whole school body - staff, parents, girls, governors - have got to feel confident in you. People say: 'Well tell me about being a head', and I say, 'The nearest parallel is Glenda Jackson: I'm a politician and I'm an actress, because there's an awful lot of performance in this job.'

Magdalen College School Oxford - Tim Hands

'The first thing you need is an understanding of children. I insist on the word management not being used in any school I am head of. I don't have a senior management team. Childhood and the primacy of the child. You've either got an instinct for the child and seeing things from a child's point of view or you haven't. Management to me is not the running of the school; running of the school is understanding children.'

Manchester Grammar - Chris Ray

'Two things. First, you have to have the capacity to win some key people over to your ways of thinking because you can't do the job on your own - identifying those people who help to move the organisation in the direction that it ought to go. Second, there is the head who knows the name of every pupil in the school, who is always about. The bigger the school, the more difficult that becomes. You can create the illusion of being everywhere, and knowing everybody, if you really care about such things.'

51

## Manchester High - Claire Hewitt

'My approach to leadership is: what do we want to achieve? Vision and values are the heart of it, but I've got to have the people with me, so I lead in a way that needs them to contribute to the vision, so it's shared. But there are times when you've got to make a decision and you can't take everybody with you. At some point, you've got to stand up as a leader and say: I really believe in this, this is what we've got to do, this is where we want to go. You listen to their concerns, you try and find a way that's going to work. That is my leadership: listening, but having the backbone ultimately to make some bold decisions.'

## Merchant Taylors' - Stephen Wright

'Coming up through the profession, one feels one can do the job better than one's superior: it's a touch of arrogance which all heads have. Confidence, and self-belief, which can for some spill over into arrogance - I'd hope not in my case, but it wouldn't be for me to judge. You've got to have a belief in your own ability. I once did a learning programme for serving heads which involved a 360 degree analysis. I came out of this as being didactic. It was a major trigger. I said to my wife, 'I'm not didactic'. She said, 'Yes, you are'. Clearly it's something that one doesn't recognise in oneself, but is an inherent quality for headship.'

## North London Collegiate - Bernice McCabe

'If you value people, people will rise to the level of expectations you have of them. I'm talking about staff as well as pupils. I am ruthless in delegating, not doing anything myself, I am quite serious about that. My team delivers the functions of the school. The curriculum is designed and staffed by my Curriculum Deputy; the pastoral side of the school is run by my Pastoral Deputy; the Bursar is the finance officer, deals with the buildings and the site; my Director of Administration deals with the functional side of the school, everything from the timetable to the calendar; and I've a Director of Franchising, another Deputy, who deals with the external relationships. I conduct, like the conductor of an orchestra.'

'Strong leadership has a role in defining good schools. I like to think that I lead by example, that people know that I care deeply: the pupils are far more important then me. It sounds terribly humble and holier than thou but there are some heads who occasionally seem to be bigger than the institutions, others take a different view. You can't tolerate poor teaching because it compromises children. It's very easy for heads to find excuses, allowing poor teachers to remain in situ for too long. That's not doing children any service, it's not doing colleagues any service because they have to cover for the weak teacher. Schools are for children, not for teachers. If you look at the recent history of education, it's easy to construct an argument that schools partly seem to exist for the benefit of teachers; perhaps children haven't always been at the forefront of some minds. Every new idea has to survive the test: what is the gain for the children? There comes a point where you have to decide either someone has got it, or they haven't. When they haven't, you have to take action.'

Radley - Angus McPhail

'I'm not an autocrat, I've always been fairly open. Some people don't like that because they can't handle debate and feel threatened by it. I don't feel status or position. There is no status really. Realising that you can't know everything, you can't get everything right. I see some people who get into positions where there is a sort of perfectionism and they can't cope with problems. You've got to find ways round that. But you've got to not beat yourself up; someone who beats themselves up is not going to last. Someone who thinks they're going to be friends with everyone is not going to last. Above all, you need a sense of humour.'

Royal Grammar Guildford - Jon Cox

'Many staff feel that they could do the job easily, but they want to be led. One of the first things you have to do as head is to reassure staff that you are someone worth working for. Being very approachable is one of the most important things about leading. A school's ethos directly follows from the ethos, personality and actions of the head. I talk, I laugh a lot, which in this business is important, I share jokes, and I'm hopefully, empathetic, supportive and visible. People will sit down next to me at lunch.'

Royal Grammar Newcastle - Bernard Trafford

'I do things in a consultative, democratic way. I use the word democracy a lot. This is my 23rd year as a head, so it's all the more important that I abandon the status, and that kids and teachers want to talk to me. You must be approachable. I walk around the whole school, between lessons or during lessons, seeing what's going on. However much you preach - please come and talk, I want to hear what people think, I want to do things by consensus - many people won't come through the door. So you have to get out there and catch them at it. Catch them doing things right. It's a nice motto: catching people doing things right.'

St Mary's Calne - Helen Wright

'You've got to keep a childlikeness about you if you're going to be really effective in what you do as a leader. You don't want to disempower people, you want every teacher a leader. That's one of my phrases, every teacher a leader. I've been very influenced by Jim Collins' *Different Levels of Leadership*. I recognise going through the stages myself and I strive to be a Level 5 Leader. The role of the head is one probably that you're required to be a Level 4 Leader some of the time, I'm around the cusp there.'

St Paul's Boys' - Mark Bailey

'It's about building trust and building relationships, being consistent, treating other people exactly how you would wish to be treated yourself, all of the time. Knowing how the common room expects to be consulted, what it wishes and expects to be consulted on - quietly questioning and challenging that, or embracing it. Also promoting the idea that there is no monopoly of good ideas, and no hierarchy of ideas or status. A good idea is a good idea wherever it comes from.'

St Swithun's Winchester - Jane Gandee

'Getting the right people is quite difficult in schools. Some will argue that to get change, you need to get others to buy into it. Some people never buy into change. You can't just say something once, you need to say it five, six, seven times and there'll still be those who say: you don't communicate with us. You do, but they don't always hear. When it is so blindingly obvious that something needs to be changed, you just have to do it. You have to push on regardless because as leader of the school you have to remember that these girls only have chance at their education and if you spend years trying to get everyone to agree, it's too late for them.'

Tonbridge - Tim Haynes

'Simply having the title of headmaster comes with huge baggage from our own childhood. Showing a degree of vulnerability, that you can get things wrong, or you cannot do things perfectly, not pretending that you're perfect, is a strength. Humility and imperfection in leadership is an aspect of its humanity. It's reassuring to know that we are not trying to mirror perfection here. Being a head, being a leader, you need to have an inner confidence. You've got to be unafraid to confront difficult issues, grasp nettles. Weak leadership that brushes things under the carpet, dodges the issues, is never going to be respected. But there are ways and ways of dealing with the difficult things. Unkindness is never necessary.'

Westminster - Stephen Spurr

'Your leaders are leaders chosen in a way they fit the schools. Unless you are a round peg in a round hole, you're not going to be much good for your school. Leaders need to be able to have a range of leadership styles to suit particular situations, or the particular organisation, or the particular stage in the development of that organisation. You've got to have that flexibility. But you've also got to be a round peg in a round hole. For me at Westminster, the headmaster therefore does need to be able to command the respect, needs to be a scholar, but then he or she also needs to have that wider sense, in my view, of what education is about, and to be of some public service or public good.'

## Winchester - Ralph Townsend

'A school needs a leader who can identify a common aspiration, express that aspiration and unite all concerned in the excitement of achieving it. The headmaster of Winchester is expected to stand for intellectual values and high academic standards in the national and international educational debate. The thing that should matter most is the person and the personality. The personality, the confidence, the intuitive qualities, the emotional intelligence that you need to do this job, are more important than whether you have mastered compliance, or not.'

## Withington - Sue Marks

'Schools have a different leadership dynamic from working in the City, where I was used to making decisions and things happened. It was a very hierarchical approach. If I said we do this, then we did it. As headmistress, you lead by gathering the hearts and minds of your colleagues, and bringing them with you. They're perfectly capable of subverting any decision you make, unless they can see why you're doing it: always begin by selling the problem before you try and sell the solution. When difficult issues are not tackled head on in leadership, it's because the balance isn't right between respect for the needs of students and the needs of staff; there tends to be a default towards the staff. We're short-changing students if we don't tackle difficult issues: their needs are paramount, not ours, the school exists for them, not for us.'

## Wycombe Abbey - Cynthia Hall

'When I start off with a change that needs to be made, you have to listen to people because if you try to carry something, with deafened ears and blindly, you may end up trying to foist something on the school which is actually flawed. If you listen to people, you may need to adjust something so that it finally fits the purpose, and if you listen, they're going to be a lot happier in accepting that. They've been given a voice.'

# CHAPTER FIVE

# SELLING THE BRAND

In receipt of tax breaks, independent schools are constituted as charities, but they are run as businesses. Highly competitive businesses. Their financial success rests squarely on the head, acting as chief executive, aided by a bursar, a board of governors, and sometimes, a commercial director. Integral to success is the art of managing the school brand, and its inherent attributes: value, trust, quality, recognition, image and identity. 'The biggest single problem a lot of people have in going on to a headship is that they have no experience of marketing a school,' says McPhail (Radley). 'Fail to fill enough places and nothing is going to get you more down, and also out of the job, probably, quicker than that.'

Effective marketing of schools goes well beyond having the right prospectus, a lustrous website and well-attended open days - selling their premium services has become increasingly sophisticated and competitive. In theory, they are open to all, like the Ritz Hotel; in practice, they have increasingly become an unaffordable luxury to most, like Krug champagne. To develop their role as effective brand managers, today's heads must also be key sales directors for their business. 'All heads have a very important role to play in the recruitment of pupils, even in those famous schools that you would have thought would market themselves quite easily,' says Speirs (RSAcademics). 'We did research asking heads if they agreed with the statement: Even good schools need marketing these days. Only one out of over 200 heads disagreed. There's recognition that a key role of the head is to ensure that their school presents well to the public. It's not a question of bowing to the needs and whims of every parent, it's recognising that parents' wishes need to be respected.'

To illustrate the cost to consumers with comparative data, it is worth looking at how school fees have changed over time, in real terms, compared to incomes and prices. Consider King Edward's School Birmingham (KES), a preeminent boys' day school in the middle of England, and former alma mater of JRR Tolkien. In 1971, the current Chief Master, John Claughton, was studying Classics in the KES sixth form, a dynamic environment, from which fifty-plus boys a year went on to Oxbridge, on a par with St Paul's or Manchester Grammar.

Comparing 1971 incomes with today as a multiple, the average income has increased by 13.5x - from £2000 to £27000. And prices over the same period? The cost of a First Class stamp has increased by 20x, a pint of beer by 29x, a loaf of bread by 11x, a pint of milk by 8.5x, a gallon of petrol by 20x, and an average house by 45x (source: ONS). And KES fees? In 1971, Claughton's education cost £135 a year. Today's annual fees come in at £10,926 - an increase of 81x - six times the increase in average earnings, and nearly twice the increase in house prices. A comparable surge has occurred throughout the independent sector, although day school fees have grown by more, proportionately, than boarding schools, where multiples of 50x are more typical over the same time period.

Independent heads have gone from selling a quality Ford with extras, to a high-end Mercedes, or Rolls Royce. The result is that each child's five to seven year stretch in secondary education, including everything from school kit, overseas trips and individual music tuition, requires total discretionary spending of between £60,000 and £200,000, at current prices. That cost has increased by 68% in the last decade alone - twice the rate of inflation over the same period. Apart from a house purchase, school fees are, for those who can afford it, the largest single investment decision that most people ever make. Although parents naturally regard them as an investment in their children's future - to fulfil their potential - they want, like any investor, to see hard evidence of their anticipated ROI (return on investment): excellent exam results; top drawer university entry numbers; and first class sport, music and drama. At a more refined, intangible level, they seek cultural appreciation, broad intellectual curiosity, self-confidence, a sense of moral and social responsibility, and good manners. Such are the performance indicators of what heads, as fund managers of their school's collective talent, must achieve from their pupil portfolio.

'We have kept our fee increase to an absolute minimum this year as we are mindful that many families may be feeling the impact of the current financial climate,' proclaims the website at Manchester Grammar, the largest independent boys' day school in Britain with some of the lowest fees. So far, the austerity years have not produced a full-blown crisis in independent education. Quietly, dozens of schools have closed, or become academies, but no big names have gone, yet. Although aggregate demand and parental aspiration remain high, the coming decade will be very exacting if the doomsday predictions of Adonis are realised.

Set against a backdrop of continued austerity, plateauing salaries, job insecurity, and unforgiving banks, there will be casualties. More independents will close, others will merge as the weak economy forces more middle-class parents to choose top state schools, especially selective grammars and top-flight academies. For heads, the future success of their businesses will depend upon how they strategically position themselves in the market - locally, nationally and internationally - when considering three key questions: How do you sell your school? How do you rebrand or reposition your service to adjust to changing circumstance? How do you outmanoeuvre the competition?

Before specifically addressing their strategic approaches, it is worth examining how heads evaluate themselves as brand managers. As guardians of their brand, history sits heavily on some shoulders in the shape of a long and distinguished heritage: 'You always feel as a head', says Elliott (the Perse), 'perhaps I feel it even more because I've grown up with the organisation: I'm just one in a long line of custodians. I've got to protect something that is very special, that's nearly 400 years old; nothing should happen to tarnish that.'

Core values define a brand's strengths. At Alleyn's, which has a strong reputation for producing actors and musicians, Savage prefers the more traditional term, ethos, and occasionally, the Greek plural, ethoi, 'We are the repositories of ethoi in our different schools, and that's quite tough.' As the new Alleyn's head, in 2009, he talked to everyone, in search of the ethoi, 'You absorb and you absorb and you absorb. You try and understand what the place is and you talk to the kids. Talking to the head boy and girl was one of the first things I did. You try to understand what it is, and where it's come from.'

How heads communicate what they learn, when shaping and reshaping the brand for external consumption, varies considerably. After twenty years of headship, and just retired at Hampton, Martin suggests, 'When younger, less experienced heads, ask me for advice: how do you market a school? I say: run a good one. If you're going to stand up in front of people and say, "Send your kids to my school," you've got to believe in it. You've got to believe that what you're doing is right, to have thought it through. It becomes obvious in the way you talk, that you've thought it through, what your school's about, what you're doing, and why you're doing it. That exudes. It's the whole package, the person, the message, the theme and the philosophy. It all fits: a logic, a reason, a rational, not short-termist, not league table manipulation, not a gimmick. But "This is the vision for our school and we're gonna do it, and we believe in it." You've got to tie everybody up: staff, governors, kids, parents.'

Immediately adjacent to Hampton is Lady Eleanor Holles, where Low says, 'Our brand is about is excellence in everything - that's why the grounds look so nice - and as well, the results. In this school, and that permeates the support staff too, there is pride - the corridors are beautifully kept. I'm also conscious on the reputation front, and it's very frustrating when there's word on the street that academic girls' schools are just an exam factory, and the girls are under enormous pressure, when I see my bouncy girls loving every minute of the school day. I am conscious that I inherited that concept of excellence. That brand, we've repackaged it, and it's got glossier.'

Hamilton (HABS) believes that external-facing communication of the brand is crucial, 'It's about going out and about: you're part of the big outreach work. The reason my school has got Foundation heads, Fundraising heads, development and advancement, is because it allows you to go and meet with prominent old boys, parents, former parents, friends of the school, to tell the tale of what's happening at school at the moment. Ultimately, yes, I'm asking for their help; but by no means at the beginning. It's about sharing the values of what you're doing, the good work that they may have experienced, either as a parent or when they were a boy here. You should be spending 20% of your time on external-facing stuff. It's not just converting the new, it's reassuring the community in its wider sense.'

So how do you sell your school? 'Don't spend your money on publicity: we don't have a prospectus, for example. Spend it on making your place better, then people will hear about it, and come and see it for themselves,' advises Hands (MCS Oxford). Nevertheless, every independent school has a website. They reach by far the largest number of potential customers, and are, therefore, a key sales tool. Image matters. Trawl through several dozen sites from leading schools, and their individuality can soon be lost. Predictable themes recur: boys playing rugby or cricket; girls playing lacrosse or hockey; boys playing instruments, girls playing instruments; girls and boys playing instruments; boys in the lab, girls in the lab; boys and girls in the lab. And so on. Surrounded by smiling children, heads, sometimes comically ill at ease, also smile. Prospectuses, especially useful for open days and in generating website requests, offer plenty more of the same. Typically over-glossy affairs, their idyllic images would sit comfortably in a Boden catalogue or *Tatler* spread: angelic faces, rosy-cheeked, busily engaged, bathed in adoring sunlight.

More potent, and certainly more revealing, are sites featuring filmed interviews with the head. Invariably, these are aesthetically backdropped by sumptuous, sunlit panoramas of splendid period buildings, rolling fields and outstanding facilities - children, at work and play, adding vibrancy. But hearing the head speak, albeit virtually, imparts so much more than a drab photograph, accompanied by a bland statement. Slick offerings from Benenden, Marlborough and St Swithun's set the right tone, while an excellent pupil voice production showcases Millfield to great effect. Sevenoaks has sound, but no film, while the 'Life at Harrow' effort is disconcertingly mediocre. A video interview with the urbane, thoughtful Hawkins might be preferable. Sporadic lack of adequate site maintenance, leaving obsolete speeches and ossified sports results, reflects badly on the schools concerned, conspicuous to any prospective parent.

'Technology, as part of our communication has become very important. Most people come to Winchester through the website, not a paper prospectus,' says the head, Townsend. The site has no video, instead presenting photos of intense-looking boys, removing books from library shelves, alongside equally studious boys, carrying books between lessons. 'Our website doesn't have drop downs, and things flashing across the screen, because it's just not consistent with the tone of the school. The image you project should be unambiguous. A good school should have limited objectives, state what they are very clearly and deliver them to the highest possible standard. It is a mistake to claim that you can do everything well!' Townsend eschews pictures of boys 'looking socially cool', or of boys covered in mud, wearing rugby shirts - Winchester does not play rugby, preferring their own football variant, Winkies. Rowers also feature. Townsend argues that Winchester is 'in business for brains, not boyness.'

On recently assuming the headship at St Swithun's, Gandee concluded that 'the previous head had not been out marketing enough, she'd been relying too much on word of mouth.' After a complete revamp of the school's marketing efforts, Gandee has been industrious, raising the school profile, writing widely and personally targeting prep schools, 'Prep school heads are very powerful. We've got to get them looking at St Swithun's and understanding what it's about now, because it had a slightly old-fashioned reputation: academic hothouse, doesn't play much sport. A lot of the prep schools we're looking at are co-ed, going up to thirteen, and they play a lot of sport. That's the type of girls they have. We therefore need to show that we play a lot of sport, that we are modern, and we're not just sitting in neat little rows in the classroom, in a rather dusty sort of way.' Gandee leads by example. A keen athlete, she is regularly seen running around the school playing fields.

Heads seek influence in circles that matter. 'Peter (later Lord) Pilkington (former head of King's Canterbury, and later St Paul's) spent a lot of his time dining in the county with people in order to acquire more property for King's and that kind of thing,' says a former colleague. At Westminster, Spurr quips that he is not always having lunch in Downing Street, despite press jokes on the subject. Clegg is an OW.

A bespoke opportunity to ply their wares comes at parents' evenings, organised by feeder prep schools: a key target audience. These occasions commonly consist of a panel, comprising several school heads talking in turn for fifteen minutes, followed by questions from the audience. Attendance can be high, sometimes exceeding 300. It puts heads on their mettle, testing their comparative fluency, wit and intellect, as they endeavour to establish a genial rapport with a large, unknown group. Strong personalities, trenchant opinions, and human understanding make their mark. A standout performer from my (limited, unscientific) experience, hearing twelve speakers on separate evenings, is the excellent Katy Ricks, head of Sevenoaks, a superb advocate for the International Baccalaureate (IB), a Swiss-based qualification that offers a broader, more rounded sixth form curriculum.

Meanwhile, the single-sex vs co-ed debate rages. A key question in the mind of many single sex heads is: for how much longer? Many former boys' schools have gone co-ed in recent years: research shows that girls are keener on studying in a boys' school than boys are in a girls' school. Of the 1,234 educational establishments belonging to the Independent Schools Council, only 21% remain single-sex. Yet, single-sex schools (with a smattering of co-ed sixth forms) still dominate the A level league tables, taking roughly 75% of the top 100 slots. In 2011, the highest placed fully co-ed school, Brighton College, ranked 18th. In 2012, that honour went to Alleyn's, which was 14th.

Alleyn's head, Savage, recalls his experience from a recent panel evening alongside a girls' school head: 'There's a bit of tension on the circuit in the co-ed vs single sex debate. Some of us in co-ed feel that single sex schools can be uncollegiate in some of what they say. You hear assertions that girls will only flourish in an all girls environment, or, if you send a girl to a co-ed school, they won't do science. It tends to be girls' schools more than boys' schools. Boys' schools say that sort of stuff a bit too: co-ed schools tend to be less assertive. I was recently on a panel with a good friend, who runs a girls' school, at a prep school. We didn't have a spat, but she made a point, and I countered it, fairly, firmly, by pointing out that at my school, we sent twelve people to do hard science at Oxbridge last summer: six were boys, and six were girls.'

Going co-ed has been a principal response to the question: how do you rebrand or reposition your service to adjust to changing circumstances? It makes good commercial sense to double potential consumer numbers. 'We haven't had to reposition, we have to strengthen and reassure,' says Hamilton (HABS). 'There are schools in certain phases of development where it's about saying, "No, it was like that then and now it's like this. We're new, we're rebranding, merging or going co-ed. Send your daughter to us." '

A recent high profile example is KCS Wimbledon, as the head, Halls, explains, 'There wasn't evident demand, but I suspected it was out there. The governors liked the idea of being fully co-ed. I didn't think King's would easily turn itself into a fully co-ed school, I thought we should take girls in the sixth form and devised a model that meant it didn't lose any boys. We expanded the sixth form. There's no doubt that taking eighty extra pupils has helped our bottom line. When I arrived, King's was a very solid, successful ship, but the surplus was miniscule. Some basic repairs weren't being done; it had quite a lot of borrowing. By taking eighty extra girls into the sixth form, we've improved the school's finances. It's probably added about a million to the surplus.' Halls concedes, 'It's the same as Westminster, which seems a very successful template.'

This was not the first significant change at King's in recent years. Having adopted the IB, in place of A levels, in 2007 - like dozens of independent schools - King's was named "*Sunday Times* IB School of the Year" in 2012. But in September 2013, the rebranding of King's as an all IB school was reversed as A levels were reintroduced. Halls explains: 'It's not that IB is not good enough, but for some, it was very heavy going. A dyslexic pupil who had to do a language or a pupil who wanted to read Maths at Cambridge were disadvantaged. It became crystal clear that Cambridge doesn't like the IB for Maths; they want pupils that have done lots of high level Maths. IB Maths is just one of six subjects.

'If a boy wanted to read Maths at Cambridge, he probably shouldn't come to King's - I hated having to say that. Then I began to see that Cambridge engineers didn't like the IB either, they want Maths and Further Maths. Some lads found taking six subjects plus two essays a tough call. I began to think: has the national system got its spurs back a bit with the A*? Yes, it has. It was embarrassing for the school: it had made a unique selling point out of the IB.' Halls adds, humbly: 'It would have been easier for me as a man to carry on and pretend IB suited everyone.'

At KES, Claughton was inspired by Halls, 'Going 100% IB at one moment - and no other school of our quality or calibre has got anywhere near doing anything so stupid - in a funny kind of way, it's turned out OK. I won't have to resign. But I spent the last six months here not being able to get out of bed, thinking I could have just made the single biggest mistake this school has made in fifty years.' When Halls reversed his decision on IB, Claughton was despondent, 'That buggered us up completely: him doing that didn't help me, because it sends out the message that IB wasn't the right thing. When we made the move, I was modelling myself on KCS, so just as we were marching up the hill, they were marching back down the hill. It was a complete bugger.'

Change is sometimes a key part of marketing strategy: being different in order to attract attention. Hawkins (Harrow) recalls how Richard Morgan used this tactic at Radley: 'He became well-known for press releases about how Radley was going to be bilingual: he said that half the lessons were going to be taught in French. He had the dons being taught French by language school experts from Oxford. Of course, it fizzled out pretty rapidly. It made a big splash and got Radley talked about. It was perhaps a precursor to the strategy that one can see certain independent schools employing now just to be on speed dial for every education journalist, just get those column inches all the time.'

For Wellington College, there could be no better ambassador than Anthony Seldon, a man who stands on his head during daily yoga sessions. Despite a diminutive stature, his column inches far surpass all other heads - the Seldon brand is never out of print. His home page offers the following: 'Dr Anthony Seldon is a political historian and commentator on British political leadership as well as on education and contemporary Britain. He is also Master (headmaster) of Wellington College.' Slight, dapper and fine-boned, he is described by many as the best-known head in Britain and much-admired, but in some quarters, the admiration is less tangible. One head describes him as being 'like that *Carry On* actor, (the late) Charles Hawtrey.' In discussing *Heads Up* with him, Seldon described himself as follows: 'I am not a leading head. I am very third rate. I am also desperately short of time.' Given that as Master of Wellington (since 2005) and previously head at Brighton College (1997-2005), he has written numerous excellent books, including three biographies of Tony Blair, more than a hundred newspaper articles and has spoken at innumerable conferences, as well as being the automatic default contact for every education journalist, it is unsurprising that he is the best-known head in Britain. Well-entrenched with the Labour hierarchy, he is surely in line for a knighthood or peerage before too long.

I watched Seldon address parents after a prize-giving: an entertaining and amusing speaker, he carried out the task with panache. As an attendee at a recent *Spectator* conference, I found myself bemused by his after lunch talk, which went as follows, 'A switch to you doing something now for the next two minutes. It's going to be the most difficult thing you have done all day: to be present in this room. If anybody has studied mindfulness, then you know this, although your body is here, your minds will have been sloshing around, not consciously, but unconsciously, all over the place. It's not a religion, it's about being yourself. I've got an important point I'm going to make out of this. You don't have to do this. I'm not going to ask you to start smoking joints or anything like that. You're not suddenly going to become a hippy or a left-winger. I risk the danger that you might start becoming more fully yourself, more fully human. Which is what the education process is all about.' Two hundred attendees then meditated briefly under Seldon's instruction.

'I have asked myself: how does Anthony Seldon manage to write a book a year, very good books too, and be a headmaster,' says Marks (Withington). 'When Anthony Seldon got round seminar tables, and was going to have group teaching in the sixth form, there was a massive feature in the press about it. At Burgess Hill, as Head of Sixth Form, in 1978, we taught round seminar tables. I don't remember it being in the press', says Gibbs (JAGS). At Eton, Little expresses gratitude, 'There is a whole other area (in my role), the level of engagement. It's shifted for several reasons. One I have to say, to my quiet pleasure, was the arrival of Anthony Seldon at Wellington. He so loves the media spotlight. If Anthony didn't exist, I would need to create him in some way. It's taken away some of that added pressure. On one level, I'm conscious of the fact that, whether I like it or not, whatever I might say, as headmaster of this place, not only has to reflect as best I can, what is in the best interests of my school, but it's broader than that. Because it does reflect a sector, a way of approaching education. Which is why, on the whole, I choose to say less rather than more. 90% of the invitations to do whatever I decline.'

Rolls Royce never advertises; nor does Eton, except for staff. There is no need: both brands are international bywords for excellence, prestige and quality on every level. Entire books have been devoted to the Eton brand and its history. Yes, there are detractors - political, social and ideological - including a few interviewees for this book, but whatever the strength or purpose of their argument, the Eton brand is stronger than ever, as is demand for places. 'I bear in mind a paragraph from an article in *the Spectator* some while ago,' says Little. 'Someone was taking a potshot at Cameron, and said: "Personally, I blame Eton - not the surprisingly meritocratic school you'd like to have your son to be educated in - but 'Eton', the byword for all social ills." I quite liked that phrase. It came close to summing up my own experience. That is to say: the place I live and work in feels very different to the four-letter word that is sometimes used, as a broad brush term. Although I once said it jokingly, I do think the fact it is a four-letter word is not insignificant, in terms of type printed. It's a punchy way of describing a whole number of things.'

Princes William and Harry both attended Eton, adding to media interest and intrusion, as no doubt will the new Prince George of Cambridge; two other OEs - Cameron and Johnson - are currently prime minister and mayor of London. Handling the media, where his views reflect a whole sector, Little is understandably cautious. 'Being able to influence the outside world isn't even something one can pretend to begin to do. You can dab away at certain little areas, then there will be a tidal wave completely beyond your control. An example is the persistent insistence that George Osborne was at Eton (he was at St Paul's), and therefore the whole government was. I see this in broadsheets, let alone tabloids.'

From the file of 'barking letters' Little receives, he cites the following example: 'One man wrote to accuse me personally, for being responsible for David Cameron, which I rather liked, as though somehow I must have sired him.' Little agrees that when Cameron and Johnson leave office, 'it will ease the pressure.' Not long after this interview, I bumped into Boris en famille, fixing his bike in Dean's Yard outside Westminster School, where his youngest son is a pupil. When I told him what Little had said, he looked momentarily crest-fallen and then beamed, asking me, 'Is your son here too?' Little adds, 'If I've learned anything at all, it's the equanimity you have to learn to develop: if it ain't them, it's going to be somebody else, or there'll be some other issue.'

Mark Bailey took over as High Master of St Paul's from Martin Stephen, another frequent media contributor. Bailey had been a St Paul's governor, while masterminding the merger between Leeds Boys' Grammar, where he was previously head, and Leeds High. The handover was very sudden, as reflected by the announcement from Stephen, posted on the school website. It followed a significant, dramatic falling-out between the head and governors over the school's renovation programme - costing £80m - the largest ever undertaken by any English school. 'Bailey's a true academic,' says another head. 'He is putting the heart back into the school. I've interviewed many people who've studied there, and haven't been very happy. There wasn't much warmth.'

Bailey is circumspect, 'As one of the oldest, and by acclamation, greatest British public schools, there is an expectation: that's part and parcel of my role at St Paul's. My predecessor was outstandingly good at it - conferences, outward facing, commentary in the media, regular response and so on. That was a strength. I've done none of it, although that might be traditionally associated with St Paul's, also with perhaps, a dozen schools, Eton and so on. The press will find their route to the tastiest quote.' Ray (MGS) talks of the rivalry between St Paul's and Westminster. 'I asked Stephen Spurr how we could we improve our GCSE results: what did you do? Spurr told me that he just waved Martin Stephen (then St Paul's head) at his common room. Of course, Martin at St Paul's was saying: Westminster, terrible GCSEs, OK at A levels, just because they've got girls. He was able to use a local rivalry to galvanise his staff.'

Westminster, Wycombe and several others can also justifiably claim widespread demand for their brands, while Winchester is determined that its reputation for academic excellence should never be devalued. Instead, Townsend sees co-ed as a potential route to preserving the brand values, 'When the market necessitates that we have to change in order to keep Winchester an intellectual school, it will be better to have girls.' He also predicts, 'It's highly probable that to stay in business, and to deliver the kind of educational product in which we believe, and at which we are good at delivering, we are going to become more international.' Westminster head Spurr, develops the point: 'Any school like Westminster that feels it can bask in the glory of being preeminent in this country, and talk with some credibility about the danger of perhaps becoming glib about it, quoting OECD statistics that British independent schools are among the best in the world, we're going to have a rude shock if we don't keep our eye on global competition.'

Boarding schools have always catered for those living abroad. Once staple fodder, ex-pat Brits are now a much-diminished minority of the overseas contingent. Today's buying power increasingly comes from newly-moneyed parents, raised in the two former bulwarks of communism: Russia and China. Visit schools and they are very much in evidence. In the capacious entrance hall at Benenden, three Russian families and their daughters sat alongside me awaiting assessment, while the charm and courtesy of Chinese boys at Harrow and Chinese girls at Wycombe could not fail to impress. 'I'm well aware of the fact that parents might come here and they might then go to Harrow and they'll prefer Harrow because they think its more multi-cultural,' says McPhail, head of Radley. 'What would really worry me, is if people came here because we weren't multi-cultural.'

Selling the brand abroad works best in Hong Kong and China. British universities' global marketing efforts have provoked substantial growth in the number of Chinese students choosing the UK as a place to study. This development is echoed not only in boarding schools - over half of Roedean girls are foreign-domiciled and learning Mandarin is mandatory - but also in day schools. 'We get a number of speculative applications from girls in China, who say they'll find a guardian, they're pretty desperate to come to us,' says Hewitt (Manchester High). 'It's about finding the right guardian. It depends how determined the girl is and our fundamental issue - that she is happy - is the most important thing. If a child just goes to somebody who's willing to put them up - sometimes it's a business contact of the parents - that doesn't work for me. So part of our contract is that they've got to be living with somebody we approve of.'

Boarding schools currently average well over 10% in overseas pupil numbers, a figure most heads publicly state is the optimum, although many anticipate it will grow substantially. At several leading independents it already has. A figure nearer 20% is not uncommon, although heads do their best not to advertise the fact: 'If you have too many overseas pupils, it can be self-defeating, the nature of a British education is diluted,' says one head. 'But don't attribute that quote to me,' he adds cautiously. On the Winchester website, there is a prominent dedicated link for those applying specifically from 'Mainland China, Hong Kong, Japan, Korea, Malaysia, Singapore or Thailand.' Interviews are done in Hong Kong.

Another route has been to internationalise the brand directly. You can easily discover the Hermes and Louis Vuitton outlets in Beijing's elite shopping malls. Down the road, you will also find Harrow. The first to export its brand directly overseas, Harrow opened a Bangkok branch in 1998, followed by Harrow International Beijing, in 2005, and Harrow International Hong Kong, in 2012. Others soon followed: Brighton College has franchises in Abu Dhabi (two schools); Dulwich in China (Beijing, Shanghai, Suzhou) and South Korea; Haileybury in Kazakhstan; Repton in Dubai; Marlborough in Malaysia (Iskandar); North London Collegiate in South Korea (Jeju); Sherborne in Qatar; Shrewsbury in Thailand (Bangkok); and Wellington in China (Tianjin). Overseas franchising helps raise additional funds, primarily to support bursaries, while providing a range of cultural and educational links.

'Setting up a school from scratch has its challenges, as we've done in Korea,' says McCabe (NLCS), who has a Director of Franchising. Last year, she made four visits to Jeju. 'We identified that we would be prepared to go into the franchising world for money without any investment ourselves, apart from our time. The fees we charge are high: the Koreans are paying us £30m over fifty years. We made approaches to embassies in London, and then we were approached by a South Korean government delegation. I lead the monitoring, the inspection of the school, I appointed the head, all the staff, trained up a team of staff from this school, so that's great professional development for them, and we've got girls going out there doing gap years. I'm developing our franchise business and we are actively looking for other franchises. Internationalism is the area of development for us now.'

At Abingdon, Lusk offers another perspective, 'Those very sophisticated Hong Kong families that send their children away and shell out £30,000, I don't think that can last. So we're looking at diversifying to other markets as well, but who knows how long we'll keep boarding going, it's full at the moment, but ten years down the track I wouldn't like to say. We're looking to diversify to Thailand, Russia, Spain and Dubai.' On opening in China or India, she says, 'It all looks very good, but it's pretty high risk.' It is the language of an international law firm or multinational company.

London accommodates many big fish in a large pool of talent. John Rae, Westminster head from 1970 to 1986, described the competition for the best and the brightest among London day schools as 'vicious.' The question - how do you outmanoeuvre the competition? - is likely to keep more London heads awake at night than in most places outside the M25. City of London head, Levin, reluctantly agrees, 'A lot of effort and money is expended on attracting the most able boys. Although this is usually denied, all of us know the game and we get on with it. We don't take what each other feels we have to say too seriously, because we know it is very intense. The word 'vicious' is a bit extreme, but it's tough. We know that's the game. Certainly, I know that I can still be very good friends with my competitors, even though they'll be telling me that they're not offering huge amounts of money (for scholarships), when I know jolly well that they are.'

Another head spoke anonymously of the bitter rivalry between two London schools: 'I've seen vicious competitiveness. When I was at school

A, the new head of School B got one of his henchmen to phone up. We had our scholarship interviews on Wednesday. On the Tuesday night, all of our scholars were phoned up by School B, saying they would have a scholarship at School B, if they didn't go to the School A interview. It was shocking. That was vicious, wretched.'

Head up the M1, and the narrative adds a different twist. There has always been a north-south divide. Economists suggest it has been widening further, not narrowing, as money discreetly leaves the north and heads south: an unintended consequence of economic success attracting success. In independent education, as in the wider economy, the overheated south is winning again, increasing its lead over northern cities more vulnerable to rising prices, frozen salaries, the stagnant housing market and public spending cuts. Of the great northern grammar schools, which once competed at the very top, only the Manchester brand still claims to. 'The temptation for any head in a competitive market place when rolls are falling is to lower the bar,' says Ray (Manchester Grammar). 'That's a time bomb that goes off five to seven years down the line.'

We return to Claughton, Chief Master of KES. 'In the south, there is massive demand, because everybody wants it,' he says. On local Birmingham competition, particularly King Edward VI Camp Hill, - a selective state grammar, and like KES, part of Birmingham's King Edward VI Foundation - he is unambiguous: 'Vicious is what it is. I am in a life and death struggle, because if Camp Hill were to get to more of the bright boys - at the moment we are almost exactly neck and neck - then we'd be buggered. Even their Oxbridge offers are as many as ours. When I was a boy here, 40% of us went to Oxbridge. When I came here as head, we were down at twelve boys. This school can't have twelve kids going to Oxford and Cambridge. It's up at eighteen now. But it is vicious. We're all part of the same family, it's like something out of a Greek tragedy: I'm being eaten by my children.'

Claughton turns his attention further north: 'It's more vicious now for Manchester Grammar. I'm a governor there, and MGS and KES have suffered very similar fates. It's got colder, it's got hard to get bright kids in, the grammar schools have improved, people haven't got the money to send their children to independent schools. At least in the south, there may be large sharks swimming around eating, but at least there are lots of other fish to eat: lots of parents with the money to pay. It's vicious 'up north', precisely because it's a much smaller pond: the number of people, in economic hard times, who feel confident that they've got their money for the next seven years because this recession has hit us locally. If someone's not even sure that they've got a job for the next seven years, well Camp Hill's a bloody good school. It's providing almost all the things that we offer - one less thing to worry about. And that's £11,000 after tax I've got spare. So, vicious is what it is, because, at least the pond is big in the south. Here, the pond is becoming a puddle.'

# CHAPTER SIX

# STATELY SHIPS

Every schoolboy used to know that Leon Trotsky was assassinated by a Stalinist agent - with an ice pick, in Mexico. Contemporary politicos recognise Trotsky's legacy as synonymous with the theory and practice of Permanent Revolution, designed to destroy existing bureaucracies. No head would declare themselves as Trotskyist, except perhaps ironically. But for nearly fifty years, a permanent revolution in education has confronted those running Britain's schools as successive governments have proclaimed, pronounced, disclaimed, denounced, reversed, re-engineered, interfered and meddled with the systems, processes and methods by which our children are educated and examined.

This has left heads with the kind of frustration that would cause, in Raymond Chandler's words, "a bishop to kick a hole in a stained-glass window." Navigating a flood of legislation and a torrent of diktats, they have routinely been blown off course by the Department of Education. In this stormy sea, there can be no such thing as a stately ship. Thankfully, examining how this maelstrom has affected British education, leaving schools and their pupils to weather the impact, is beyond the remit of *Heads Up*. Suffice to say, a tome far longer than *War and Peace* is required.

Instead, this chapter will address heads' management of internal, sometimes radical change, required by their schools in order for them to flourish. Wary of the adage "if it ain't broke don't fix it," wise heads recognise that schools are never set in aspic. Permanent revolution may not be the answer, yet they must constantly adapt in order to compete and survive - otherwise, they might end up on the rocks. 'You have to be a transformative person to be a head,' says Wright, formerly in charge of

St Mary's Calne, 'because institutions develop bureaucratic structures; you have to take them apart.'

Even where such change is attempted through building consensus and prolonged negotiation, there can be difficulties. After five years as head of Wycombe, Hall says, 'In my previous school, the change that I made was more radical: it is very heady stuff to feel that you've put a distinctive stamp on a school. Perhaps the more distinguished the school, the less likely it is that you will affect it in quite such a profound way.' She has, however, renegotiated many staff contracts at Wycombe in common with many of the leading boarding schools, as a precursor to more staff living on site.

Hall found it 'quite tricky' asking people to change their practice. 'When I was changing the tutor role, deepening it, that took me about four months of consultation to go through the whole argument for: the benefits to the staff as professionals, the remuneration that we were going to offer for the change of role. As a result, we had staff who understood what they were being asked to do, why they were being asked to do it, and who were in agreement with the change.'

She offers the following advice in implementing change, 'You have to know what you're wanting to do, you have to be able to offer that vision, you have to be able to say: I think this school needs this for these reasons. This is the bit I find tricky because I know there are some heads that are much more ruthless than me. I can't work in any other way, I will always say: I think it is only fair, therefore, for us to offer you this. So, if I am asking people to do more, unless the school is on its knees, and I was having to say we will close unless we do this - and I know some heads who have done that - I have to say to people: because I'm asking you to give more, therefore the school is going to acknowledge that. It can't be great riches, but it is a gesture, an acknowledgement that we're asking you. You have to win the hearts and minds first of all. It's not money. Money is the way of showing people that you are treating them fairly, but you have to win the argument first.'

No ships can be considered more stately than Eton and Harrow, as reflected in their annual Lord's cricket match - a fixture since 1822 - and by their combined provision of twenty-six British prime ministers. Current score: Eton (nineteen), Harrow (seven). But even stately ships face issues that threaten to blow them off course. Most recently, the university application process has been problematic. Harrow head, Hawkins, explains:

'As soon as I arrived I perceived, and this has been backed by others in my team, that our preparation of the boys for university was lacking. These days, university entrance is a highly technical process, the system that Harrow was running is that the twelve housemasters were effectively acting as a separate autonomous head of sixth form for boys in their house. All very bright people who know the boys well. But I said to them: I cannot expect you to understand the difference between the requirements of the admissions tutor for English Literature at Durham as compared to Exeter or Oxford. So we have got to, whilst retaining the strength of having the housemaster's knowledge of the boy, have centralised our collective school knowledge of universities.

'UCAS forms were going out far too late; the left hand just didn't know what the right hand was doing. It's more than just sorting that out, we're aiming to become preeminent in the sheer quality of university preparation starting right from the shells, working through the new head of university. There's a team of people working with the houses and already, just in one year, we've dramatically improved our UCAS related process and our foreign university advice. So early offers and far more desirable Russell Group offers by this point than has been achieved in more recent years, but of course also the selective universities, above all else, are looking for evidence of extraneous reading and ability to research.'

Central to every UCAS application is the personal statement: approximately 500 words in which potential students have the opportunity to sell themselves to their five universities of choice. Eton head Little reflects upon how experience has radically altered his school's approach: 'The pressure for us is university entrance. I will say to boys, certainly fifteen year-olds upwards, I will stand in front of five hundred of them and say: What I'm about to say, I regret saying; in fact, I'm appalled that I'm about to say it. We've just got to face up to the reality: all that you need to get into a top university are paper grades. Nothing else matters in the slightest; don't pretend that it will. Indeed, when you come to do your UCAS statement, we'll help you make sure you don't inadvertently refer to playing football because we know, as a fact, it does you a disservice if you're applying to a top, competitive university. It is bizarre, but it's true. And let's also face up to the fact that from the moment you leave university, the only thing that will matter is everything you ever did outside the classroom. I describe it as Orwellian doublethink. They're bright enough to be able to play that. It's a trade-off and I do think about this. In being direct and honest - saying things, describing things as I see it to them - I'm also introducing them to an adult world of cynicism, which you need to mitigate in other ways.'

Little reached this view based on experience, as he recalls, 'We had a boy, when it really dawned on me we had to change course. He didn't get into Oxford, outstanding mathematician. He was a concert level pianist, and also a first pair tennis player, a real Renaissance figure. When we enquired privately through the Maths Department, checked it out, it was because we'd been stupid enough to talk about the piano-playing and the tennis-playing - on the grounds that he clearly wasn't a serious enough mathematician. And those two activities - piano-playing and tennis-playing - are middle class. So on every level, apparently, we did him a disservice. That's a one-off instance, and I'm making it sound more cynical than it is. We're just very careful. The line is: what a boy says about himself and what we say and what we write about him must be focused on the course he is applying for, and nothing else.'

Spurr (Westminster) adds, 'I think it is absolutely right, what Tony says: by all means talk about your extra curricular or co-curricular activities, but you have to show how it links in to what you've said in the rest of your statement. So you might have wanted to say: your Grade 8 Diploma in the violin is something which therefore shows how you could be really concentrated and passionate about something, or the quartet that you're in, or the orchestra and you're doing some directing of that, shows how you can do team work, you have to tie it back in - in a way which at Princeton doesn't necessarily ask you to make that rather tendentious connection, they just want to see that you are first class at something else beyond the classroom.'

The Eton and Harrow examples can be seen as fine re-adjustment of the rigging compared to the full-blown hurricanes experienced by some. Few heads will ever openly discuss real internal difficulties. Dr Christopher Ray - High Master of Manchester Grammar (MGS) from 2004 to 2013, and 2012-13 chair of the HMC - is an exception. As catalysts and drivers of change in difficult circumstances, heads face their greatest challenge from that most hostile of opponents: the enemy within. Nowhere is this more evident among leading schools than at MGS. 'I want to be up there with Manchester Grammar,' proclaims Felix, the fictional head of Cutlers' Grammar in Alan Bennett's, *the History Boys*. As a former pupil, I must confess personal knowledge of what MGS used to be in the 1970s: an academic powerhouse on a par with St Paul's, Winchester and Westminster, sending seventy or more boys a year to Oxbridge. MGS remains a great success story, with the highest achieving output of any boys' school north of Oxford. But it is not quite what it was. Results and national standing are of a slightly different order: Oxbridge numbers have more than halved.

Ray had monitored what he describes as 'the long slow decline' of MGS, before he became High Master, a position he held for nine years. Others encouraged him to apply. 'I was interviewed for the Marlborough headship. Nick Sampson got it - he had tons of boarding experience. I didn't really try in the second round. Then Martin Stephen let it be known he was leaving MGS', says Ray. 'At the HMC conference - in Dublin, early October - two people came to me: James Miller, my former head at Framlingham, who was then at Royal Grammar Newcastle, and Tony Evans, head of KCS Wimbledon: pincer movement, they pinned me to the wall, and told me that I was applying for Manchester.' Ray then spoke to the appointed headhunters, Spencer Stuart: 'They pulled me in immediately.' The message was clear: the new head would have to effect cultural change.

'I'd been forewarned of some of the problems I would encounter', says Ray. 'Two quotations: "1) The MGS common room is the nearest thing to Old Labour, outside Winchester; 2) I have never encountered such disloyalty to a headmaster from staff in any school I have ever visited." Both were said to me before I decided to go for the job.' He accepted the offer. 'It's difficult to refuse a job like MGS, even when you know what the warts are going to be, because there's going to be a huge amount of joy and pleasure alongside it. Anybody who was trying to deal with the issues at MGS, and was determined to carry it through, and not give up - and this is not arrogance - it would have destroyed most people.'

In implementing change, Ray faced hardline resistance from what he labels 'a vociferous, relatively untalented, but supremely arrogant minority.' He offers the following critique, 'The talent that was brought into the school in the seventies, left for the most part in the eighties, to go on to headships, inspectorate jobs, university careers. What remained were people who liked others to think they were clever. A number of MGS staff would speak for a long time, but say nothing whatsoever, continually pulling into narrow ground of which they were single-minded specialists. Sadly, there were rather too many of those. One member of staff, at the height of any tension between me and others, said: "Well, if the High Master says white, we shall say black; if he says black, we shall say white." '

What they disliked, according to Ray, was management: a resentment about being managed. 'Some staff believed the High Master's job was simply to create the conditions so that they could get on with their jobs. Younger staff, forty down, wanted career opportunities; they didn't see their lives always being at MGS. The school was not in a healthy financial position because the governors had been running it on the smallest fees possible. Regular classroom teachers were paid incredibly well. We were paying, and do pay, London salaries. Low fees, high basic wage bill - that leaves very little room for manoeuvre to create positions of responsibility, beyond heads of departments.'

Ray's first priority was pastoral care. 'Pastorally, the school was at risk', he says. 'The most important thing was to accelerate what Martin Stephen had started, to strengthen the pastoral structures. That had to be accelerated pretty rapidly. I also wanted to appoint the very best person for each job. This is really what caused a major problem: I kept appointing women. The feminisation of MGS, it was called. Not only was I appointing women, I was appointing women to positions of responsibility over men. This core didn't like it. "If you have women in the school, how are they going to run the sports?" they asked. Some very misogynistic attitudes were being played out. Furthermore, the common room renegades told me, "High Master, you are absolutely wrong when you say: if you get things right for the boys, you'll get things right for the school. You should be asking what needs to be done for the staff. If you get things right for the staff, you get things right for the school." The worst thing of all for this group was when a number of their members, in their view, were seduced by the new system, and they took on positions of responsibility. Betrayal. Treason. Things got very bitter.'

Ray worked hard with those who supported him. 'Being on the side of staff demonstrates the inaccuracy and the poverty of those who described things in quite a different way. The MGS common room was passing motions so frequently, it's as if they'd been on senna pod. Generally speaking, they were totally unrepresentative. They saw themselves as having a political role. Not only did you have unions representing the interests and rights of the staff, you also had the common room acting as a trade union. It was a very politicised core. There were members of staff actively working against me, some of them skilfully, some of them ineptly. The ones that are inept, they play into your hands. I had seen the problems at KCS Wimbledon and how Tony Evans dealt with them.'

Ray removed the Second Master. 'Between my appointment and my arrival, without consulting me, Martin Stephen appointed a Second Master. That's not on. I would not have appointed him.' Ray also tried to focus teachers' attention nationally rather than locally: 'I continually referred to the competition as St Paul's, Westminster and Haberdashers. The majority of teachers were talking about how much better MGS was than Bolton, Cheadle and Stockport. They were much more parochial, whereas my focus was national. If MGS wanted to retain its position, it needed to see itself in national terms.'

Soon after arriving, Ray's strategic plan met with the following response at a senior management meeting: "Only failing organisations need strategic plans, High Master." Ray says, 'I send staff to Westminster, to St Paul's, to HABS. They come back absolutely enthusing. They find it hard. I haven't got the critical mass yet.' He enlarged the MGS intake to 1400 boys: 'Expansion of the junior school created bitter hostility: "High Master wants a junior school, so we don't," I was told.'

Ray also had 'huge issues' with the way MGS was marketing itself and set about a positive campaign. He recalls the response to his initiatives was: 'Barricades up. Inaction. Inertia.' In merging the two school libraries, he faced combined resistance from staff and boys. 'There was a two-pronged attack on me. One misfired badly. A student was persuaded to write on behalf of other students to (the children's author) Alan Garner, because the junior library was called the Alan Garner library, saying this new High Master was wrecking his heritage. The interesting thing was that the student had Garner's private email address, which only two members of staff had. So I know exactly who had pushed it. The student was very loyal and said: 'I'm not going to say who told me to do this. But yes, I was advised to do it.' It was a member of staff who's still in the school: one of our people who likes to think himself more intelligent than he is. The other thing that was hugely amusing, was the poster campaign comparing me with Goebbels. Book burning. But Alan Garner had endorsed and supported my plans.'

Ray says that it was 'not just a tough job for me, but a tough job for my wife. Partners of heads in schools can have a lot to deal with. They will be got at. There will be attacks and attempts at humiliation by staff.' His wife suffered. 'Many wives in many other schools are suffering far worse,' he suggests, darkly. Ray concludes, 'I've achieved as much as I can at MGS. Any head going into a school trying to consolidate what has previously been done, is headed for failure.' His successor, Dr Martin Boulton, who started in September 2013, came from Westminster, where he was Under Master (Deputy Head) with a reputation as a tough disciplinarian. Boulton should understand how to get the best out of MGS boys: he was educated there.

Making changes can mean making unpopular decisions. But an unpopular decision is not always a bad decision. One man who knows how it feels to make unpopular decisions in order to change direction is Andrew Halls, the current head of KCS Wimbledon. He remembers the frosty February morning in 1972, when Arthur Scargill's flying pickets successfully descended on Saltley Coking Works, for what became known as the Battle of Saltley Gate: his father was then head of Saltley Grammar, Birmingham. Scargill's unlikely triumph was the turning point in militant strikes over national pay restraint: within two months, Heath's government was defeated.

In 1998, when Halls sailed into Magdalen College School Oxford (MCS) as the new Master (head), he knew he had a rather different battle on his hands. 'Magdalen is a great school and was a great school. I picked it up at a time when, there's no real doubt, it was in difficulty. It was like a fifties grammar school that had just gone to seed, with pretensions of being posh, partly because of its name and location,' he says. But in looking back on his decade at MCS his feelings are decidedly mixed. 'I partly bear the scars of that school,' he confides. Performance had deteriorated. MCS was 170th in the league table - a once academic school, no longer in the fast lane. Halls recalls, 'Magdalen was struggling, with fair exam results, but very poor buildings and no money. Anyone in Oxford at the time would have known it had quite a difficult common room. I learnt quite quickly at Magdalen, which was a very difficult school initially, because it was so antagonistic to management. Some of the staff were utterly poisonous and malevolent. They found me very hard.'

Halls advanced with all guns blazing. 'I probably went too hard in on certain things, but for me, the issues that needed to be dealt with were: an unconstructive common room, under-achieving pupils, a very poor surplus, and low numbers. There was quite a lot of replacement pretty quickly. To be fair, I appointed an excellent usher, i.e. a sole deputy, who joined me in my second year: Richard Cairns, now head of Brighton College. He is an exceptional man; he was only 32, but very tough and I needed that. To be fair, and I should instantly be fair, there were plenty of excellent teachers and people could see things were wrong. Magdalen was stuck in a time warp, so merely having staff appraisal was a shock to the system. For the head to be doing every appraisal himself, which I would never do now, I don't know how I did it frankly, even with a smallish common room. Appraisals I just brought in as a fact. I did every one myself because it meant I went in to see people teach and I talked to them about their aims, which some didn't approve of. They weren't evil. There were one or two very malevolent members of staff, but they weren't, by and large, evil. These were heads of departments. They just took it upon themselves to hurt: they were pretty awful to my two predecessors. One of the most notorious of them, not in my time, but with my predecessor, stood up and humiliated him in a staff meeting. It was really nasty.'

'When I said, "Look, I've got complaints from parents," or "These boys have been to see me in a delegation," I'm sure I was sometimes rude. But I tried to be courteous, yet firm. It's interesting that if a colleague feels that the head has some reason, in his own mind, for being disillusioned with that colleague's progress they sometimes will just move on. Quite a lot of people took early retirement. Once people saw that what I was doing was working, and certainly the local parents liked it and the number of applicants grew, the story just kept getting better. The good thing was that Magdalen changed gear extremely rapidly. By and large, the staff came on side with me. After five or six years, the great majority of them were very supportive.'

Halls got rid of those who were not up to scratch. 'He boasted to me about sacking 42% of the staff in three years,' says a rival. 'That was very much his style. Shake the place up. He was very hard.' Another comments: 'Andrew was an absolutely tremendous hirer and firer and getting rid of people at the end of their first year. A very driven man.' But for Halls, evidence that his approach worked lies in the numbers. 'We had 510 boys, when I got there; by the time I left; it was 700. The IQ had gone up from an average of 118 to 131'. In the year he moved to KCS Wimbledon, 2008, MCS was number one in the league tables. He may have been a tough, abrasive commander, but Halls was widely noticed for the right reasons. A fellow head gets to the heart of his achievement: 'Of all the heads of our generation, Andrew Halls is the only one who has really, really changed the academic profile of a school. Many people go in and say: I will raise it by this, that and the other. They don't accomplish it, but Andrew did, he altered that school completely.'

# CHAPTER SEVEN

# STAFF: GETTING THE BEST

We know them when we see them, or are fortunate enough to be taught by them: we never forget a good teacher. One of my A level English masters was Nick Rawson, a published poet and a close friend of Samuel Beckett. On 23rd February 1977, Ash Wednesday, he strode into the classroom, opened a book, and announced, 'Gentlemen, *Ash Wednesday* by TS Eliot.' Rawson proceeded to declaim the poem beautifully. The recital complete, he smiled, turning dramatically on his heel and exited without another word. End of lesson. No comment, no analysis, no discussion. Yet his performance worked. It got us talking. He made us think. By turns anarchic and eccentric, he devoted other lessons to his experiences as a German psychiatric hospital orderly, his work as a farm-hand in Argentina, his enduring friendship with Beckett, and his wife's collection of carved stone phalluses, tidily deposited in a kitchen drawer. Heady stuff for a fifteen-year-old schoolboy. Smoking a pipe throughout, he broke nearly every rule in the book, but he was also our John Keating, firing imaginations, inspiring a love of literature and of learning, just like the Robin Williams character in *Dead Poets Society*.

What therefore is a good teacher? Answers to the question, never definitive, arrive heavily laden with positive abstracts: passionate, inspirational, innovative. Rawson personified these adjectives, forging a durable impression in the classroom. To assess their staff, heads use carefully calibrated criteria, evaluating them individually and collectively through micromanagement of performance by numbers: turnover, retention rate, diversity, remuneration, average age, average duration, test scores and exam results. But in appointing, the best heads look for much more than those who simply teach to the test to get the grades, instead seeking out Rawsons and Keatings whose carpe diem philosophy enables pupils to think for themselves.

Or at least they should in an ideal world. Trafford (RGS Newcastle) speaks for many of his counterparts in other schools by describing teachers in his real world experience as 'a fascinating, charming, entertaining, contradictory, frustrating group of people.' So what do they seek in interview? Marks (Withington) says, 'The first thing I look for is a real enjoyment in being in the company of children and young people. When you go to other schools, and you walk around, you sometimes can't help but wonder why some of these people went into this profession when they manifestly don't like children.' She offers one simple mantra by way of advice: "If in doubt, don't appoint."

Perse head Elliott recalls, 'I always remember the first question I got asked in a job for teaching, "Well, we see Mr Elliott that you like Geography; you've got your first-class degree. Do you like boys?" And I was thinking, "Is this an early sort of prototype safer recruitment question? What am I supposed to say?" But it was done by a very old world schoolmaster and the key thing was, "Look, you've got to like working with children. You've got to be able to think like a child, you've got to engage with children, you've got to be able to have that sparkle in the eye that really excites them." 'Gibbs (JAGS) says, 'The biggest secret of good headship is to appoint really good staff.' Empathy is at the heart of what she seeks: 'I need staff who actually care about children and their learning,' she explains. 'That is the most important thing. You can be the best, most well-informed person in the world, but if all you're going to do is perform your subject, and not take an interest in how it's being received, then no.' Gibbs' sentiments are further echoed by Oulton (Benenden): 'I look for warmth, for how much they care and mind about the pupils. If you take as read the teaching and learning skills, which obviously you test extensively at interview through all sorts of questions, beyond that, I'm looking for people who enjoy the company of teenagers, know how to bring out the best in teenagers, and all the accompanying qualities.'

Human understanding underpins the art of successful recruitment, as Hawkins (Harrow) confirms, 'I've developed the experience and the confidence sometimes to say no, when the head of subject and others, all they can see is: gosh, they're brilliant at this, or brilliant and that. But you can just detect something that isn't right, usually in terms of character and ethos. I'm looking at why are they doing the job, what motivates them, because that's going to be important, when they're under pressure, when it comes to it, what is driving the work they're doing. Wanting the best for the pupils, having a holistic view of education, seeing, wanting to develop the right sort of character and enquiry, and having an attitude towards scholarship, which is absolutely right. Also, that they are, at least, sympathetic with the school's foundational ethos.'

For many schools, finding the right person is not straightforward as Wright (Merchant Taylors) explains from his past experience running a state grammar: 'Here, it's generally easy, but in my previous school, recruitment was very difficult: we just could not get the best people. You just couldn't find teachers sometimes. Looking for a Maths person, having no applicants, I didn't go as far as going into Tesco with a soap board saying, 'Come and teach with us', as some heads have done, and remarkably, had success. There was somebody called Adebayo Big Boy, whom they were tempted to interview just out of interest, but didn't.'

At KES Birmingham, 'recruiting good staff is not easy,' says Claughton. 'It's easier in London, and in the great boarding schools. I'm not recruiting the kind of school masters I would like here, who are going to provide other things, particularly sport. I'm really struggling in that regard. I can only recruit what comes to me.' He is brutally honest in admitting mistakes. 'I've made some really bad calls because I haven't thought hard enough. I've found myself bounced into bad decisions. With people who are weak and not doing a good enough job, I remain absolutely useless and although on occasions, I have finally got rid of people who are useless, my biggest mistakes have been - it's taken three years to do it. I've been scared of the consequences, and when it's happened, it's been ok. You think to yourself: why didn't I just get on with it three or four years ago.'

While some independent schools face acute problems, the reputation of the leading players is usually a sufficient draw - an advertisement in *the Times Education Supplement*. other trade press, or using headhunters produces a good selection of suitably qualified candidates for most positions. Choosing the correct fit for their school is another matter. 'Appointments is the biggest area in which you can make mistakes,' says Hands (MCS Oxford). 'I spend a lot of time interviewing and I would never allow an appointment to be made here without me being personally involved. I would never allow someone to come in to the College, whom I did not believe was the equal of the person leaving it. So, I'm a great believer in the second advert, if it's needed,' says Spence (Dulwich). The Gibbs secret rests not just in appointing the right candidate on the day of interview, but for the long term.

McPhail (Radley) highlights a much-improved environment for recruitment, 'There's a higher status in teaching than there was, the money is better. Clearly in a place like this, you've got a package, plus accommodation. There is increasingly - maybe it's just amongst the people we meet - a focus on quality of life, which is quite reassuring. The thing that attracts many people coming for interviews is that they immediately see there's a lot of young staff, a buzz about the place. Again, it's creating a virtuous circle. We're well placed, near Oxford, not far from London. You get ambitious people who've got time to give.' Hall (Wycombe) adds, 'Radley is a wonderful example of community life. Whenever I went over to Radley for meetings, we'd go up into the common room and staff were sitting around. All the family houses there. You just felt that people were living there, living the education that they were providing, and the pupils living amongst them.'

So what does it take to become an Eton beak? Little explains: 'There are a number of things that become self-selectors on the teaching staff here. The fact that you have to live in school accommodation is actually a very good deal. But nonetheless, there is no choice about it. You're coming in to a community. You wear funny clothes. So, even from the start, there are plenty of teachers, who would baulk at that straightaway. You've got to be prepared to sign in to what we are as an institution. I'm always looking for new avenues to explore increasing breadth of access to the school. The qualities I look for in boys coming here are in three areas: First, any boy coming here must at least be academically comfortable - we're an academically selective school; second, he must have something else to bring to the party - not really fussed what it is, football, clarinet, something, because it becomes something to share, it's a language of exchange, coupled with the fact this is part of the point of being in a place like this; the third thing, as best we can judge it, is that he has the resilience to cope with being in a residential school, full time, all male, which is therefore, by definition, fairly competitive. Take two steps back from that, it's not so very different when it comes to the staff, in truth. Except I expect a rather higher level academically than I would from the boys.'

Heads often canvass opinions widely before appointment. Marks (Withington) ensures that potential recruits go on a school tour with an existing member of staff to meet the girls, 'Often the most telling piece of information comes from the person who did the tour, who said: "They didn't engage in eye contact with a student all the way round, or they didn't have a question to ask." ' Retiring Hampton head, Martin, goes further, 'I always ask the front office staff what they think of people because they can behave like angels in here and gangsters when they're talking to the support staff. Were they rude? How did they treat you? Did they talk down to you? We get boys to show them round and I always get feedback - did they show an interest in you? what did they ask you? The boys here are pretty astute, and they'll give you a view, whether that person was interested in them or not. We don't want anybody who is shown round by a couple of senior prefects and just grunts at them. I would expect them if they're going to be a good teacher to show an interest, to ask what they're doing, what their ambitions are. It's extraordinary how people don't realise that all that is part of the selection process - it's so important, the soft stuff.'

McPhail (Radley) says, 'What are we looking for? We're looking for the fact that they either can teach, or have the potential to teach. We appoint quite a lot of people who haven't taught. When we're looking at the potential to teach, in one sense, as much as anything, you're looking at the ability to give a performance - there's a strong overlap between the best teachers and actors to some extent in classrooms.'

Other heads stress different priorities. 'I'm looking for people who are inspirational, because my girls relate well to personalities. So it's got to be somebody who has personality. We also want variety. It's an important life lesson, because we have to relate to lots of different sorts of people. So quirkiness, yes.' Hewitt (Manchester High).

'Passion about their subject is more important than anything and much underrated in teaching. Then the ability to communicate, which involves the ability to establish a good relationship with young people' says McCabe (NLCS). 'I look for reason, the capacity to reason. I prefer reason to faith. I like people to have reason and to be able to think independently, to weigh up alternatives,' suggests Levin (CLBS). 'I want people who are comfortable to commit well beyond the classroom. The staff is overwhelmingly male - I'd love in many ways to appoint more female teachers, but very often the best teacher is a male,' says Haynes (Tonbridge). 'Most of the best appointments I make seem to be of bright young women,' says Spence (Dulwich), also an all boys' school. 'You're not going to appoint anybody whom you wouldn't want to teach your son or your daughter,' suggests Hamilton (HABS). 'That's really what it's about, appointing: do I want this man or this woman standing in front of my kids. Because if the answer to that is yes, then you're not going to worry too much.'

These automatic responses to the question differ according to the respective demands of each school and of those running them. Since people tend to recruit in their own image, or some partial reflection of it, then it is no surprise that appointment criteria can vary so much. So do the heads themselves. Compare these two responses from different heads to the question of staff recruitment:

School One

'I want well-balanced human beings in my staff. Yes, of course, I want their academic qualifications. I want the knowledge of the subject. I want people who can teach well, that's obvious. I also want people who are fun to be around, will make the staff room a good place to be, who are positive people - not whingers - who are going to enhance life. It's very interesting when you're interviewing, when you ask people about their current job, because the worst thing anyone can do is start being negative: "Well I'm looking for another job because I don't get on with the Head of Department." You think: well that's exactly how you're going to be if you come here. We are looking for people who will contribute to the wider life of the school and it doesn't matter if they're a Maths teacher, but they're happy to run debating club, that's brilliant.

It's the willingness to go on trips. If the History Department doesn't have enough staff to run the trip, oh well, someone else will come along, or run the club and just make sure that the girls have every opportunity that they can. It's just having that broader of view of what it is to be a teacher. You're always looking for passion for the subject, because that's got to be there. But they've got to want to be a teacher, and you want people who can take the normal stresses. Teaching's a funny old job because you have these very intense terms, then the holidays. Terms can get very intense. The last couple of weeks before Christmas are not good, because you've got reports, carol services, this, that and the other. Everyone's tired. But it's about just having that balance to deal with that, and being, just interesting people.'

School Two

'We talk about the primacy of the classroom. So one needs to be a subject specialist and have the ability to inspire the pupil in the classroom. I always start from that. If you then decide, that actually the school needs to develop its pastoral care and social welfare, you need to explain to your teachers who are brilliant subject specialists, that the act of teaching has a great pastoral dimension to it as well, because how do you develop the right sort of rapport which is going to transmit the spark from the teacher to the pupil? Well you do it in more than just the subject. You are engaging that young person and helping him or her develop in social confidence and confidence as a young person in general. So you have to have a strong pastoral element.

'Then if you think: right, well in addition to love of the subject, being able to be confident through that pastoral care in the class, so that you can respond confidently to questions and debate with others, so you develop a kind of Socratic cut and thrust and that's enjoyable in the classroom. You then decide that you want your privileged young men and women, highly intelligent, to be able eventually to use their education for the public good. Then you would want to be able also to talk to your members of staff or choose members of staff, who share that view of education as well, and therefore might be interested in getting involved in what we call 'civic engagement' - a very serious engagement with the local community, and the raising of social responsibility and social consequence. So, start with the primacy of the classroom and then build out from that in a coherent way. That is always the approach that I take.

'If you start from the academic point, you are looking for top academics who are interested in teaching young people, and you are providing an environment of scholarship, where you are encouraging both pupils and their parents to look upon learning as something of intrinsic value in itself, and not instrumentalist in necessarily thinking about careers or the two things can be combined. Or you can convince pupils and parents that it's not instrumentalist in the way of just teaching to the test. If you can create that kind of environment and belief in your wider community, parents, pupils and teachers, then in my view, you are always going to be in the fortunate position to attract men and women of calibre. Not necessarily huge quantities, but the right calibre.'

Both responses are from prominent London day schools. The first is from Gillian Low, head of Lady Eleanor Holles; the second is Westminster head, Stephen Spurr. Yet they present distinctly different views. It is not that Low does not adopt the Westminster approach - she lived in the school's boarding house for several years when her former husband was a Westminster Housemaster - it is simply that she articulates a different set of priorities.

The attractions of independent schools are obvious. Money, reputation, prestige, bright pupils, bright colleagues, and a congenial working environment help them get the best staff. Westminster does so, in part, by paying the highest salaries, as reflected in their fees - up to a third more than comparable London day schools. Many boarding schools - Winchester, Eton, Radley and Benenden - provide first-rate accommodation on site, in a wonderfully attractive location. Recruitment at Tonbridge, another similarly attractive boarding school is equally rigorous, as Haynes outlines, 'The process that we go through, when we recruit, is pretty thorough. They have interviews with me and my deputy together, with the Director of Studies and the Director of Teaching and Learning together with the Head of Department. They teach a lesson, observed by the Head of Department, and there is feedback from the boys on that lesson as well. They have lunch with the boys in a house, and there is feedback from the boys on that lunch.'

Townsend (Winchester) presents something of the Rawson/Keating perspective in his requirements, 'Most English schools, and particularly boarding schools, are really sports clubs, with some other things on the side. They like to have good exam results, music and drama, but really, the beating heart, is sport, one way or another. That is not the case here; this is a genuinely intellectual place, where the priority of the teachers is their love of their subject; their delight is in infecting the boys with their love of their subject. That is what is special about Winchester. It's OK to be brainy here, geeky even, and there is a lot of affection around the place. There's no other school quite like it.'

Diana Ellis, headhunter for many headships, delivers the following critique: 'Some heads recently have completely rewritten the salary contracts of all their staff, which has been very difficult, because they maintained that a lot of the bigger boarding schools, most staff have accommodation, it's so cushy. They never move on, they're not developed, they stay in one place. They perhaps move to head of department, then they go on and do a stint as a housemaster and they do perhaps a second stint. Then, they are there, sitting in the common room a few years off retirement, the chair they always sit in, and they don't want change. It's very hard for a young head coming in and dealing with some of these people and perhaps they've got a First from Cambridge, perhaps the young head hasn't.'

In common with most schools, many Harrow beaks have been there for twenty to thirty years, since the day they left university. Hawkins says, 'Harrow is a difficult place to leave. It's great if you've got a spine in the school of people that know the school, and love it, and have been here for a long period and can refer to your three predecessors as heads.' At City of London Girls', Vernon takes a pragmatic view. 'I would rather appoint good people, and get the best of them for however many years, and then encourage them to move on. What I don't want to do is be seen as a backwater, where no one ever grows and flourishes and moves on.'

But old hands can present problems. 'The worst part is mediocre staff,' says Gandee at St Swithun's, 'because they're not bad enough to get complaints and yet you just don't want them in your school, but it's so hard to change them. They do a bit of teaching, they do some marking, but the girls don't come out thinking that was a really good lesson, and that's so difficult to deal with. If they're only forty-five and they've got children in school in the town, a partner who works locally, they're never going to go anywhere, they've got no ambition. For me just annoying. And parental complaints which are fully justified because a member of staff just hasn't done her job properly, she hasn't got the marking back, that type of thing, it's just so avoidable, it really, really irritates me.'

Martin (Hampton) recalls the following episode, 'When I took up my first headship, the bursar said to me, "Well, you can't sack a teacher, you know, they are a protected species." Firing can be just as important as hiring in business, quickly dispatching under-performers and replacing them with fresh blood. Most schools are less ruthless. David Smellie is Head of the Employment Team and Schools Group at Farrer & Co, which advises more than 100 independent schools, often on child protection issues involving a member of staff. 'They'll almost invariably get on the phone to us saying: crisis, we need to deal with it,' says Smellie. 'Whereas, if it's a performance issue, quite often they will seek to deal with it themselves.' But increasingly, he advises on disputes for 'simple underperformance: a teacher who is not teaching to the requisite standard, the lessons are boring, the pupils are worried that with the quality of teaching, they're not going to get good enough grades. There's a pattern of sane and rational parents expressing concerns.' In these circumstances, schools' reluctance to reach for lawyers can exacerbate the problem, as Smellie explains, 'It's quite easy to focus on the cost of dismissal, what schools often don't quantify as much is the cost of inaction.'

He paints the following scenario, 'The soft damage which can happen, once you have one, you start having three, then five, then you have fifteen underperforming teachers, so there's a huge cost of inaction. There is, of course, also a cost of going through a performance process, because, generally speaking, to do it properly, you probably need to spend the better part of an academic year going through a full performance process with someone. Quite often the member of staff might end up going ill, or they file a grievance because they think the management of them has become akin to bullying. And at the end of the year's performance management, you still end up with a blasted tribunal.'

Judging each case on its merits, Smellie cautions, 'Schools have got to pick their battles and choose which cases to fight and which to settle carefully. It's dangerous to routinely get into the habit of settling lots of cases. So you do need to fight some: where you've got a member of staff who hasn't behaved properly, or who's performed badly and you've followed a decent procedure, even if you stand a chance of losing, sometimes those are the cases which are worth fighting. Equally, employment tribunals are notoriously unpredictable fora for justice, you just don't know what's going to happen until you get there. And it's an expensive process. So if an amicable resolution can be found, and an amicable one will tend to be one which leaves no one happy - the employee's unhappy because they haven't got as much as they wanted, the school's unhappy because they've paid more than they wanted - but it's almost invariably better for all concerned in those circumstances, as long as the schools aren't doing that routinely.'

Once appointed, the majority of staff are not problematic. The head's role, according to Levin (CLBS), can be summarised as follows: 'You invest huge effort in making the appropriate, correct appointments, then you give them the power and the authority to get on with the job. You ostentatiously back them at every turn so it's very clear to all the constituencies of the school that this chap or chapette has your total confidence and your backing and that that person is making the decisions.'

# CHAPTER EIGHT

# HAPPY STAFF

'The principal task of a head is to look after the staff, teaching and nonteaching. If you fail in that, you jeopardise the welfare of the pupils and the whole school.' The words of Colin Diggory, former Alleyn's head. While some may instinctively oppose reductive statements on principle, it is hard to oppose Diggory. The head's interaction with the common room and their relationships with individual staff are of paramount importance. Working with the Senior Management Team (SMT), heads develop close relationships with their deputies, heads of department and heads of year. Getting the best from them, encouraging them to implement change, and maintaining common room morale tests a head's powers of persuasion and management skills. Balancing professional distance with avuncular familiarity, attitudes are critical. So is recognising and rewarding talent, even if heads can't always deliver. While bad heads may hold back talented, ambitious staff from moving on to better opportunities elsewhere, the good head not only lets go, but encourages it.

'The power of the common room is very strong in boys' schools,' says McCabe (NLCS). And probably in girls' schools too. Go into any common room and ask the staff about their head, and there will be three distinct factions. First, you find the loyalists. They typically like and support what the head is doing, believe him or her to be fair in their approach, providing good leadership and making sound decisions. Next come the indifferents. Ambivalent or diffident by nature, voicing neither criticism nor praise, they get on with the job of teaching, comply with instructions and make few if any complaints. Finally, there are the malcontents. Irrespective of merit, they dislike change. Decisions are disparaged or derided, and however unjustified, they articulate their dark displeasure quite vociferously, as evidenced by Ray's account of Manchester Grammar. Usually the smallest faction, they often make an impact disproportionate to their size because they shout loudest as they actively seek recruits to their cause. Assumed in all of the above is that honest answers are given to the question: what do you think of the head? Like plotters in the court of a Tudor monarch, the reality is that some malcontents secretly masquerade as loyalists. What they say and what they think may be quite different.

Staff can and do change sides. Make bad or unpopular decisions and a loyalist or indifferent may soon become a malcontent. Conversely, make what are perceived to be consistently good decisions and indifferents, even malcontents, might transfer to the loyalist camp. When applying the Diggory dictum, heads do not purposefully set out to create blind loyalists - no head wants to be surrounded, like a Tudor king, by unthinking sycophants, nor do they want grumbling servility achieved through fear. Instead, most try and build broad consensus, and where possible, prefer compromise to confrontation. Heads therefore focus their energies, not in courting popularity, but in getting things done while trying to minimise the siren voices by addressing individual concerns through dialogue. At least, that's what the textbooks say they should do.

Day-to-day, heads work very closely with their SMT: it is their primary window into the common room to see the impact of wider decision-making. 'Relations with staff need the most sensitive and careful handling', says Levin (CLBS). Great care is needed in explaining things,' according to Bailey (St Paul's), 'because different words are interpreted differently by different people. There are times when staff get tired towards the end of term and minor issues suddenly become major ones; you have to manage that storm whilst keeping your own perspective.' He recommends consistency. 'Treat others exactly how you would wish to be treated yourself. People make their own mind up. You need to build trust with the SMT because they are your eyes and ears and antennae in the Common Room.' Managing staff is 'like herding cats,' he concludes.

Teachers certainly constitute a highly intelligent and often opinionated group - to influence their thinking requires strong powers of persuasion and unremitting effort. Good heads know how. The current Alleyn's head, Savage, develops Diggory's thinking, 'The old adage is 'value the staff and love the kids', and there's a lot of truth in it. If you have an undervalued or demoralised staff, teaching and support, then the atmosphere of the community will be hit and the kids will suffer. You want staff going into classrooms feeling stimulated, content, well looked after and valued. Then they're absolutely on their game and the kids feed off it. You also want gardeners, cleaners, catering staff and admin people, who really enjoy being part of a community.' In coming as a new head to deal with an established common room, Cox (RGS Guildford) says the following, 'Staff were deeply suspicious when I arrived. There's a great quote: "Taking on a headship is like shagging an elephant. If you're successful, you don't know about it for two years; if you're not successful, you'll get shat on from a great height very early on." There is fear, and staff are naturally suspicious, because staff here are unbelievably bright, sharp and quick, and they have to be confident in you as a leader.'

Boarding schools present a different challenge. 'Boarding wasn't in my background at all, so to come and run a full boarding school, I knew that I had a lot to learn,' says Hall (Wycombe). 'I was immediately very deferential to all the residential and boarding staff, and set myself to learn from them what the priorities are in boarding. What I gradually picked up was that there is quite a divide between the residential way of looking at the school and the ordinary teacher without residential responsibilities.'

In his Eton SMT, and among his beaks, Little recognises 'various different types, not necessarily people I would choose to go on holiday with. I can think of a head of another well-known school who appointed the deputy as someone he liked, someone he'd have a drink with, because life's tough enough. And I want a mate. I want a chum. I've never taken that view. I've some vague idea of my own many weaknesses and omissions. The people I have round me need to be able to plug those gaps. My current deputy, for example, is genuinely good at all the policies and structures stuff. He loves it. He's really good at it. It's the kind of thing I'm not terribly good at.' Little believes that treating all staff fairly and with decency is integral to his approach, 'It's who you are, how you live, how you deal with people, must, at some level, percolate through, or influence the atmosphere or the tone of the school. I try to encourage people with good ideas.'

Marks (Withington) came into teaching in girls' day schools after thirteen years heavyweight experience as a senior corporate financier. 'I am more collegiate in my management style than most heads that I've met and certainly heads that I know well,' says Marks. 'I was used to delegated authority in the City, and the concept isn't always well embedded in schools. The heads often are, or were, very powerful people who didn't necessarily want control to be delegated to anybody else. My expectations of middle management, of the heads of department and heads of year, carry a fairly high degree of delegated authority for their own budgets, for appraisal of their own staff. That has been quite a steep learning curve for people who've worked with me. You might have thought that the reverse applied, that in the City, when you said, "Do it", people just did. But it's not the case. We always had collective decision-making. So I've found that it's been necessary to empower, awful jargon word, but empower people in the SMT and people in middle management, to take more responsibility for their own areas, which they've enjoyed ultimately. But they've found quite frightening to start with in many cases.'

The confidence of experienced heads can be measured by the degree of power they give to others: 'I am a much better delegator now than I was when I started,' says Gibbs (JAGS). 'I still know what's going on, and I see the notes that come through. Staff will talk to me and come to me, but I trust implicitly my senior team and my deputy, and there will be things that I only hear about afterwards, if that's appropriate, and I trust them completely. I delegate down to my SMT and we have a lot of confidence in our heads of departments to run them.' Loyalty is crucial, says Savage at Alleyn's, 'I would be pretty unhappy if any of my SMT publicly questioned what we had collectively decided, and they don't. You must be loyal to the head and back him. You can be a critical friend in private; good deputies are and should be - but you, absolutely, publicly back him.'

To develop new systems or ideas 'you need consensus but you can't please all the people all the time,' says Hewitt (Manchester High). 'I put down ground rules: open door policy, call me Claire. But really getting to know staff, letting them get to know a little bit about me, so that they know what I'm about, and it's really in everything you do, you are conveying who you are'. Hall (Wycombe) is similarly open, 'Have I been blown off course? Hopefully, such blowing off course would happen within the confines of this office with one of my senior managers saying to me: you must be joking. I like to run a very flat SMT and I will often say to people: it seems to me that we need to do this. But please now everybody, what is wrong with this, why should we not be doing this? Tell me.'

After recently joining St Swithun's, Gandee says: 'I want people who are going to be up and at it, who are going to opt into things at school, who enjoy spending time with the girls, because my predecessor used to say to staff: 'Oh, it's a day school, you don't need to do anything apart from just teach.' That's mad. I found staff who were straining at the leash. Sadly, my academic deputy was desperate to take responsibility for things and hadn't been allowed to. For her, it hasn't been a question of training, it's been a question of letting her get on with things. You get so much more done when you do that. There is no point in appointing good staff if you then ring them up every two seconds to say, 'Are you doing this, are you doing that?' It's just irritating, it slows everything down. That's the thing, not for them to feel that I've abdicated all responsibility and I'm saying: it's up to you and if you're in trouble, you've got to sort it out. Absolutely not, but saying: you can make these decisions, you can do these things and report back to me when you need to.'

When it comes to the common room, Hamilton (HABS) says, 'Sometimes, it might be a very grudging acceptance that the head does know what he's doing. They need to see you enough in action in some of the trickier parts and some of the nicer parts - to know that they're in safe hands. It's a bit like riding, they need to know that you, sat on their back, know what you're doing. Nobody asks you to be loved, but people need to know what you're talking about and that you've got the track record to prove it. Therefore, if you do make decisions after proper consultation - it doesn't mean of course you agree with everybody, and it might be a decision that some people don't go with - but at least they know that you've thought, listened and heard, that you know that this is not an act of madness. And the confidence to do it.'

At KES, Claughton confesses, 'I'm weak as water. I'm a bleeding heart. I'm very weak with weak people, but I try to run a praise culture. I spend as much of my time telling my staff I think they're doing a good job because in a school like this, the vast majority of people are doing a good job, they're very loyal, very committed. I try to run this great school on trust and respect: we trust our teachers, and we respect them and we're not saying we just let them loose completely. We try to give them autonomy.' Claughton is self-deprecating, 'I delegate badly. I've got better at dealing with the minute particulars and paying attention when I need to. You have to micro-manage. I'm better at that than I was but if you asked what the common room felt, they'd still say: well there are too many bright ideas, not all of them have been thought through, are we consulted enough? I've been better at ideas than I have been at implementation.'

Prime ministers are often seen as primus inter pares in the cabinet room, although even her most loyal lieutenants would not have described Margaret Thatcher as prima inter pares among her colleagues. So how do heads shape up in the common room? 'When I came to Eton, I discovered that its SMT structure was in the traditional form, that is to say: the headmaster is a kind of primus inter pares,' says Little. Claughton initially says no he is not, then says he is, to some degree. 'It would be very depressing for staff if they thought they couldn't have an argument with me,' responds Halls (KCS). 'I am probably primus inter pares,' says McPhail (Radley). 'The tribute would be, and in fact it has happened, the school runs well without me. It may be different and there may be (hopefully) something lacking, but other people will assume responsibility and do things. I'm not a control freak. I like seeing people doing things well.'

At Tonbridge, Haynes also signs up to being primus inter pares. 'I don't set out to put a distance between myself and the common room,' he says. 'I hope I would be seen as accessible, that I will listen. I go into the common room almost everyday and usually several times a day. There was a time when the headmaster had to be invited in. That sort of thing is just unthinkable here. Some headmasters used to have to knock before going into the common room. In one or two schools, it's still a bit like that.' He also acknowledges the value of praise. 'There are getting on for 500 people who work at this place - if I praise one person a day, it's still only every other year. Kindness and generosity are massively important qualities.'

Perse head, Elliott, offers a contrasting view. 'Heads who think they're first among equals are probably a bit self-delusional in the sense that if you ask the teachers out there, they'd say: no. You always sense if you sit on your own at the lunch table, no-one is going to come and sit next to you. I make a point of going to lunch with different people every day. I always make the joke that I have no shadow to cast when I sit down at their table. You're always going to be a bit remote because you have so much power potentially - you can shape their careers and all the rest of it. But they know that I'm accessible, I think they know that I'm fair, that I'm honest.' Elliott is clear on decision-making. 'You want to have discussions, you want to allow people to articulate their points. But there comes always a time where you have to say, "Enough is enough, we're going to make some decisions. We can't shilly-shally around this forever and a day. Some of you are playing quite a cunning procrastination game anyway." Most people will accept that and go with it. But you've got to allow people the opportunity to get engaged in the debate and the discussion.'

A more nuanced response comes from Spence (Dulwich), 'I'm always hopeful for corporate leadership and cabinet responsibility, in a world in which, I'm encouraged to believe that I should be sharing leadership with my SMT. My position is to try and encourage that, but absolutely, to realise where the buck stops, and therefore, at least be primus inter pares. Knowing that there come moments when, even among those who say they want to be involved in decision making, they always want you to be the person, at the end of that debate, to make sure it's action-orientated by saying what we are now going to do.'

Alternating between autocrat and democrat personas when dealing with staff can be precarious. 'Obviously no one in your book, unless they're mad, is going to say, proudly, that they're an autocrat,' says Halls (KCS). 'But it helps, when you try and change something, you write a paper, which is a proposal for people to fight. Rather than have some open thinking, much better for busy to staff to see what you're thinking and then fight it on both sides. I like the idea of dialectic and debate. It's the responsibility of the head to be clear with his staff what he believes in and, when it comes to a proposal, you've got to lead from the front. That's not quite the same as autocracy, but it comes quite close to it.'

Townsend (Winchester) believes the head needs to be 'somebody who appreciates the dons (masters) for their passionate interest in their subjects and who enjoys the eccentricity or quirkiness that often accompanies high intelligence,' adding that Winchester has 'a very interesting, stimulating, humorous common room.' None of the headmistresses interviewed admit to modelling themselves on Thatcher's autocratic style, although McCabe (NLCS) and Wright (St Mary's Calne) both pay tribute to her as an inspiration. Their management style, as stated, appears much more collegiate. But Hall (Wycombe) concedes that you have to be both an autocrat and democrat in headship, adding, 'Sometimes you're a mediator because you've got two perfectly good members of staff who both have something reasonable to say and you need to create peace.'

One of the key responsibilities of headship is to do develop staff, to mentor them and prepare them for additional responsibilities. Beyond internal and external training, how do heads nurture their talent? 'All heads are constantly trying to encourage other people to be heads because they do feel it's the most wonderful job in the world,' says Evans (KEHS). Do heads tap staff on the shoulder and say: you should think about being a head one day? 'I don't think I have ever said that to any member of staff,' says Trafford (RGS Newcastle). 'Maybe that's a burden I don't want to put on them.' Although Hawkins would like to develop future headmasters, he says, 'Harrow is quite notable for the absence of those people, partly because Harrow is a difficult place to leave.' At Tonbridge, which has a similarly attractive regime for resident staff, Haynes counters, 'I've never been frightened of losing good people. One of the things about being a head is that you need to have an inner confidence, and part of that is: I may lose a good person, but I'm confident that I'm able to replace them with a good person of a different sort, who brings something new to the table.'

Until 2012, Gandee (St Swithun's) was deputy head at City of London Girls' under Vernon, who is noted for her staff development. 'I have one-on-ones with the people working directly for me,' says Vernon. 'Inevitably, part of the discussion is not only what they're doing here, but how can I support them? Then, what are they thinking about longer term? I'm very happy to put them in touch with educational headhunters. It's always a difficult one because what you don't want them to think is that you're desperately trying to get rid of them. I quite pride myself in the fact that I can go to conferences and there are quite a lot of people there, who have, at some stage, been on my SMT. It's important for everyone sitting in the staff room, if they've got ambitions, that they can talk to me about what should they be doing and how should they be doing it.'

Lusk also sees it as her obligation at Abingdon, 'I deliberately go through the list and have a sense of who it is that I need to nurture in a particular way and encourage them to start making applications,' she says. 'I give them coaching: how to get through a job interview, what they should be putting in their letters and CVs, what heads look out for. It's absolutely crucial and it's a duty because so many of us are now coming up to retirement. Where are the masses of young heads following? It's a tough route and so to be able to identify those young teachers who've got the potential is a great trick.'

It's not aways easy to satisfy ambition, as Hands (MCS Oxford) explains, 'I have a member of staff at the moment who would very much like to be a head. If you saw his CV, starred First from Cambridge, etc., you would say well that person will be a head. I can't actually get him into a deputy headship. Why? Because governing bodies spot that last thing: he's not got the human instinct to deal with, to understand kids who find things difficult.' Spence (Dulwich) points to a future head among his staff, 'I've got a really good young female head of department, in her early thirties. In a funny kind of way, she could go from her job here, into being a head, rather than having two stops, having to go to a SMT, she should go all the way. It's my job to make sure that she knows I'm aware of that. I'm trying to give her chances to develop so that she doesn't feel stalled here and maybe in a few years' time, she can go and be a head.'

At City of London Boys', Levin highlights a wider concern, 'You know the saying, "The strength of the school is it's a happy school, and the weakness of the school is it's a happy school." One of my worries is, that we have very able, dynamic, great young staff, but they enjoy it here, they're well paid and they're quite happy and don't want to move through a number of different schools to get a headship. Not all, not exclusively, but I'm quite surprised at how few are ambitious in that respect and would rather, as they see it, stay here where they're comfortable. They enjoy the boys, enjoy the subject, in the centre of one of the greatest cities on Earth. I don't want them to wake up in their mid forties, and suddenly think: "It's too late." '

# CHAPTER NINE

# HAPPY CHILDREN

Every parent wishes their child to be happy, not like Shakespeare's 'whining school-boy, with his satchel and shining morning face, creeping like a snail unwillingly to school.' And every head hopes, like Gibbs (JAGS), that their pupils 'come into school on the worst, grottiest February morning, in the dark, carrying their musical instrument, and a bag of books if necessary, with a smile on their face, and go home at the end of the day with a smile on their face, because they've been happy, and they've had a good day.' Happy girls make a happy head. 'But,' she adds, 'If that's not happening on a regular basis, then something's wrong. We need to sort it out.'

So what makes for happy children? And what is the head's role in that process? There is no automatic answer to either question, as demonstrated by the 100,000+ items listed if you type the words 'happy children' into the Amazon search bar. One short chapter on the subject, supplementing the wealth of published information, may not do much to add to the sum of human knowledge, but it does allow heads to answer the question which should be at the forefront of every teacher's mind, every morning: how do I keep my children happy? The word 'my' is used deliberately, for while they are at school, teachers are in loco parentis: they should regard the happiness and well-being of the children in their care as if they were their own, be they eight or eighteen.

Hamilton (HABS) believes that 'happiness has a lot is to do with getting the right child in the school. That's not just about academic selection. If you know the ethos of your school, if it's highly academic, please don't put somebody who's not up to it in because they'll have an awful time, and it won't be good for them, it won't be good for us and it won't be good for the parents.' Once boys are in the school, he adds, 'You really just need to work very hard at the extra stuff, the hidden stuff, the co-curricular stuff, making sure that you've got a wide enough variety - it doesn't really matter what it is: games, debating, bridge, theatre, music, so that you've got that holistic approach. The kids, when they come, need to be busy, happy, doing lots of things, lots of stimulus and input with people who are working for them, working with them and that includes their peers.'

Serving the same north London constituency as Haberdashers', Wright (Merchant Taylors) has a different emphasis, 'Happy boys are busy boys, happy boys are boys who aren't slogging at their books the whole time, but are doing lots of other things. If pushy parents want an exam factory they'll go somewhere else.' Hands (MCS Oxford) argues that happiness comes with a combination of 'sympathetic teaching, a range of extra-curricular activities, and constant concern into their welfare, especially when they first arrive.' Levin (CLBS) adds, 'The joy of schools like ours in London, is that we offer so much. It's got to be a pretty switched off young man who can't find something that he's genuinely enthused by.' Also catering for north London's intelligentsia, McCabe (NLCS) agrees that happy girls are busy girls, 'You make sure there's a niche for every-body: the forty different clubs and societies, the thirty-six productions every year, the plethora of magazines and things that happen here. That channels energy: they find their niche, they make their friends, it's a way of affirming themselves, it's a way of experiencing success, identity. All of those things then help them deal with their hormones, their boyfriends, their relationships, their work.'

Beyond interviewing McCabe for nearly two hours, I had an extended visit to NLCS. The whole operation was impressively slick: the Marketing Director (an urbane former US attorney) outlined the school's international strategy before I was shown round by two bright, articulate and naturally enthusiastic girls, both eleven. They were keen to answer my questions, as were several other girls I talked to in various classrooms, in the dining hall and in fundraising activities for charities. Leaving me free to question in this way showed great confidence by the head in her girls. On my way out, walking along the corridors with McCabe, it was noticeable how many girls smiled at her. It must be said that many other schools, such as Tonbridge, do the same thing: willingly handing over visitors to boys as tour guides. But if happiness can be quantified by natural enthusiasm, infectious laughter, and an obvious thirst for knowledge, then North London Collegiate girls score top marks on all criteria.

Assemblies are the primary opportunity for heads to set the tone and shape the mood - for most pupils, this is their most common form of contact with the head. 'I take assembly, which tends to be for the recognition of achievements. I never like to moralise at the boys,' says Lusk (Abingdon). 'I don't like to be the matriarch around the place, I work very closely with my senior team and inspire them: they're the ones who do all the work, they're fantastic, they go out and they make all the policy happen.' At KEHS Birmingham, Evans says, 'I try to give the girls lots of opportunities to talk to me. Assembly isn't one. My assemblies are pretty didactic. I just stand there and talk about something that I care about and that's how it goes. But I do, with different year groups, have question and answer sessions, where we discuss a topic. With the second years (12 to 13 year olds), I do a session on why girls feel they need to wear makeup. That just seems to be the age where they start slapping it on, and it just breaks my heart. I can't bear it!'

Smart, smooth and self-contained, Hawkins (Harrow) suggests, 'Often the best communication is done by placing emphasis rather than sermonising, although there is a place for that, just occasionally, topics like the prevention of bullying or major disciplinary matters, or the way that we treat one and other: a carefully crafted message has an effect. But more effective is placing value on things that happen, to be emphasising "Look when you did that, that was very well done, that was just right and this is why. Great and congratulations to these people for doing that." Even the little things. This is where one is in a position to wield great power. If all I talk about is the first fifteen rugby result and I barely mention anything else - a classic, but easily done as a head, reflecting one's own passions and interests - if one isn't careful, these are the only things mentioned.' Hawkins pays tribute to drama, music and debating as much as sport. 'It's really important that I have a love for those things too. Certain things can wither and die if one is not careful, just through neglect. So we must, as heads, spread ourselves in the right way. In speech room, I deliberately have a random order to the list of successes and results: Badminton before rugby and so on.'

At St Paul's, the ever-genial Bailey elaborates, 'Assemblies are principally the way in which you articulate and reinforce the values of a school. You can do that by a five minute philosophical piece, using whatever hook is appropriate. You can also do so by celebration; that is hugely important. By listing, describing, presenting to those who have achieved, and you consciously ensure that there is a balance: that the presentation and celebration of success weekly or at the end of term, in different sort of gradations of assembly, represent the full range and panoply of activities within the school. Therefore, you are almost subconsciously reinforcing that no one activity is implicitly regarded as higher up a hierarchy, but they all count.'

Elliott (the Perse) broadens the argument over happiness, providing lessons for the world beyond and developing aspiration, 'You need a school where the children are at the centre of everything that you do, the children are respected, they're listened to. We do a huge amount here on the pupil voice through school councils, study buddies, peer listener schemes. You need to have a very broad range of activities and a clear understanding that no one activity is more important or more valued than another. I remember the bad thing about my school was that rugby was the be all and end all, and if you didn't do rugby, you felt like a second class citizen and you just did a cross country run for five months. What you need to tell the children is, "It doesn't matter what you do, it's what you get out of it. All forms of achievement are cherished and recognised and what the Lego robotics people do is just as good as what the first fifteen does." If you keep hammering that message home, particularly with bright kids because Lego robotics is the sort of thing you might make a bit of a joke about, but you can say, "Well, actually, those Lego robotics, you might call them geeks but some of them are going to be internet millionaires. Who will be laughing then?" Kids here are bright enough to realise, "Yes, that's true, and I'm probably never going to be a professional rugby player."

Combining youth and energy with a warm, friendly manner, Gandee (St Swithun's) summarises her approach, 'I do assembly once, sometimes twice a week. It is important for me to talk about the things that I think are essential such as resilience or compassion or intellectual curiosity or not always believing *the Daily Mail*. I would like some of the girls saying, 'Do you know what, I want to be prime minister,' because to me that would be a success. I don't particularly want them saying, 'I want to get married to a rich investment banker.' I want them to say, 'I want to be an investment banker!'

At Merchant Taylors, Wright is a genuinely caring man, who has often used assemblies as an opportunity to 'talk about the school's very tolerant and accepting community because we've majored in on it particularly pupils with disabilities. The Marks and Spencer's Christmas campaign featured a beautiful little boy with Down's syndrome and I did an assembly on that. I also decided that there was too much homophobic banter with rather than vindictive language going on. I said, "Some of you will look back on the language that you use in terms of being homophobic and you will regret it, like I do." One of the prefects told me that boys he had tackled on this came up to him the next day and apologised. I thought it's not often that you're aware that your assembly has had an impact, but it clearly did. So one occasionally inspires people to think and that's always useful.'

Vernon (CLGS) regularly hands over presentation to her pupils, 'I structure assemblies in terms of who's going to give them. Humour will come through. If I get things wrong, the girls will laugh. At Harvest Festival, we were singing 'We plough the fields and scatter' …. verse, chorus, verse, chorus, verse, chorus. They were all ready to sit down at the end of the final verse. Half of them sat down before we carried on the chorus, so there was a certain amount of giggling, which is fine. The whole school comes together in assembly, everyone's there, everyone's hearing the same things. They know that we're one extended family, and for me, that is very important'. Low (LEHS) adds, 'You take what opportunities you can, private and public. Both are important. We make a big thing about the Monday morning assembly. I hand out every certificate and medal. Those are public opportunities for celebration.'

Although assemblies are the primary source of pupils' contact with the head, celebration has a wider dimension as Spence (Dulwich) says of his boys, 'Celebrate them. Make sure that you celebrate those who are engaged in those esoteric activities, as much as, if not more, than you do those in the big profile things. Because in the big profile things, they get the adulation from their peers, their parents and a substantial number of teachers anyway. Making sure that you've found your way into those little stories - of someone who thought they were doing something that was not recognised - is very powerful. Being happy, in the best sense of what happiness should mean - in yourself, in your role - creates a happy school. Your demeanour is everything.'

Celebration and demeanour apart, sometimes just being there has great value as Martin (Hampton) exemplifies, 'I'm here pretty well every Saturday on the touchline, or away. My wife and I drove down to blooming Canford ten days ago to watch the away rugby fixtures. Now if you turn up on the touch line ninety five miles away to watch - we had half a dozen teams away in their extensive grounds - so if you're there on the touch line at two-thirty on a Saturday afternoon to watch your boys play rugby away, that's motivational. You wander round, and I saw every team play: firsts, seconds, under sixteen A, Bs, under fifteen A, Bs. If you do that, parents say, "Thank you so much for coming." I like doing it. You can chat to boys. It means you can stop somebody in a corridor and say, "I thought that was a really good penalty kick, or it was a great tackle on the line, or a great goal that you scored." That kind of stuff just lifts everybody.' Trafford (RGS Newcastle) adds, 'You can't beat yourself up because you can't get to everything but get to as much as you can without killing yourself. It's all about taking pleasure in it, so there is pleasure and enjoyment, that is the happiness part: you need to be happy too.'

A happy head does not always guarantee happy children - their needs are generally more fundamental than spiritual or philosophical. Good food comes pretty high on the list. 'Well-fed girls are happy girls,' says Marks. Over lunch at her school, she explained how she requested the revamping of Withington's menus, making sure that everything was provided for the girls with fresh ingredients, freshly cooked. The fish cakes and salad offered on the day of my visit would not disgrace a restaurant. From pupils and parents I have spoken to, most schools have similarly good food with plenty of choice, particularly for those boarding. It would be invidious to mention them by name, but there are a few listed in this book where complaints abound: the food is stodgy, the vegetables soggy, the meat fatty, the portions meagre and the mash still lumpy. Also worthy of mention are two boys' schools - one day, one boarding - where I was offered neither tea nor coffee during lengthy interviews with the heads, after travelling some distance to get there. It would be equally invidious to name and shame them, but it struck me as odd, and created a distinctly unfavourable impression.

Gandee (St Swithun's) uses food to engage, 'I have lunch with the girls. I'll plunk my tray down next to them. I choose the children with the most food left on their plate so they can't escape!' At City of London Boys, Levin regularly eats with the boys, 'I started off with breakfast, now

I have lunch. It was based on birthdays in Year Six, Seven, Eight and Nine. I now do it by forms, so I have about a third of a form in and we just have a chat. Usually, over a doughnut and a Coke - not very correct, not very nutritional, but I know that I will get their attention with a doughnut and a Coke. We'll have about a 45 minute chat about what their interests are, who are they, where do they want to go? I try and listen, I ask questions, and then get a conversation going.'

One head who manifestly put herself in loco parentis as mother to all her girls is Claire Oulton, the retiring head at Benenden. On arrival, she says, 'The girls needed their boarding accommodation improved, they needed their food improved, they needed their weekends improved, they needed a bit more warmth and care and nurturing. I'm not saying these things weren't here before, these were things I wanted to work on. This was fine tuning, not major surgery, so the girls very quickly realised that I really cared about them.' Benenden food received the biggest overhaul, an improvement likely to have an even greater impact in a boarding school. 'It was radical, completely radical,' says Oulton 'because I wanted them to look forward to every meal. We completely redid the dining room, got in a new catering manager, who's still here and is absolutely wonderful. One of the ways you show people that you care about them is you feed them well, that's always been the case. For a mother not to feed her children well is one of the hardest things; it happens when people are very poor, or in war-torn areas. It impacts greatly on their well being. The fact that I've really minded that they had really good food available, that they could enjoy it, was important to them. It's really hard to work out how they recognise it, but teenagers are quite intuitive: they know who cares and who doesn't.'

The key to happiness, says Low (LEHS) is confidence, 'You need to give girls opportunities to develop and shrine. For some girls that's not going to be in the Maths or Latin class, but it might be on the lacrosse pitch, or in debating. Or it might be in being head of house. That's going to make them feel happier about being in school, even if they are struggling a bit with Maths. It's just going to make them feel better about themselves and probably more confident about asking for help, or just feeling they've got their place in this school, even if they're not at the top academically.'

Marks (Withington) believes that heads need to be very alert to maintaining children's self-esteem and self-confidence, particularly in academic schools, 'I try to tackle the fact that in a school like this, with such a narrow ability range at the very top end, there is a tendency for the girls who aren't top to think of themselves as not very able. In a national context, it's nonsense, but they don't see that, they only compare themselves with girls here. There can be self-esteem issues which lead to under performance and all sorts of other personal concerns because they feel that they're not very bright. I try to encourage the girls not to compare themselves with each other but to look at their own individual progress. We've taken away the median mark when we report. Some parents found that quite difficult: their daughters tend to be above the median. I feel very strongly that it's not necessary to motivate somebody by pointing out how many people they have beaten. That isn't a kind way to motivate; it's very demotivating for those below the median. The best way is to say: where were you last time, how much progress have you made, how much progress can you make next time? In our reporting system, we're moving away from a comparison with our rather unusual cohort to a measure of progress of that individual child from the last point, and tracking it against what might be expected of a child of that ability using national norms.'

Wright (St Mary's Calne) argues that happiness comes with confidence plus courtesy, 'There is a lot about example, and making sure that teachers deal with respect. When I came to the school, I noticed that girls weren't opening doors for people, there wasn't a sense of common courtesy. I was a little surprised. I didn't say anything but I just started opening doors for people. Then if I was late for the girls, I'd say, "I really am very sorry that I'm late," because I was sorry. Girls now open doors and apologise for being late. I smile when I see that. There is role modelling for confidence, safety, security, being yourself, having freedom to be able to speak out. You can teach it as well. We have personal development lessons which have several different strands, also providing opportunities for people for leadership. When I came, the head girl's team was quite narrow, small and they used to do practical things like hand out hymnbooks. I changed all of that. I took lots of staff out of running chapel and put girls in there. A senior member of staff used to read the notices, I got the head girl's team to do that. It gives them confidence to be in charge, doing something, part of the running of the school.'

Giving children freedom to take the initiative is crucial says Gandee (St Swithun's), 'I've got somebody that wants to do archery. I said to her:

go away and find me an archery coach. Scottish dancing they wanted to do with boys from Winchester College, we've got that going now. Battle of the Bands they wanted to do with boys from different schools, we got that going at the end of term. So, they quite often come to me and I think they know that I will tend to say yes. My default setting is: yes.'

Heads cannot make every child happy, although they can ensure that each teacher does his or her best supplemented by strong support structures: housemasters and housemistresses, counsellors, the school chaplain, nurse or doctor, so children feel valued, cared for, and that people are interested in them. 'But,' says McPhail (Radley), 'you can have all the systems you like, what you've got to do is to prepare individuals to be open to them. To know the limits of what they can and cannot do, and what they should do.' Wright (St Mary's Calne) agrees that essential to the happiness of the overall school community is setting clearly established boundaries which everybody recognises.

On a personal level, Bailey (St Paul's) summarises what heads can do, 'It's about personal exemplification. It's one thing to be presenting and shaking hands, it's another thing to be exhorting and trying to articulate a philosophy. Adolescents respond to actions, they want to see that you care, and if they see that you care, and this is true of any teacher, they will respond well. You do it in lots of subtle ways. You attend as many activities as possible - even if it's just on a touchline for five minutes, at plays. And even some of the less prominent activities - smaller ensembles, fringe plays that boys might have written, or put on; little things like that. A note afterwards perhaps for two or three. Not too many; you don't want to dilute the currency! But a little hand-written note that praises. A word on the corridor, as you pass them.'

At Eton, Little puts the pastoral above everything, 'I'm absolutely convinced that the point and purpose of schools is human communities, and that relationships are the most important thing. If I had to say, and it took me some while to identify this, the single most different and better thing about Eton compared with any other school I've worked in, is the quality of relationship between teachers and pupils. That comes about for a whole variety of reasons. The centre - the stuff and substance of what we're doing - is pastoral. If you get that right, there's a fighting chance you'll do well academically, and in every other area.' He explains the fostering of self-confidence for which Eton boys are renown, 'I have this open house every morning, from eight to eight-thirty, a chat with any boy can pop in. A boy did wander in one morning, and said in a quite airy way: he'd written to the Dalai Lama and got an audience, got four or five of his chums to go with him. The Dalai Lama's people said: would the head go as well. So we did. We met him in London. That's great. When you have bright young people, and it's not peculiar to Eton, we have the great privilege where a number of them are brought together and live, is they haven't really learnt the constraints. Sometimes, that can be in a bad way. Mostly, it's in a good way.

'We have this extraordinary tradition at Eton where, at the age of seventeen, you'll run your society, and you'll invite the speakers to come and talk in a whole variety of different ways, different subjects. We're talking over a couple of hundred each year. I can't think of many school environments where seventeen year-olds, without demur, will think it perfectly normal to do something like that. Without a doubt, that's the best part of it: it's the variety and quality of what one sees young people doing'. It creates a virtuous spiral: Little derives obvious pleasure from the happiness of his boys' activities. 'I can have a day stuck in this office, routine meetings, or things are going pear-shaped with people moaning at me, that's all part-and-parcel of the job,' he says. 'Then I go to a concert in the evening. I can think of no other job where you have such an immediate positive.' Happy boys also make a happy head.

# CHAPTER TEN

# UNHAPPY CHILDREN

Sex, drugs, and rock 'n' roll. The very phrase puts shivers up the spine of most parents who have teenagers at a certain age or stage. And with good reason - they are vulnerable. Many children have problems, some become problem children. For teachers, and ultimately for heads, they can create genuine difficulties, but the greatest impact of problems is usually felt by the child concerned. Where identifiable, the principal root cause is unhappiness. Adapting Tolstoy: happy children are all alike; every unhappy child is unhappy in his or her own way.

'The boy had to leave, although I never threw him out,' says one head, referring to a recent episode. 'He was one of the naughtiest boys they'd ever had at his prep school before he came here. The problems he had, and they were many, seemed to be caused by a reaction to his parents, particularly his mother (a public figure). It was horrid. He is still a very troubled boy, and she was, I'm afraid, a dreadful parent in some ways, but I hear that things are getting better now.' At school, problems can manifest themselves in unusually poor academic performance, disruptive behaviour, bullying, drug use, eating disorders and a variety of other ways, each of which schools do their best to resolve by working with parents, and sometimes outside agencies. Some problems can be solved or worked out over time; others remain intractable.

By far the worst, although relatively few in number, involve sexual abuse by teachers of their pupils: the ultimate betrayal of trust. In the independent sector, this is more frequently an issue in boarding schools. Although no published statistical data is available, a thorough trawl through online newspaper archives over the last twenty-five years reveals scores of perpetrators and hundreds of victims. Many historic victims have come forward since the Savile revelations. Of the thirty nine teachers reported in 2013 to Operation Kiso, the police investigation into sexual abuse by teachers in Manchester's music schools, the police are concentrating on "a pool of about ten offenders," who taught at the independent Chetham's School of Music.

Offenders often evade detection for decades. In July 2012, Bruce Roth, a Maths teacher, was jailed for eleven years after being found guilty of sexually assaulting five boys over a twenty-year period: three at Wellington - where he had entered the boys' dormitory at night and molested them - and two eight year old boys at King's School Rochester, where he taught between 1987 and 1994. He had been investigated and suspended at King's after relatives of the boys reported him. At the trial, the court heard that Roth was exonerated at an internal inquiry after the head decided it was his word against that of a boy. He was finally arrested in October 2010 after one of his Wellington victims phoned the children's charity, ChildLine. Wellington head, Anthony Seldon, said afterwards that he was 'sickened and appalled by his employee's vile crimes.'

Without hysteria, one has to ask how many more Roths are there operating in other schools, who have so far escaped detection and circumvented existing vetting or investigation procedures? 'I can't imagine that child protection is going to get any worse because I don't think that in society there is more of it happening, it's more just paranoia about it which is growing, and certainly Savile has caused an increased number of complaints of issues in schools, particularly historic complaints,' says Smellie (Farrer). 'There's been a bit of a surge.'

Problem pupil management is an everyday issue. On the one hand, heads provide strong pastoral care to help wherever possible; on the other, they have the needs of the wider school community to consider if they are jeopardised by unruly or inappropriate behaviour. Heads are generally made aware on a need to know basis. Major problems are notified immediately. Most are initially delegated, unless the problem is so serious that the head needs to become involved directly; more frequent minor problems, which often subside at an early stage, may be dealt with entirely by others. Only when things are serious or remain serious do they become personally involved.

'It's a collaborative exercise always,' says Marks (Withington). 'I do try not to play God,' says Trafford (RGS Newcastle). 'It's very tempting for heads to try and sort things out, whereas in fact, the person they deal with most is the form teacher; that is where those things should happen, or the head of year. There is a temptation sometimes for us heads to play God and be "big time" about it, wave magic wands for people. I try not to do that, I really try to make sure that it's done at the right level.' Early intervention is sometimes necessary. 'Children will come to me with their problems from time to time,' says Gibbs (JAGS), 'particularly the really intractable, very difficult ones, where there are confidential child protection issues. I might well be dealing with them, because there's a need to know basis, and then the buck stops with me. It's a question of working as a team, but making sure they've got plenty of places that they and their daughter can have conversations and try things out, before it escalates.'

High achievers at leading academic schools rarely come from troubled backgrounds of poverty or deprivation, but privilege is no guarantor of happiness, nor of good behaviour. Among those interviewed, one head revealed that on appointment to a school featured in this book, 'The thing that hit me most was our exclusion rate: seventy pupils a year were being excluded from school for a few days at a time. That's huge. It was for bad behaviour, terrible behaviour.' Seventy exclusions a year is a figure which ranks among the highest - not a league table where you would expect to find any independent school featuring prominently, let alone a school best-known for its academic prowess. 'I've never had to exclude anybody here,' says Hewitt (Manchester High). Because the school in question is independent, it does not appear in any published data for exclusion; the comparable figure in recent years is much reduced.

Home is the source of most problems. 'You go as far as you can in a way that will be of benefit to the boy. It's boy-driven. We have no interest, nor should we, in anything that's going on within a family,' says Little (Eton). When determining jurisdictional limits, the paramount concern for schools is preserving their own reputation - a word heads project with the intensity of an Othello character. McPhail (Radley) says, 'Our jurisdiction clearly goes beyond the school gate at term time and everything else, if the school's reputation is affected. Other than that, I don't think it does, enormously. I don't think it should.' For day schools, it goes well beyond Monday to Friday in term time. 'If I hear of anything that has happened in the holiday, or at a weekend, I feel I have absolute right to get boys in here and ask about that, and act upon it,' says Spence (Dulwich). 'When they go out, they are still a member of this community and if they behave in a manner that will bring this community to disrepute, and we are aware of it, I don't care how old they are and what they're allowed and not allowed to do, there will be a conversation,' says Hamilton (HABS).

Schools may not intrude too deeply into family life, but they see the consequences, particularly of marital breakdown and parental conflict. 'Quite often, for the most troubled girls, we are an oasis in their life and coming here is the best bit of normality that they have,' says Hewitt (Manchester High). Low advises caution on boundaries set at home, 'You've got to be careful because every family has the right to have its own values and make its own decisions about what they're going to allow. We take the line that if something is going on outside that is having a negative effect on things in school then yes, we do have to get involved.'

Of most common concern to parents and to victims, and often least visible to the school, is bullying: the biggest single problem affecting most children. According to NSPCC research, 38% of teenagers claim to have been the target - staff have a statutory duty to prevent discrimination, harassment and victimisation. However well-conceived their policies, procedures and monitoring processes, most bullying goes unreported and unpunished, creeping under the school's radar. When it does become visible, there can sometimes be institutional denial and a systemic failure to deal with the problem adequately. 'You go to any school, there's going to be bullying', says Cox (RGS Guildford). 'If the head says there's no bullying in the school, they are lying. Boys and girls they all get it wrong, but the way you deal with it, that's the important thing. So, if boys feel that if there's a bullying incident it comes straight to me and I deal with it. Then they're on safer ground, they feel much more comfortable, because we deal with it and make sure that it doesn't happen again.'

Wright (Merchant Taylors) says, 'There are a variety of approaches. You have to respond to an individual situation. Most of our bullying takes place within year groups, generally low level name calling; nonetheless it's insidious. Some situations are very difficult because we have younger ones who go looking for and are encouraged by parents to look for issues of bullying that aren't there. We have to protect them and we have to respond very quickly and very efficiently. It can be just saying: 'What you're doing is upsetting this individual person'. Quite often, the kids will say, 'I didn't know, it's general banter, we'll stop it.' Occasionally, we have to take more robust action because it's clear that they're not going to stop. But some are irresolvable and it's usually the parents who have the issue, not the boy.'

Physical and verbal bullying are problems for which schools have well-established procedures, although they often go unrecognised. The offline and online worlds of bullying converge thanks to technology: cyberbullying, the scourge of our age, presents new difficulties for heads everywhere. 'We're at a watershed moment in learning to use, rather than live in fear of social media. That whole world of email and social media has transformed things,' says Spence (Dulwich). 'There's been a lot of internet bullying, people able to say things behind that screen that they'd never be able to say face to face: the whole world of social media from the Facebook generation, what they say to each other on Facebook, and dealing with the problems that come from cyberbullying as the new bullying. Insecure boys, they're very likely to be either victim or perpetrator, and so often, they can be both.' Boys have recently been expelled from Dulwich for Facebook abuse.

More than a third of teenagers experience bullying; two thirds of abuse is in cyberspace, via technology like mobile phones or the internet. Of those teenagers who have reported cyber abuse, 87% said they were targeted on Facebook; those most frequently victimised were teenage boys (source: knowthenetsurvey 2013 - Opinium). Asked for their initial reaction, only 17% said they would tell a parent and only 1% per cent would inform a teacher. Huge pressure is also put on some girls by teenage boys who send naked or semi-naked photographs of themselves via mobile phones and ask girls to reciprocate - commonly referred to as sexting. Some comply. Talk to teenagers and the problems are greater than many heads appreciate.

Elliott (the Perse), recalls the change he noticed after his school went co-ed in 2012, 'When we were an all boys' school, I don't think I'd have had to deal with parents coming in wanting to talk to me about sexting in the way that they do now, but I would have been dealing with boys behaving in a more boorish fashion than they do now because boys do tend to become a little bit more civilised and reflective with girls around. We probably deal with less girl catty issues than you might find in an all girls' school because girls moderate their behaviour as well. Boys don't get why it is someone will fall out with someone for the rest of their life over something very small.'

McCabe (NLCS) summarises her experience, 'When I was deputy head responsible for discipline in a comprehensive, the boys would thump each other and it would be all over the next morning. If you tell a boy off, facing him down, absolutely fine, no grudges. Girls are much more insidious to each other, they'll fall out with each other in a very different way, it's all going on under the surface. If you handle them in a disciplinary way, in the wrong way, then they will bear a grudge for ever, and if you don't know who they are, they take things very personally. You have to spend a lot more time with girls, valuing them, encouraging them, being positive about their achievements, praising them, I'm sure everybody responds well to that, but girls in particular. Cyberbullying and the eating disorders, they're all to do with issues of esteem. People with sharp elbows finding their space, that's the cyberbullying side, issues of control around eating disorders.'

In 2010, a new site called LittleGossip.com allowed teenagers to post anonymous online comments - frequently abusive, vicious or sexual - about their peers. The site was disproportionately popular with independent school pupils: regrettably, the comments from several former pupils at schools such as Benenden are still available to read online. Commenting at the time, Gibbs (JAGS) told *the Daily Mail*, 'I'm just so angry that this vehicle for cyberbullying exists. I can't imagine what kind of person wants to set up a site like this. It must be some kind of sick person.' Reportedly shut down in 2011, although the site remains online, the founder was subsequently named by *the Sunday Telegraph* as Ted Nash, a 19-year-old former public schoolboy. Twitter and BBM (BlackBerry Messenger) have their fair share of bullying too, while the newer ask.fm, a question-and-answer social networking site, also allows anonymous comments and abuse. Extremely popular with teenagers, it has approaching 50 million users worldwide. One of the most prominent ask. fm victims, Hannah Smith, 14, committed suicide in August 2013, after receiving continued abusive messages. A 15-year-old boy, Thomas Mullaney, hanged himself following repeated threats on Facebook.

In dealing with the problem, Savage (Alleyn's) explains, 'If some cyberbullying takes place between members of the school community, that's our business. We would intervene, and do intervene. Kids do respond to punishment. Parents, usually, can be persuaded that it's appropriate, if they believe that you share, with them, the best interests of their son or daughter. Because it is of no use to anyone being allowed to have a bullying attitude, and to go through life with such a one. You talk to parents, you talk to children, you punish. The key thing is to make parents understand. A lot of parents wish us to intervene. So we educate the kids, not just for their behaviour in school, but for their behaviour in life. We intervene where we can in order to help them learn those lessons. Cyberbullying is a case in point. It's difficult. In some ways, they have the right to say what they want over social networks, but if it creates a problem, in terms of the relations and dynamics at school, then it is our business. We also have a moral imperative to intervene if someone's being made to feel unhappy. What I tend to do in practical terms - they might be in serious detention, they might be suspended, they will come back. I will talk to them, I will look them in the eye and say: what lessons have you learnt? They will talk to me about that. Pastoral staff will keep an eye on things, and help them, guide them towards learning from that lesson and being reintegrated. I see it as a pastoral thing. We have from time to time incidents, which can be hugely pressured at the time, and parents can become partisan. You can get caught in a cross fire, and you have to hang on to your convictions. There must be room for atonement, restoration and learning.'

As with sex, every generation thinks it has invented drugs. Heads know better: they come from a generation well-versed in the problem. In adult life, Little (Eton) has 'come across a fair number of casualties who were here with me in the sixties.' Referring not just to drugs, but to the lasting influence of Eton upon some of his contemporaries, when he was himself an Eton boy between 1967 and 1972, Little says the experience 'has certainly influenced me.' Substance abuse - legal drugs, notably cigarettes and alcohol, and illegal drugs, ranging from cannabis to cocaine - is of perennial concern to heads. Smoking or drinking in school grounds, or in uniform outside school, carry obvious penalties, and habitual offenders, as with repeated contravention of any important school rule, can expect suspension and ultimately, expulsion.

Discretion and human understanding can play a part in what sanctions to apply. Hands (MCS Oxford) recalls, 'When I ran a boarding house, it was a very difficult year group to take over. My father (who had been a headmaster) was staying with me. One boy had made life particularly difficult throughout the year. After his final warning, I found him smoking with about three days to go, and he should have really been packed off and not taken part in any of the celebrations. It's difficult in those kind of situations. I said to my father: "Well now I can get rid of him"? My father said: "Your problem is, you've never been a smoker." On the basis of that, I let the boy stay.'

Views on how to deal with illegal drugs appear clear cut: any dealing and you are out. 'I've actually only expelled one boy; he appeared to be a kleptomaniac,' says Haynes (Tonbridge). 'Three boys left earlier this year, it's the first time in seven years it's happened. They were withdrawn because we discovered they'd been smoking cannabis - they were caught doing it three times, and all three boys were involved, in one way or another, in the procurement of the stuff.' It's a perennial problem. In 2001, forty Winchester boys were disciplined for drug and drink problems, eleven were suspended for a week. Following sex and drug scandals, police with sniffer dogs raided the Marlborough dormitories. Many state that the taking of controlled drugs, if caught, carries a mandatory penalty of expulsion, but the reality is more nuanced. It's an unspoken truth, but at the head's discretion, some schools, particularly with first offenders smoking cannabis, will caution, suspend, drug test, counsel and rehabilitate rather than eject automatically.

The public voice is a little different. 'Drugs are a big NO,' says Hamilton (HABS). But, a school counsellor, if you're worried about a friend, or if you're worried about somebody, please go and talk about it because that is the right way to go. But do nothing and get caught, that's probably the wrong way to go. For me, the bottom line is the reputation of the school. Reputational damage.' Wright (Merchant Taylors) thinks differently, 'We try to resolve Saturday night issues if we feel that we can do something useful, if we can't then we won't. If it's the anonymous letter that says your children are taking drugs or naming boys that are taking drugs at local night clubs then I might share that with the parents, but I'm not going to do anything about it.'

Hawkins (Harrow) is unequivocal, 'We have a zero tolerance policy that says that if any boy, whilst a Harrow boy, even during the holidays, is known to have or is proven to have or strongly suspected of, beyond reasonable doubt, having used or supplied, or had any sort of direct involvement with illegal drugs then you're straight out. Experience shows that you just need a very clear policy. The only exception is that if a boy, who is not under suspicion or investigation for this, comes forward and says: 'I've got a bit of an issue here, can I go on a testing regime and can I have support?' Then the school and the parents work together, those are the only mitigating circumstances. We find that parents really appreciate that because it's an anxiety for them. We all know what the dangers of alcohol are - in many senses, they may be even greater than what they describe as recreational drug use - but illegal drugs, quite rightly there's a real stigma, and there are reputational issues for schools and individuals. Someone could spend the rest of their life living with the fact that: Oh yes, he was expelled from that school for this kind of thing.'

Provoked by a once-wider problem, Harrow's zero-tolerance policy has its origin in the school's prominent drug casualties over the last thirty years, including both the Marquess of Blandford and the late Marquess of Bristol. Their persistent drug taking exploits were well-documented, invariably prefaced in press reports by 'Old Harrovian' when detailing their numerous court appearances. 'I'm always likely to be someone who wants to give another chance. I have no tolerance for the phrase 'zero tolerance' because I think it's antithetical to what we should be doing as teachers,' says Spence (Dulwich). This reflects the private sentiments of many.

Heads' views can certainly change, as Halls (KCS Wimbledon, Master MCS Oxford 1998-2008) explains, 'I was really impressed when I came here by the way that drug issues are dealt with very pastorally. If a pupil was dealing drugs in King's or Magdalen, in both cases, I'd intend to exclude him permanently without a doubt. When I came here, a boy came to tell us about his drug usage. At Magdalen, in my first few years, when I was very concerned by the over-liberal ethos, I'd have been pretty anxious to lose that boy, probably. I learnt from the way that King's dealt with this case that it was very much a pastoral issue. I've grown up a bit and I've realised that he wasn't a boy who was of harm to other pupils, he was a boy who was hurting himself - he'd come to us with a problem. I'd never had someone do that for me at Magdalen, but I thought it was a strength of King's that this boy felt he could do that; nothing to do with me, but that was the character of the school. We did help him, we got counselling. He went to the Priory - it was quite serious, his addictions. He got through, he got his IB and he was a bright, amusing boy. I liked him.'

Sometimes, one pupil can present a multiplicity of problems, as McCabe

(NLCS) recalls, 'There was a challenging girl, who was practically my nemesis here, a very difficult period and a very difficult individual.' Vernon (CLGS) had a similar case, 'It was my first weekend ever as a head (Woldingham 2000-2007). It was absolutely ghastly. We'd known this girl was incredibly ill. Bizarre things: a pair of jeans vanished, the kettle vanished, the kettle was found in her room. The father wasn't in the country at the time, and the girl should not have been in school. I didn't expel her, I just said she needed to take time out and then we'd accept her back again. The way that girl looked at me. If looks could have killed, I would not be here talking to you today. She was terribly ill. But I needed, we as a school needed, to do something, to make her realise how ill she was. She had to get help. Sometimes, the school does have to present itself as the big bad wolf, because we might come down with some home truths, but it's in the long term interests of individual girls. The girl concerned, I saw her quite recently. She's been back to visit. She said: 'It was the best thing that happened to me.' '

Back to Eton, where a current pupil is the focus of Little's attention, his attitude notably much more understanding than heads of his day would have been, 'I've got a boy at the moment who's had all kinds of problems, becoming a real pain in the house, and exhibiting some very odd behaviours. In effect, we've arranged for him to be a day boy to get him physically out of the house. We've arranged this with an onside master, who checks him in in the morning, uses his home as the base. It's transformed him, certainly transformed the atmosphere in the house. We're prepared to be flexible where we can be to try and get to an end result. It comes back to our central purpose which is about relationships. If we don't take the time and the trouble to get that right, even if we fail sometimes, then we're just not doing the job.'

Some heads take a firm stance on problem children when entering a new school - pour encourager les autres. Marks (Withington) did so in her first headship at Tormead, 'I suspended a large number of girls in my first week because of something they'd done on a hockey tour of Barbados. They'd absented themselves and gone off and had a good time. But I was putting down a marker very early on about expectations of behaviour and it worked very well. It wasn't very popular with some of the parents who were affected, but it was with those parents whose daughters weren't affected.'

In his first term at Hampton, Martin resolved, 'I'm not going to do anything but listen for a term, not take any action, or introduce new initiatives. I saw all the staff individually. I said I'm not going to do anything, no changes unless there is something I really feel strongly about. Then I chucked nine boys out in my first term: I didn't like their behaviour in school very much. That was the thing on which I decided to set my stall out quite quickly. When I say I chucked them out, I take one step back from that, I didn't expel anybody, but I had conversations with parents and assisted those boys to find alternative places for their education. As head, you're in a powerful position: you can exercise quite a degree of power over somebody's career and future. You must use that wisely. That was my big statement. I had members of staff coming through the door, privately, unseen, saying, "I just want to thank you for doing that, because it's about time. It's going to make it so much easier for us to act as teachers, when we know we've got someone who is going to take that line, and support high standards in the school." I even got thanks from boys.'

Smellie (Farrers) sees another growing concern, 'Disabilities, I'm using the legal definition, and broadly speaking pupils with learning needs, more often than not, are actually deemed disabled in law. So a child who's pretty much anywhere on the autistic spectrum within reason, dyslexia, dyspraxia, all of these things, parents possibly quite rightly, are expecting schools to make more and more provision, and if they don't get it right, arguments result. So that's definitely a growing area of potential conflict between schools and families.' Eating disorders are among the most difficult problems encountered predominantly by headmistresses of girls' schools and co-ed headmasters. 'With eating disorders, which every school of our sort will come into contact with at some point,' says Marks (Withington), 'it is often the school that will notice it first and often the parents who'll be the people you need to be persuaded there is an issue. Sometimes they will be aware of it, but won't want the school to know. In my experience, it's always most effectively tackled if we're working together and supporting the girl. They need to buy into whatever the medical professionals suggest as do their parents.'

Low (LEHS) describes her approach, 'If we're concerned, we will always contact parents. It can get picked up in various ways in school - by PE staff, by other girls sometimes - coming in and saying "we're really worried about x or y not eating," because staff on duty notice that girls are not eating and concern will be expressed. We will offer parents advice about what can be done. One of the things with eating disorders in particular, and I completely understand this so it's not a criticism, is when we do contact parents, there's denial. Because you don't want to think your daughter's got that problem. It doesn't happen every time, but it is quite a common reaction. "No, she's eating fine at home", or "She's just going through a growth spurt" or "She's always been a picky eater" or "Don't worry about it, don't worry about it." We will keep tabs on them - we will go back to the parents and say, "Look, we are still concerned." But you can only go so far. We don't go back on a daily basis, we'll watch her because in the end it is down to the parents to get the girl off to the GP. We invariably come to the parents' recognition, we work with them. The whole eating disorders thing in girls' schools does get blown out of proportion because they're everywhere naturally - the roots are not in the school. It's very rarely to do with pressures at work, it's external issues. On one occasion, we said, "We can't move forward on this one, she isn't physically up to doing PE anymore." Just because it wasn't safe.'

Wright (St Mary's Calne) has a different approach, 'No school can solve an eating disorder, it's a mental illness. What we can do is to have a clear policy that says that we will require young people to get help, because otherwise they cannot be at school. Sometimes you need to be quite firm, to say this is what you need, it's not just an option. This is essential if you're going to be part of this school because these are our boundaries. If you have somebody with an eating disorder, then their traits of perfectionism mean that it's very important for them to stay at school, therefore they're more likely to: we can contribute to their recovery in doing that. Our policy, which I created at my last school with the help of psychiatrists, is to get that - to be really clever. As a head, or as a school, you should never think that you can create all the answers, other people have got to be part of it. You've got family, external care givers, school, all working together, each has different roles to play. We can't deal with the illness, but we can deal with the behaviour.'

In a critique that does not apply to Eton, Little says, 'You can make an academic institution deliver some pretty tight results by being top down, highly selectively focused, chucking people out who don't meet the mark.' Reticent in discussing the minutiae, academic schools do cull: removing weak performers who cannot keep up with the pace and are going to produce poor GCSE or A level results. It happens in most high-flying schools, as Gibbs (JAGS) explains, 'We are a selective school, so if a child is struggling by the end of Year 8 or 9, then they'll probably be more comfortable elsewhere. Or, as they come to the end of the GCSE course, if we think another place - they need a safety net, so that occasionally happens.'

More routinely, although the numbers are still small, are those who are asked to leave because of behavioural or rule-breaking issues. Despite best endeavours some children have to go: expulsion is the nuclear option in every head's arsenal. 'There is such a thing as a bad apple, who if removed, can transform a form, a year group, almost a school,' says Spence (Dulwich). Among all secondary schools in every part of Britain, far more boys then girls are expelled (or permanently excluded, in modern parlance), the ratio typically being four to one.

At Radley, McPhail says, 'You'll get this from all heads, the areas in which the problems can arise, are not only growing, but the other really difficult thing is just the speed at which a situation can develop. That's a big change. The hardest situation is where a boy has been involved in low-level incidents, but of a repeated nature. The question of when you are going to say "one more time and that's it," that's difficult. It's always difficult thereafter because it can look to many people that you've got rid of someone for something that seems quite paltry. There needs to be a confidentiality between you and the parents of a pupil in a disciplinary thing, which means that you're not going to talk other people about what's happened. That's quite difficult. I remember talking to Tony Little about this when he was deputy at Brentwood. The head had seen some boys smoking in the schoolyard, and he just booted the lot of them. I remember Tony saying that would be about two weeks work: the interviews and so on. If you're at somewhere like Eton, all the other aspects as well.'

We do not live in the world of 1928 when five Eton boys were seduced in turn by American film star, Tallulah Bankhead, including one son of a lord and another of a baronet. The head, Cyril Alington, kept the scandal secret, refusing to cooperate with a police inquiry after Bankhead had entertained the boys at the Cafe de Paris hotel in Bray. Today, consequences and the attendant stigma of expulsion are much more serious. 'It's a very time consuming process. If you just think you're going to boot 'em, this can be a very significant change in someone's life,' says McPhail. Never a pleasant task, he summarises how it feels to expel a boy from Radley, 'I find I don't worry about most things in headship, but I still get that sort of 'pre dentist' feeling, when you're about to see parents and say, "I'm sorry, he's got to go." And you should really feel like that.'

Prior to expulsion, schools investigate the circumstances thoroughly, as Smellie (Farrer) explains, 'Given that one is dealing with children, one has to be particularly careful about the quality of the evidence, the corroboration. If something bad has happened in a school and one boy, for the sake of argument, is in trouble, there is a good chance that by the time the relevant member of staff has got to him, he's spoken to his six or seven best mates and they've got their story straight. So the issues that arise: one, is the quality of the evidence; two, maybe the quality of the investigation, because the older school teacher, by which I don't mean age, just old style, probably has grown up in a tradition where you don't really need to investigate these things very thoroughly. You develop a gut feel and you act pretty swiftly, and that doesn't sit comfortably with modern day parents.'

Smellie concludes that process and procedure can obscure the solution to problems, 'The quality of investigation and the thoroughness of investigation is often not as good as it should be, although schools have become better. They're alert to the danger, they know that they've got to follow the rules of natural justice in reaching an important decision, which means that they know that statements have to be taken and shown to the parents and the boy or girl who's at risk of being expelled. They know that if it's a shambles, or if it doesn't hang together, they're definitely going to get an appeal to the governors and they may get lawyers' letters. That's been a big change, progressively over the last twenty years. They may slightly resent it because it's all negative, in the sense that it's defending against the risk of a claim, rather than actually dealing with what the problem was.'

# CHAPTER ELEVEN

# PARENTS

In an ideal world, schools cater for the needs of two generations, building a strong relationship with parents, while allowing their children to learn and flourish in a caring, responsible community. Regrettably, the world is far from ideal. Burdensome legal obligations and practical involvement with parents in contentious situations require the head's jurisdiction to stretch far beyond the school gate. Simultaneously, the modern parent-school relationship, integral to our education system, has made parental involvement universal in almost every aspect of school life: as supporters, consumers, and participants. Accordingly, the head's interaction with parents has come a long way from the annual gowned appearances on speech day and a line or two in the school report. Expectations are high, scrutiny constant, delivery imperative.

Over-ambitious parents are certainly well-represented throughout the independent sector: 'We have pushy parents', says Wright (Merchant Taylors). 'But I don't want, we don't want parents who see this school as a route to getting their son into Oxford, Cambridge, UCL or Imperial. We filter them out because our message is so clear and has been for the past thirty years: we want boys coming here for the experience, not jut to pass exams.' For parents, the competitive process involved in winning a place for their child at a good school causes much anxiety. Bamboozled by a wealth of league tables, websites, prospectuses, visits and entrance exams, they turn to guidebooks, newspaper articles, and to each other - all in an attempt to furnish themselves with, they hope, the right informa-tion, before making their choice, assuming the choice is theirs to make. Often pivotal in that decision is what parents make of the head. 'Market research shows that the first, most important thing is whether you trust the head', says Hands (MCS Oxford).

From the moment when prospective parents first meet the head, a relationship is formed, opinions fixed. 'Parents are extremely judgmental,' confides one head, 'they make up their minds in the first thirty seconds.' Behind the friendly smile, the warm handshake, and the engaging manner, heads are ever-mindful that parents routinely reach decisions about schools, based upon such perceptions. It works both ways: heads routinely make instant judgments on parents. 'I can tell as soon as some parents walk through the door, that they're not going to get what they want,' says one head witheringly. 'That's the key really, it's the parents more than the pupils. We always take into account the parents.' Variously described by interviewees for this book as clients, customers, and jokingly, punters - the latter epithet making heads akin to bookmakers - parents are care-fully evaluated, sometimes for their capacity to pay fees, plus extras. Full Harrow kit comes in at over £2000, for example.

Although it has an anti-independent schools reputation - unfairly deserved - Mumsnet, Britain's most-trafficked website for parents, is replete with threads about which leading brand is best for their dd (darling daughter) or ds (darling son). One is headlined: 'If Winchester College don't accept ds1, what about Charterhouse?' Specific comments on heads include: 'Dulwich has always been a good school, and there's a real buzz about the headmaster.' Advice on meeting the head flows freely, addressing posts such as: 'Are the heads interviewing the parents to see if they will fit in?' and 'Be yourself, and wear a nice blouse?' One recommends: 'Leave the LV (Louis Vuitton) bag at home,' provoking the response: 'Depends which school, a LV bag might be a prerequisite to get a place.' Among the practical tips for Mumsnet mothers: 'If you wear a skirt, make sure it exits the chair at the same time you do when you stand to leave/ do a tour. Nothing more embarrassing than accidentally flashing your knickers at a prospective school headmaster.' Sharper minds suggest the following: 'Remember that they are the people with something to sell - not you!' and 'The meeting is to see if you like the head, not if the head likes you.'

At Tonbridge, Haynes says, 'Unusually, of the big schools, I see any prospective family who wants to see me: 300 families a year, at least. We do not have a view that the parents are a nuisance here. Which is not always how it is.' Others adopt the line taken by JAGS head, Gibbs, 'At secondary school level, you're recruiting the child into your school, and therefore, we interview the children, not the parents.' One Mumsnet post affirms: 'When my ds was interviewed for St Paul's we were also "interviewed" separately.' Describing Radley parents as 'generally well off, they travel, they tend to be quite open, so I don't find them parochial,' McPhail is, however, periodically surprised at their gaucheness: 'You get some parents, who come in and say, "Oh gosh, I haven't been in the headmaster's study before." You just think, "Crikey, you're fifty now. Please! Get over it."'

For every parent who would choose independent education - 57%, according to the latest Independent Schools Council research - only 7% can support the fees. '35.6% of pupils in HMC schools across the UK received help with their fees in 2011/12 totalling £119 million in assistance,' states the HMC website. Despite one in three independent school children receiving some form of fee remission, many scholarships are nominal; full bursaries aid only a small minority - most pay the full whack. Although some grandparents help in footing the bill, or part of it, parents invariably call the shots when choosing the school, subject to their offspring passing the relevant exams and performing well at interview. Many struggle to afford the fees, as Hands explains, 'These people are making sacrifices from their pockets. Sure, there are those that have lots of money, but we have a lot of parents, who are scrimping and saving, because it's what they believe in.' The reality is that a significant minority regularly forego holidays, or re-mortgage their home, to fund their children's education. City of London Girls' head, Vernon, explains, 'Whilst we have girls of very highly paid City and legal professionals, there are an awful lot of parents for whom the fees are an enormous stretch. They all learn that everyone's got something to offer - whether or not, you've got two houses, winter in Barbados, ski in Val d'Isere, or frankly, you sometimes go to Brighton for an awayday.'

In common with many independent schools outside the affluent south east, Manchester High has seen an increasing number of parents in financial difficulties, as the head, Hewitt explains: 'The hardest thing is dealing with people who can't afford the fees, either because they hit hard times, or they've come into the school thinking: well, I'll just get my foot in the door and then I'll try and get a bursary. At the heart of everything I do is a girl. I want to do everything I can for that girl to have the very best possible start in life. It's very difficult if the family can't afford the fees. I look at what point they are up to in the school. If it's a mission critical year, GCSEs or sixth form, I've got to find some way of keeping them here. You do sometimes wonder whether parents are trying it on. We really drill down into their finances, ask questions. We have a bursary fund. I've got to make sure that that money is being spent wisely. I feel a moral duty. So, it is academic merit and looking at the need. If funds are limited, you've got to decide who it's going to have most impact on. Before we allocate the monies, we do home visits. It's got to feel right. It's not a black and white thing that you can set out. But I've got to be totally convinced. The hardest thing is a girl who has only just started, maybe a year in, both parents made redundant, what are you going to do? Realistically, you've got to find six years of fees; it's an increasing problem. Some rely on families to help. Sometimes we put in temporary hardship funding and help to find them another school.'

Where selection is deemed imperative, parents, as well as children, can be discreetly assessed at the outset. Townsend, the 57th headmaster of Winchester, our oldest public school (the first was appointed in 1382), suggests that respect for learning and knowledge is the dominant culture. 'I have tried to communicate that very clearly to our customers, without any ambivalence,' he says. 'Part of my job is to put off the people who are never going to understand or appreciate the school's core values and ethos.' According to Townsend, Winchester has a natural unworldliness, affording a learning environment which can only exist in the peculiar culture of England. The school's tradition has been described as 'intellectual, moral: providing the power behind the throne rather than the throne itself, the traditional characteristics of the English intelligentsia, less obvious or pronounced compared to their more flamboyant European counterparts.' Townsend agrees. Winchester parents apparently like the idea of their boys being able to spout a bit of Virgil in Latin at a dinner table.

Housemasters, reveals Townsend, still have complete autonomy in offering Winchester places, two years before entry. 'The housemaster will also take into account the parents,' says Townsend. 'He will make an assessment: do these parents really understand us?' Before rubber-stamping each housemaster's decision, Townsend sees the boy, plus parents, a year later. Being the product of an Old Wykehamist does not guarantee anything: entry is entirely meritocratic. 'We have a relatively low number of sons of OWs for two reasons,' says Townsend. 'One, because they tend to go to professions that don't make them rich. And bright fathers don't necessarily produce bright sons.' He would like to have more OW offspring 'because their parents are in tune with the culture of the school.'

Up the hill from Winchester College, Gandee describes St Swithun's parents as 'very sensible'. There are some schools, she emphasises, where there are more 'flash with cash' parents, who are 'less sensible'. She considers her 'current parents are really important because so many people come to us through word of mouth, and if they feel really warm towards the school, that's a very good way of reaching out to prospective parents.' Gandee is glad to have 'less of those rather over-anxious parents' who dominate some London schools. On assuming the Dulwich headship, Spence confides, 'I was warned about London parents and their demands.' Wright, at Merchant Taylors, offers a contrasting frame of reference, 'I came to north London from Sittingbourne, with the warning that north London parents are incredibly pushy: you're going to have a hard time. That's partly true, but the only difference is that some parents there tended to threaten you with violence; here, they threaten you with litigation.'

For parents with more conventional concerns, such as exam results, years before they happen, Low at Lady Eleanor Holles, offers perspective, 'One of my lines with prospective parents is, "There comes a time, not long after you've left university, when no one cares what you got for Geography GCSE any more. They are just hurdles to the next stage." '

At the entry stage, a universal caveat applies in selective independent schools: make sure your child is up to it. Not wishing to blunt justifiable aspiration, most heads vigorously deter the unrealistically over-ambitious. 'I say to parents all the time: "There are lots of great schools out there; the most important thing is to get the correct fit, not the dinner party fit, but the correct fit for your child" ', says Hamilton at Haberdashers. This is echoed at the Perse, in Cambridge, where Elliott cautions prospective parents: "Don't waste your money, and don't take up your child's Christmas holidays with intensive coaching for entrance tests, because you could be doing them a disservice in the future. You need to be the right child in the right institution."

To help parents choose, Vernon advises: 'The head has got to inspire confidence in a parent because otherwise that head is unlikely to inspire confidence in the child. Parents have got to feel happy in the choice of school, and choice of the head. Children will recognise that if parents aren't happy, then the child, however subconsciously, might then think: well, hang on a minute, so I'm just allowed to go to a second best school. That's no good.' Once the school is chosen, the parent-head relationship evolves. Day school parents, whose children sail through effortlessly, are greeted with warmth and familiarity. They see and hear only good things from the head - at concerts, plays, prize-givings, or on touchlines. 'They see fragments of you and they generalise from the fragments,' says Elliott. 'In a day school, you physically see parents a lot, which has its benefits, in that things like concerts are well attended during term time; whereas here, you won't find many parents coming,' explains Hawkins, head of Harrow. 'The frequency of parental communication is naturally lower, but these are, very often, very sophisticated, very busy parents.'

A minority are relatively disengaged, overseas or overworked, leaving everything to the school. From his seventeen years as an Eton beak and housemaster, Claughton recalls: 'You go for years without seeing some parents. I was amazed when parents of boys at my house rang up to say: "Can we take him out on Sunday?" And then not even have a conversation about them. I never quite understood that.' In 'a completely counter-intuitive' analysis, Haynes believes that 'a good boarding school has a stronger relationship with its parents than a day school.' He points to the dozens of parental emails every housemaster receives daily. Sue Marks, head of Withington, recalls her visit to Eton, 'I remember asking Tony Little, "How many parents do you see a term, and what do you see them for"? He looked at me and said, "Well I tend to see them if the boys are in very great trouble, and I'm about to ask them to take them home for a while." '

In dealing with Eton parents, Little says: 'We go as far as you can in a way that will be of benefit to the boy. It's boy-driven. If we've done our job right and created the right kind of relationship with parents in the first place, there should be people here who have a way in to the parents, which doesn't mean it's a formal situation. In terms of disciplinary issues, my default position is that we have a moral obligation if we have taken a boy, to see him through. So, we absolutely don't hoik people out because they don't reach a certain academic standard. We initiate a conversation so that everyone knows where we are, to talk about the options. We spend quite a lot of time trying to get things right.' The importance of devoting sufficient time and energy to parents is underlined by Bailey at St Paul's. Since Bailey succeeded the high profile Martin Stephen as High Master in

2011, maintaining a low profile has been a conscious decision. 'At present, I have judged the needs of this school to be for me to communicate with parents, assuaging any concerns they may have about an extraordinarily complex and challenging rebuilding program, and attending to that.'

A challenging parent demographic exists in some schools, as Claughton, KES head, outlines, 'It's not always entirely easy because we are 60% Asian. We have a lot of Muslim boys. Could I honestly say that I understand the family circumstances and the cultural contexts of all of my kids? No, I couldn't. When we have our Eid party, and there are 200 Muslim boys and old boys praying with an Imam, I'm really moved by seeing my school - this is Enoch Powell's old school - being one that's successful at being multiethnic. But I couldn't say that I understood. Similarly at parents' evening, when the parents come along: mother has a covered face and won't shake you by the hand, and the daughter has to be there to translate, because the parents, particularly the mothers, don't know any English. There are lots of pockets where that's increasingly common.'

Where necessary, Savage (Alleyn's) suggests that 'Kids do respond to punishment. Parents, usually, can be persuaded that it's appropriate.' He was previously in charge of discipline, as Westminster Under Master, 'busting the skivers and the smokers.' Most heads, like Savage, work very hard to resolve problems with parents; they all have problem parents. Certainly, the number of issues they typically encounter, and the nature of parental response have changed. Spence believes that 'the death of the deferential parent' happened in the 1990s: ' "Oh, thank you" became "Why don't you?" and therefore, I'm having more examples of people sitting here, saying what their expectations are, as expectations have grown, notably of teaching, and the extraordinary demands made on teachers'. RGS Newcastle head, Trafford, highlights 'particularly sour parents that you can never satisfy: they grind you down.' According to Elliott, 'When Perse parents have a grumble about something, it's very easy, as the head, to say, "Silly parents, they don't understand." But if they don't understand, I've failed in my communication systems.'

Pushy parents populate many high-performing schools. Benenden head, Oulton says, 'We have parents who are very ambitious for their children, but then that's a parent's job, isn't it? If they are too ambitious, and it's causing the child damage, then you say it, if they knock their child too much, and her confidence needs to grow.' McCabe (NLCS), who regularly advises Michael Gove and Prince Charles, thinks differently: 'I'm more likely to have difficulties with staff who say the parents have unrealistic expectations for their daughters. I always say, "Isn't that great that they've got such dreams for their daughters and that's why they've sent them to this school." They have that fantastic belief, particularly in Asian cultures, that if a girl's not very good at Maths yet, it's because the teacher hasn't found the right way of teaching them yet. I'm really sympathetic to parents who are incredibly aspirational for their children because I can see this in Korea (where NLCS has a franchise school). That's why the Korean economy is so successful; that's why educational attainment is so high there.'

Schools employ a well-established protocol to ensure that most day-to-day concerns can be dealt with by others, preventing heads from being swamped by parental anxieties and minor issues. By the time a situation reaches the head, the problem is usually quite serious. Hands (MCS Oxford) summarises a typical approach, 'I say to parents when there are difficulties, "Look, there are three parties: child, parent, school. If all three move in the right direction you can accomplish near miracles. If one isn't in line, then you've had it." ' When they have to see her, suggests Vernon, 'parents are emotional about their children, whatever the situation, terribly upset, if they haven't done well, or they're in trouble. Sometimes, it's very difficult for parents to see beyond that, at how we deal with things. People will respond emotionally, and when we respond emotionally, it's not going to be as constructive as it could be.'

Dealing with onerous and challenging circumstances requires intelligent risk mitigation, as Hawkins explains, 'Often it's about process. A parent makes a certain kind of complaint. What are we going to do with this? Are we following our policy? Frequently, it's our initial response that will just set something off. It can require a very sophisticated response, well thought-out and pertinent. In any school of this size, at any one time, you've got potentially three or four issues that could become a serious legal matter. Thankfully, very few of them do. But they could, so you've got to spot the pitfalls to prevent litigation arising'. Claughton (KES) says 'In seven years, I have only been involved in one formal complaint or appeal of any kind with a parent. I think our parents are more forgiving than down south: the litigious world hasn't come to us.'

At Wycombe, Hall has to deal with 'some of the most powerful and resourced families in the country, and indeed internationally, who bring their daughters to be educated here. Therefore, it is very important, where I think that something is right, to be able to press for that to be the outcome, and to be supported by resources in order to do that. I also have to protect the school. Because some of our parents are quite powerful, they will sometimes want very individual concessions to be made for their daughter, which frankly would not be fair to other girls, not a fair distribution of resources, and also, although parents don't see it at the time, can actually bring social criticism from other girls from which their daughter might suffer. When parents start off aggressively, it does such damage to the relationship with the school, and one is always trying to get a reasonable dialogue going, in which both parties are listening to each other, and trying to see what the problem is, to work it out. At Wycombe, I have felt it very important to use various tools to support what I feel is right in the face of sometimes quite powerful parents: having very firm and clear policies and having had those very carefully lawyered.'

Smellie (Farrer) routinely gives legal advice to heads in this situation, 'The head's position can be quite a lonely one at times; disputes with parents can be very emotionally draining for them. There are a lot of alpha males and alpha females amongst the parent bodies (of leading independent schools): they're very intelligent, they've been very successful, and they don't like not succeeding. They particularly don't like it when it relates to their children; that really gets their goat. In those circumstances, when they've got financial resources, they can put the school to an enormous amount of aggravation.' When it comes to expulsion, Smellie points to a changing culture, 'Twenty years ago, a head could quite safely expel a pupil with no realistic expectation of an appeal, of a solicitor's letter; whereas now, at the very least, for every ten pupils you expel, you will probably get at least one solicitor's letter and two or three appeals.' Causes of expulsion, he adds, are comprised of: 40% bullying, 20% drugs, and the remainder for sex, persistent smaller breaches of rules, and failing to work.

Smellie highlights parents who become 'emotionally preoccupied and wedded to whatever outcome they want to receive, that simple emotional energy can put the school to huge amounts of effort. Headmasters and headmistresses who have busy lives, can be getting five, six aggressive and unpleasant emails a day. There they are, trying to take strategic decisions about the curriculum, finding that they've spent two hours or more dealing with these really aggressive emails, trying to construct a response which sticks to the line, is not placatory, but equally, is not going to fuel the fire. If things escalate,' says Smellie, 'it's like a chemical reaction, it gets worse and worse. At that stage, when it's a battle between an alpha head and an alpha parent, it's inevitably going to end up with the governors, at the very least, having to adjudicate.' Sometimes, he says, schools do reluctantly 'settle carefully,' i.e. back down and give way in the face of possibly protracted, expensive litigation, particularly from overseas billionaires and oligarchs with infinite resources, who are used to getting their way, whatever the cost. If money talks, here it bellows.

In 2012, when addressing a conference, Sir Michael Wilshaw said, 'Teachers often have to instil traditional values in pupils to make up for wider failings within the home. Schools have to fill this vacuum, even if it means being unfashionable, counter-cultural and setting good examples where few exist at home. Schools - particularly those in poor areas - have no option but to be surrogate parents so that children can achieve.' Independent school parents do not come with a rule book. Simply being able to afford the fees is no guarantee that they will always behave appropriately or with decorum. Heads use their discretion. Gibbs (JAGS) says: 'I have had parents coming in who've had fights at dinner parties at weekends. They said, in the olden days, heads would have leapt in, and I say 'no'. Also, where girls fall out at sleepovers in other people's houses on Saturday night, then one has to draw the line. Sadly, we have a generation of parents, in many cases, who would prefer to be their daughter's best friend, rather than the parent.' When heads believe, or suspect, that parental conduct is harming the child, they regularly do step in, as Wright (Merchant Taylors) explains, in his study, 'I'm very used to dealing with parents doing things that might damage their children, and I'm quite happy to tell them so. They take notice, a lot of them. Others take exception to it, go away and think about it, and say they might mend their behaviour. That box of tissues is there for a reason: we have some difficult conversations in here.'

One of the great challenges for any school is to be singing from the same hymn sheet as parents. 'The clearer you are able to distinguish what the school stands for, the less likely you are to have areas of misunderstanding,' argues McPhail. He highlights a recent episode at Radley, 'A boy was in breach of an important school rule with the connivance of his parents.

They knew. I spoke to the father and said, "We're pretty cheesed off." Parents look for guidance from you more than they used to. Ultimately, you have to say, that the boy is responsible for his behaviour: he knows the school rules. So you deal with the boy. You're clearly not punishing the boy for his parents, you're punishing the boy for what he has done. You then deal with the parents. I deal with them on their own. If you try and upbraid a parent with the boy there, they're going to get defensive. Some of them don't have an answer. They're weak, terribly weak. Ultimately, they've been asked, "Can I do this?" and they say, "Yes", and they shouldn't have.' Spence (Dulwich) had similar experiences in his previous headship at Oakham, ''In a couple of cases lifestyle, as allowed by a parent, has led to me asking someone to be taken away from the school. Because if you're living that, and letting your fourteen year old daughter live that, I cannot. I like you. I think you're great. You're fantastic fun, and good luck to you, and may your form of parenting work, but it will not work within this school.'

Understandably, heads will not speak publicly of individuals, but accounts of parents not just allowing their teenagers to take drugs, but facilitating their purchase or directly supplying them to their sons and daughters make them wince. Too much money, too little time is a not uncommon problem, especially among some of London's elite. And it spreads to the leafier suburbs. One local mother was recently overheard saying to her Dulwich friend, 'Sending my daughter to x (a well-known boarding school) was the best thing I did, gives me more time for my tennis.' Whether it is an all-consuming, high-powered career or a high-maintenance social life, high-flying parents can lead to low self-esteem kids.

Clarissa Farr, High Mistress of St Paul's Girls', provides seminars to parents on setting boundaries for harmonious family life, explaining that 'being a parent is the role for which people have the least training. I have a lot of parents in powerful professional roles who nonetheless find parenting a challenge.' A report in 2011 found that almost half of all parents spend less than five hours a week bonding with their children. Farr believes that parents can overcompensate for being away for long days by failing to be tough enough with their children. She told *the Sunday Times*: "We're deceiving ourselves if we think we can bring up our children through an iPhone. Some busy parents give their children everything except the boundaries they need to find their secure place within the family and at school."

Some heads caution over what to expect in the teenage years. Low tells parents, when their girls reach thirteen, 'Brace yourselves now for the parties'. She believes it is very important 'to pre-warn them about things like parties and alcohol. Otherwise, there can be a problem because we have these lovely sweet little girls, and suddenly there's a party, and you discover there was a whole load of vodka there - because that's what happens. Check that the parents are going to be there. It is important for parents to know if their daughter is doing x, y or z, that it's normal, and she will be alright in the end.'

Occasionally, there are terrible consequences, when parents ignore warnings about serious issues. David Levin, City of London Boys' head, says, 'If, in my view the boy's career, wellbeing is imperilled, I will be pretty intrusive.' His robust attitude stems from experience during his headship at a previous school: 'Some parents were going to their country cottage, leaving their sixteen year-old boy in sole charge of the house. I knew he was dealing drugs - okay, it was out of school, he didn't bring it into school etc - and that there were some pretty wild parties going on. I called the parents in, and said, "We think you should know this. I know it's not part of our remit, but we think your son and his friends are at risk."

The guy tore a strip off me and said, "Your responsibility is for when the child leaves home until he gets back. Otherwise, he's my responsibility, and I'm quite happy with the way A is conducting himself, and how things are going." About five weeks later, he sold an ecstasy tablet to a friend, who collapsed in a nightclub and died at seven in the morning. The parents of the boy who died had a real go at me because I hadn't slung this chap out for dealing drugs in an empty house, or at least, hadn't made every attempt to tell every parent in the school. I said, "Are you suggesting that I should write to every parent in the school and say: so-and-so is dealing drugs in an empty house every weekend. Tell your son to avoid it." They said, "Yes." I said, "Well, my remit doesn't run that wide. I can't do it." Such events are, fortunately, very rare. But this tragic episode illustrates how heads can find themselves in very challenging circumstances when dealing with parents. Ultimately, heads want to work with them for the common benefit of the child; they do not want a battleground, nor unnecessary confrontation. While most parents enjoy largely good relationships, underpinned by strong mutual respect, some have unrealistic expectations, placing unreasonable, sometimes overwhelming, pressure on the head and the child. Children feel that acutely. So do heads, although it is seldom acknowledged.

Vernon (CLGS) summarises what many heads regard as the essential elements for a productive partnership, 'I don't think that schools and parents can bring up children in isolation. You're not the one bringing up the children, but in order for the children to be settled and happy, it's essential for them to feel happy, settled, comfortable with who they are, otherwise they're not going to be able to thrive and flourish. Often parents say to me, 'Diana, for you, what's the most important thing?' I say, "That your daughter's happy. We can do everything, if she's happy. Then we can encourage her in all the right directions. If she's not happy, then it's going to be much more difficult." '

# CHAPTER TWELVE

# HEADMASTER VS HEADMISTRESS

*Men are from Mars, Women are from Venus* is 'the all time, best-selling nonfiction hardback' title, claims HarperCollins. But why has John Gray's book been so popular? Perhaps because the title is so well-conceived, the theme so universal or because its central tenet is so simple: Gray's 'golden key to better relationships' rests in the acceptance of differences by both genders. Whatever the reason, his magnum opus resonates across cultures and age boundaries, placing it among the most successful self-help titles ever published.

Since headmasters and headmistress are not usually in relationships with each other, how is this relevant to headship? The answer lies in their respective relationships with, and approaches to, staff and pupils. The genders can and do differ - in Gray's narrative, each gender is best understood by their distinct responses to stress. Which provokes the following questions: how are headmasters different from headmistresses, and what do those differences mean in practice for the way in which they execute their responsibilities? Underpinning these questions is the separate, but related issue of managing boys' schools as opposed to girls' or co-ed schools. Of the twenty headmasters interviewed, fourteen run boys' schools and six run co-ed; among the twelve headmistresses, eleven run girls' schools, and one, Felicity Lusk is head of the all boys' Abingdon.

Some may disagree with such a chapter, in particular the belief upon which it is predicated, namely that there is any difference at all between heads, as determined by their gender. They will say that it smacks of sexism and stereotyping. While acknowledging that viewpoint, earnestly held, there are also those who agree that differences do exist, and that they are worth examining. From the views outlined below, there is no suggestion that headmistresses are better than headmasters, or vice-versa - just different in some respects.

Ask headmasters how they differ from headmistresses and an uncomfortable look descends on their faces. The question provokes not just reticence, but fear. A typical answer comes from Bailey (St Paul's), 'I have no view. That's not a diplomatic response. It's cats and dogs! Some are more empathetic, some aren't.' Cox (RGS Guildford) is palpably defensive, 'Gosh, that's a really difficult one. In the same way I've seen some pretty average female headmistresses, I've seen some pretty average male headmasters. I honestly can't really comment because I don't know enough about that particular aspect. In terms of empathy and approachability, that's just a natural thing, it doesn't matter if you're male or female, or young or old, you've got it. All I can say is: I have, I think, the best director of studies in the country and she's a young lady, and the headmistress of my prep school, one of the few headmistresses of a boys' prep school, and you appoint, not because they're male or female, because they do a great job, they're fantastic and so....I've slightly evaded your question.'

If most headmasters do not comment about differences in approach between genders, then most headmistresses do. Independent single sex schools invariably follow a traditional pattern: boys have headmasters, girls have headmistresses, while most co-ed independents are headed by men. Before 2009, no woman had ever run a boys' public boarding school. Until Felicity Lusk arrived at Abingdon in her black Jaguar, after twelve years as head at Oxford High School for Girls. On being appointed, she said, 'Women don't apply for these jobs. I hope more women will. Headship is not about gender, it's about a capacity to lead.' Lusk hates stereotypes. Acknowledging that her determination comes from her father, Stewart, who flew fighters during the Battle of Britain, she firmly rejects the idea of any gender difference in her approach, 'I would say that I do the job in exactly the same way as men and that the requirements are the same, there's no differential agenda at all. Leading a school must be similar to running any business or company where you're trying to encourage people to give their very best so that the organisation can be at its peak. I don't think there are different skills necessarily.'

At Eton, Little argues that in dealing with boys, they are more emotional than girls, 'I don't mean emotional in the sense of weeping and dabbing their handkerchief. But in terms of reacting in an impulsive way, in a way that's driven by the emotions rather than by the intellect, boys are more emotional. Girls at fifteen are much cannier.' He regards teenage girls as more emotionally intelligent and more mature. 'They are able to see how the way they are behaving is affecting a situation, whereas boys will just react emotionally and not think about the consequences.' Lusk disagrees. 'What that tells me is that girls sit there quietly and consider before they let rip, but I'm afraid that's not the case,' she says. 'I would say that boys and the men who work here are equally emotional as girls, young women, female teachers, and need a great deal of looking after pastorally. I'm dealing with human frailty, human nature, human potential.'

McCabe (NLCS), who has been head of both girls' and co-ed schools, develops Little's view, 'When I was deputy head responsible for discipline in a comprehensive, the boys would thump each other and it would be all over the next morning. If you tell a boy off, facing him down, all the rest of it, next morning, absolutely fine, no grudges. Girls are much more insidious, they'll fall out with each other in a very different way, it's all going on under the surface. Also, if you handle them in a disciplinary way, in the wrong way, then they will bear a grudge for ever, and if you don't know who they are, they take things very personally. You have to spend a lot more time with girls, valuing them, encouraging them, being positive about their achievements, praising them. I'm sure everybody responds well to that, but girls do in particular. I have focused a lot on those sorts of things during both headships, but particularly here.'

Lusk's approach is certainly empathetic. 'What has surprised me at Abingdon is the number of boys or my male colleagues who have dropped in for a chat and told me about very difficult and painful circumstances in their lives. There's been no invitation to do that, quite often young men who are coming out - that seems to be a bit of a feature of boys who drop in and talk to me for some reason. I don't know why. Or colleagues who are having marital problems, there's always personal stuff. Now I don't know whether that's because it's easier for them because I'm a woman. I would have thought not because the fact that I'm a woman here can be quite scary for them. Those are just surprising events that happen: the knock on the door over at the house on a Sunday morning and there was a male colleague weeping. Well you just have to be there for that person. It's instinctive, it's called emotional intelligence, you either have that or you find talking about those things very, very difficult.'

In lengthy interviews with twenty headmasters, none talked of dealing with the emotional problems facing other male staff or pupils, such as weeping colleagues or boys coming out as gay. Perhaps they are not seen as empathetic. It is hard to envisage many teenage schoolboys knocking on the headmaster's door, followed by, 'Please sir, I think I'm gay.' Maybe they do face these issues, but they chose not to discuss them when asked about the various issues they encounter. And yet collectively, they were significantly keener to be interviewed than headmistresses. In approaching heads simultaneously for this book, fourteen men agreed to an interview and confirmed a date before any headmistress even responded.

Vernon (CLGS) was the first woman to say yes, 'I will always say yes, do it. It's probably why I was the first female head to say yes to you.' Appointed as head after only six years in teaching, Vernon exudes confidence without arrogance, 'Most people will tell you I've probably always wanted to run things. I stand in the queue at the airport and I think I can run this. I can do it so much better.' Her words, accompanied by laughter, have a sense of engaging self-belief. More serious, yet naturally maternal, Oulton (Benenden) recalls from her teaching career that 'there was a certain pettiness in girls' schools, some rather old fashioned petty rules. I went to Charterhouse (a co-ed school) and there I just thought: my goodness, why can't a girls' school be more like this, why can't it have this kind of atmosphere?'

McPhail, head of the all boys' boarding school, Radley says, 'I don't know that the head's job is automatically that different, teaching is different. You do teach boys in a different way in an all boys' class. You can be more direct, you can use different sorts of humour. You're not making a compromise that is going to appeal to girls as well as boys, but also meet the potential anxieties of the boys being in a co-ed class. You might call that escapism, but it works really well. As a head, the jobs are pretty similar, whether you're in a co-ed or an all boys' school. I don't think there is a great deal of difference.' Townsend (Winchester) recalls from his headship at the co-ed Oundle, 'When it came to the execution of discipline, I found that girls were inclined to take things more personally than boys, more inclined to argue the toss, more determined to have it their way. Boys tended to shrug their shoulders and say "fair cop." One thing I learnt about co-education is that many parents have doublethink about their children: what they're prepared to allow their sons to do, they don't necessarily like their daughters doing!'

Evans (KEHS) has researched women and leadership in education, taking a lengthy sabbatical to complete her thesis. She offers an overtly feminist critique, arguing 'that there are still an awful lot of leaders in education who are totally ego driven, very much on the male heroic model of leadership. So it is creating scenes of themselves, where they appear to be brave risk takers, succeeding. Then when things go wrong, everything's completely and utterly and hopelessly wrong. That heroic model is still very deeply embedded. If you look at where power exists, it exists, by and large, where there isn't very much emotional intelligence.' Her alternative thinking - at least for the independent sector - has manifested itself at KEHS. Sport is optional. There is no head girl, no prefects, no house system, no prizes, no streaming, no sets. But the academic results are first rate.

McCabe (NLCS) has a fundamentally different approach: competition is uniformly encouraged; success is visible and openly rewarded. She also sees herself as being different from some of her male counterparts, echoing Evans' thoughts, 'From talking to heads of boys' schools, I think the power of the common room is very strong in the long standing boys' schools. From my years of working with people in this country and in other countries - in boys' schools, governors and heads work together more like a club. I've watched male heads of boys' schools operating with their staff in a way that I would conceive is pretty impossible. Watching male heads operating, sometimes they feel the need to occupy a lot of air space with what they say in meetings. Male staff here don't do that. When I've been at HMC type meetings, I don't really go to those any more, but there's sort of a clubby atmosphere there, which I just don't recognise, a sort of: I'm going to have my say now and I'm going to talk potentially for ten minutes. And you just think: oh for God's sake. Women are more used to having a much quicker interaction in conversation and just sorting things out, rather than making statements. My perception is there's a grandstanding that goes on by some.'

As a measure of how far headmistresses have come, two former North London Collegiate girls recall their heads: Madeline McLauchlan (1965-85) by Low (LEH), 'She had enormous authority and presence in a rather lady-like way. Her dog was always in her office. We had enormous respect for her, but practically no contact with her,' and McLauchlan's predecessor, Dame Kittty Anderson (1945-65) is remembered with affection by Hall (Wycombe), 'I definitely carried my daffodil (on founder's day) for Dame Kitty.' Hall explains that for women teachers at Wycombe before the war, 'the assumption was that the housemistresses, even the headmistress would be spinster ladies who might have a parrot or a dog, so their accommodation was single flats.'

Speirs (RSAcademics) highlights further differences that still apply today, 'Female heads are much more likely to read their speech or talk from notes than male heads,' he says. 'There will be exceptions, but the gags, the jokes, just sound that little bit more spontaneous when they're not being read off the page. In the context of headship recruitment, men are more likely to spend time networking, building, developing connections with colleagues, whether it's through formal committee structures or just informal grapevine, telephone calls, chatting at the bar at conferences. They're more likely to want to feed those networks and recommend colleagues for headships and generally recommend colleagues from other schools, people we might talk to, not necessarily their own colleagues, that's quite different. Female heads are just as supportive of their own staff and their development as male heads.

'The other thing that we've noticed is that women who are interested in applying for headships, perhaps a second headship, seem less likely to want to move, up sticks, move house, move their friends, move their family, move their husbands or partners. There are all kinds of reasons for that to do with the way society has developed, social networks that people are plugged into in their home areas. Women are more likely to have stronger roots where they live than men. It affects people's mobility.' Gibbs (JAGS) goes further, 'There are sexist issues, gender issues in headship. You get a lot of young male heads in their thirties, who come up from almost no experience, and there are many, very successful women heads who get their first headship in their fifties. That's partly to do with the way that men's and women's lives, their career patterns, are very different.'

Ellis (Odgers) identifies problems, 'It's much harder to find heads of our girls' schools because a lot of women don't want that ultimate responsibility and time commitment.' The most common reason is families. For boarding school heads, the role of headmistress can have extra difficulties compared to a headmaster, as Ellis explains, 'In a boarding school they get involved in a house because knowing the stresses and pressures on house staff, even if you haven't been one yourself, and being sympathetic is very important because it is tough. The majority of the boys' schools are far better equipped: they have nicer houses for them to have their families, they have better structures, and the staff expect to have evening duties and to be doing extra curricular activities, be going round the dorms at night. That's much harder in a girls' school because you'll have a lot of staff with young families who come in on a daily basis and just feel they can't do it.'

Oulton (Benenden) reveals the difficulties, 'My children were very young and I went to every possible effort for them not to suffer in any way because I was working. I don't think they did and they tell me they didn't. But it was really, really hard. I found it hard, I don't think they did. I took them to school every day I was always there collecting at the gate. I would block out the collection time in my diary so I was always there and I took them home for tea, but then I went back to work and I would work very late at night. I suffered as a result of trying to make life as lovely as I could for my children. When my younger daughter was nine, I saw her reading a newspaper at the kitchen table and the headline was: 'Children of full time working mothers do much less well at school.' I could see her focusing on it, and then she looked up and said to me, "Mummy it's lucky you don't work full time." And I thought: that was my success. I was there at all the important times. My husband always says I am temperamentally unsuited to be a head.'

All heads work hard. Hands (MCS Oxford) offers a typical headmaster's response on working hours: 'I never start before 8 unless it's really exceptional and I often finish late. I would like not to work on Sundays, it's always something that comes up in the appraisal, and I say: yes I'm going to try that out. But it doesn't often happen.' Are headmistresses even more conscientious? Do they work harder than men? 'I hadn't thought about it before,' says Ellis. 'But you're right, although they would not like to be told that. Men probably delegate more - I wouldn't be surprised if they delegate more - and they have the facilities, because the structure is there in boarding schools, with the house parents taking much more responsibility. They're such important communities, they're the home, the family the boy has in his school life in the house, so they're very important people. I don't think there is another job the same, nothing like being a head of a boarding school where your house is in the centre of the community and you and your family are in a goldfish bowl and you never get away from it.'

Hall (Wycombe) develops the point, 'I've observed that girls' schools, perhaps not Wycombe Abbey, tend to run on a tight budget. The senior management teams tend to be smaller, and headmistresses tend to be more involved in daily discipline and logistics, than I observe fellow headmasters to be. In boys' schools, the senior management teams are either larger, or members have delegated more responsibility in the male structures. It's the same with housemasters and housemistresses. So heads of boys' and co-ed schools tend to get out and about more. They tend, particularly boarding schools, to travel more. They tend to sit on committees and the school copes without them. Headmistresses tend to be much more on their turf, dealing with minutiae. Also, when you talk to parents as well about this, girls' reactions to other girls, to things they don't quite like in a school, to staff who they feel maybe have offended them or don't value them sufficiently, tend to be quite emotional and parents tend to get quite involved in those anxieties. That means that you have quite a lot of concerns from parents triggered by girls phoning them about these sorts of things that they want put right. My understanding from talking to heads of boys' schools and co-ed schools, is that boys don't wish to bring their parents in to fight their battles for them quite as much. In fact, they prefer them to stay off the premises. So maybe that's an explanation for why headmistresses feel that they can't leave their schools as much as headmasters do, but I observe that headmasters seem to feel that they can leave the camp more easily to go and do big important things and return to base.'

At Withington, Marks also points to 'a difference in parental expectations of the head. In a girls' school, parents expect to have access to the head for all sorts of reasons. Over the years, I've had a number of people say to my PA: don't fob me off with the deputy head. Parents of boys don't have the same concerns as parents of girls. A lot of the meetings I have with parents are about girls' social interactions, it's not about their academic progress.' Further echoing Little, she adds, 'Girls vocalise their feelings more and understandably parents get concerned about them. It's interesting that friends of mine who are male heads in boys' schools raise their eyebrows in amazement when I tell them some of the things that parents insist on coming to talk to me about. Because they never experience it.'

Someone who understands these demands well, after thirteen years in headship, is Helen Wright. According to her website, 'Wright is a leading commentator on education and a well-known headmistress.' Until January 2013, she was head of the girls' boarding school, St Mary's Calne for nine years, and in 2011, she was President of the Girls' Schools Association (GSA) succeeding Low (LEHS). Shortly after Lady Thatcher died, Russell Brand wrote, 'When I was a kid, Thatcher was the headmistress of our country.' She certainly did much to inspire a future generation of headmistresses in her country: exactly half of those interviewed cited her without prompting, Wright among them. A phenomenon of positive thinking, she describes herself as being inspired by Margaret Thatcher rather than Germaine Greer. 'I've always been driven,' she says. Pushed from an early age by her devout father, a Scottish minister who regularly changed denomination, Wright became a head at the age of thirty - one of the youngest ever to be appointed in the independent sector. She personifies a phenomenon more frequently characteristic of headmistresses: a passion to inform of her phenomenally long hours.

'I don't think I ever stop working,' says Wright. 'I was very miffed in the last census that they only had two boxes to write an answer in for hours worked per week so the maximum you could write was ninety-nine. I get up at four in the morning so I can exercise, sort out email, get the children up. I need a maximum of six hours sleep, sometimes less, but I can cope. At the moment, I'm on a rhythm of about five and a quarter hours. If I'm being driven somewhere, I easily have a cat nap in the car. People often say to me, "Oh Mrs Thatcher used to do that." Great, well she achieved a lot.'

In 2011, Wright had her third child on a Wednesday morning shortly before Christmas during term time. Nothing unusual. But as Wright recalls, 'I was back at home from hospital before lunch. Just after lunch, I was back in school. You feel so proud when your baby is born. It was kind of: I did that, and look at this amazing baby, isn't she fantastic. I wanted the girls to know at chapel. I got the message back to school because she was born at about twenty to seven in the morning. We came back and when you've got two other children, you don't just lie down for a week, you can't do that. My husband went out shopping and I thought well, I want to share this. This is my wonderful baby and this school, this community, is part of this. So I put her in her pram and we came down. I will never forget walking down to the sixth form house, there were a couple of girls at the window. I waved and they looked up. It was joyful surprise and they came running down; by the time I got to the front everybody was there. "Ah Dr Wright, look at this baby." This was my life, this was my family, there wasn't anything instrumental in it, it was just this is what you do because it's right. I went around school and ended up back here (in my study). I had to sign a few things and why wouldn't I?'

Replete with photographs of Wright and baby Jessica, she gave full access to *the Daily Mail*, which reported her story extensively under the headline: 'Headmistress goes back to school…7 HOURS after giving birth.' Two years on, Wright told me, 'I was a bit surprised. Our PR woman said: this is an opportunity because you can say very clearly what you think about women and babies. Obviously, it was presented in a sensational way, so you have to rise to that and take from what was a potentially controversial standpoint to say: well this is what I do. This is about women's choices. It's not about saying everybody should do this, this is about me and my baby and the possibility that flexibility exists, and understanding that is so amazing.

'It's the next step we need to take. We're locked down so much in really restrictive boxes and if we're going to achieve our full potential as the human race, then we need to get outside those boxes and not be afraid of thinking broadly. I thought it was very good for the girls, because they could see that you don't just have to listen to the news you can make the news - that's really important for them. They got really worked up, engaged. There were even girls posting things like: "I think my headmistress is inspirational," That was lovely. It's been very good for the school because it put us on a platform, broken free from the impressions people may have had. When you think: girls' boarding school, Wiltshire, you might suddenly have a picture of something that we're not. To be able to challenge that in a very clear, explicit way has been very good, and good for education, for people to see schools as places where they are challenging society.'

Wright points to a guest speaker at St Mary's, the sixty-two year old Lord Lucas, owner and editor of *the Good Schools Guide*, 'Ralph, Lord Lucas, came to speak to the Upper Sixth. He talked about how women were always going to find it difficult because they need to take ten years out to have babies. One of our deputy head girls, who wants to be a doctor, came up to him afterwards. She was shaking with rage, but she spoke very articulately and said: "We have in our headmistress, we have this person," she was using me as an example (of women having babies and going straight back to work). He was a bit taken aback, describing it as "a bruising experience". It's difficult for people - at a certain stage, they've come from a certain background - to change their minds. I understand that, but you have to recognise we've come a long way in a short time as a society.'

But not in all respects. Thanks to Sheridan's comedy, the combination of 'school' and 'scandal' remains popular with headline writers. A recent example is that of Dr John Triffitt, 54, whose former wife, Jayne, is the head at Woldingham, a prominent girls' boarding school, where Triffitt also taught part-time. His inappropriate relationship with a girl at the school was investigated in 2013 by the Government's Teaching Agency. Other well-known schools have encountered similar problems involving several independent heads, according to press reports in recent years: in every case it has been a headmaster rather than a headmistress at fault. Governors have sometimes been slow to act, with their hands only being forced after stories were leaked to newspapers. Early retirement soon followed.

Five of the seven headmistresses aged over fifty interviewed for this book are divorced. The figure for the twenty headmasters is 10%. Is this very small sample size representative of a wider picture? "I'm afraid it is,' says Ellis (Odgers). 'I'm not surprised. It is a terrible strain.' That strain, she says, is greater for women than men, especially for women running boarding schools because 'there is the whole business of: is there a job for the other half.' One head points to her hours of work, 'It is certainly over seventy a week. When my ex-husband left, one of the things he said to me was: you are married to your job.' In interview, not one headmaster talked about work consuming his life, even if it does.

At their 2012 conference, Helen Fraser, CEO of the Girls' Day School Trust, which comprises twenty-four independent girls' schools and two academies, said that women should be 'ambitious in their relationships,' by choosing a husband who would 'act as a cheerleader for their careers.' One husband who was cheerleader was Lord Hall, the BBC director general. His wife Cynthia Hall (Wycombe 2008-2013 and St Helen and St Katharine 1993-2008) pays tribute, 'My husband was working for the BBC, and then the Royal Opera House, and was very kindly commuting every day because of the decision that I'd made to go and work in Oxfordshire.' Fraser followed up her cheerleading speech at the 2013 conference by saying that headmistresses 'need to build girls' confidence and resilience to help them blow their own trumpets in the workplace and weather the tough times they will invariably encounter.'

Sympathetic to that argument, Clarissa Farr (St Paul's Girls') had previously written a newspaper letter, suggesting that girls educated in a single sex school have more time to express "the distinctive female point of view," adding: "In future society, collaboration rather than competition is going to matter. The special skills of women, understood and honed in girls' schools, will be ever more crucial." Farr was responding to Lord Lucas, as mentioned above. In 2012, he angered many headmistresses by writing that single-sex girls' schools risk going out of fashion, that they are no longer the best place to prepare girls for 'a world of men, marriage and career' and that they will not survive. He concluded: 'Girls are going to be competing with men all their working lives and need to find out how to do that from the beginning.' Watching Lucas speak and reading his authoritative commentary, criticism of him seems somewhat misplaced, originating perhaps from the perspective of self-justification. He may not always be right, but his views, far from being obsolete, appear objective and well-informed. ISC figures show that the number of single-sex independent girls' schools fell from 209 in 2007 to 157 in 2012.

Although they may secretly agree, very few headmistresses articulate their thoughts quite as candidly as Evans (KEHS), 'Women are much more modest than men! You see it at the most simple level: when I get applications in, men will often say in their letters of application "I am an outstanding practitioner." They write very powerfully about how wonderful they are. Women just don't do that. It's extraordinary. Very few women, however much the evidence and what their referees say about them, just won't say it. It sounds as though I absolutely can't stand them, whereas in fact I adore my husband, my son and my father, all of whom I look after. For some reason, women think other people will promote them because they're good, they don't need to say that they're good. That's wrong. That's a mistake. Men can overdo it, but the idea that just being good is enough does limit some women in moving to the top levels.'

In headship, as in life, women and men may indeed be as far apart as Venus and Mars.

# CHAPTER THIRTEEN

# THOSE CURSED LEAGUE TABLES

In the anonymous waiting room at St Paul's Boys' School, a framed newspaper cutting has pride of place above the coffee machine. The banner headline proclaims: 'A Level Record as passes reach 110%,' by Michael Grade Inflation. 'The schools' minister,' it states, 'is thrilled that more people have passed A levels than sat the exams,' citing Maths in particular: '87% got A star grades, 42% got A grades, and 78% got Bs or above. Overall, the girls did better than the boys with the average sixth form girl getting 17 A levels and 52 AS levels. The average boy, on the other hand, managed only one pass grade, in cycling proficiency, and a fail in the fifty metre swimming badge.' It is a satirical spoof. Because their results in the real world are so superlative, St Paul's can afford to laugh. Combining GCSE and A level results, *the Sunday Times UK Top 100 Schools* in 2013 listed St Paul's Girls' as the highest ranked girls' school, and St Paul's Boys', the highest ranked boys' school. Their latest Maths GCSE results speak for themselves: of the 171 St Paul's boys who sat the exam, 167 got A stars, the other four got As. To describe these as outstanding, a much overused word in the modern lexicon of British education, is a genuine understatement.

Our national obsession with exam results, and the relative standing of individual schools, is surprisingly recent. The concept of school performance league tables - to provide transparency and consumer choice - was introduced by the Education Reform Act 1988. The first published results appeared in 1991. Masterminded by the Conservative education secretary, Ken Baker - educated at Hampton School, then St Paul's - the Act envisaged that published league tables of GCSE and A level results, by school, would give parents free choice in deciding where to send their children. GCSEs began life in 1986, replacing O levels. A levels have a longer history, starting in 1954, when only about 3% of children achieved 3 A-level passes; by 1981, this had risen to 10%; and by 1996, it was 23%. Today, it exceeds 40%.

League tables were a blessing for newspapers, generating acres of good copy: think of those substantial schools' supplements with uplifting titles such as *Parent Power*, which grew ever-weightier during the 1990s. In 2002, state and independent school heads joined forces to demand their abolition because they were "damaging the education service." Edward Gould, then HMC chairman, and head of Marlborough, said: "The tables serve neither pupils, parents, heads, teachers nor the general public." In an attention-grabbing soundbite, Martin Stephen, then High Master of Manchester Grammar (and later, St Paul's) branded the mentality behind them "a cancer on the face of education." They failed. Beyond the rhetoric, a succession of Labour education secretaries - David Blunkett, Estelle Morris, Charles Clarke, Ruth Kelly and Alan Johnson - were acutely aware of the political reality: the majority of heads may not want them, but most parents did. They repeatedly endorsed Baker's vision, adding greater transparency along the way. The present incumbent, Michael Gove, has gone further still, increasing the level of available information about each school's comparative performance.

For the modern generation of teachers, pupils, ex-pupils and parents, school league tables are almost as much required reading as following the comparative positions of clubs in the football Premier League. 'It is extraordinary how much store people set by them, other than education-alists,' says Savage at Alleyn's, London's most successful fully co-ed day school. 'We don't tend to, but others do: governors, parents, everyone. If I had a pound for everyone who has said to me, "Wow, you're beating Dulwich College, you're beating JAGS. You're 14th in the league table." I have to say, not least to the governors: hang on, we've done tremendously well, but any school will do this, and if broadly, over time, we're doing that, that's wonderful.'

Despite serious educationalists not putting much store by them, they continue to provoke strong opinions from many heads, particularly when separate league tables - published by different newspapers and research guides, using re-calibrated criteria - produce different results. Wycombe regularly sits in pole position across league tables, published by the Telegraph and Independent newspapers, while North London Collegiate has been number one in *the Financial Times* (FT) IB table for five successive years. The superior aggregate performance of girls' schools is uniformly visible in every table. Crunch the numbers from all the published data for A level/IB/pre-U, and the composite top twenty comprises: ten girls' schools, five boys' schools and five co-ed.

The highest ranked co-ed sixth form is always Westminster, which takes boys only, lower down the school. The head, Spurr says, 'Westminster is regularly at the top of the league tables. You have to understand why you think it's at the top, and then you have to think: what is going to keep it at the top, which is really very difficult. The fact that Westminster has been at the top of the most serious leagues tables (FT) for the past six years, means that you are constantly evolving and developing to stay there. There are two ways you can go: you can go down, or you can go up (in standard and performance) in order to stay where you are.' More than 90% of Westminster pupils routinely achieve all A star and A grades at A level, or pre-U equivalent: the highest in the country. To put this into context, of all state secondary school pupils sitting A levels in 2012, 10.9% of candidates scored all A star and A grades; in all independent schools, the figure was 31.6%. Among all A level candidates, the 18% who attend independent school sixth forms account for more than 50% of A and A star grades (source: DfE).

The thirty-two heads interviewed for this book manage highly selective schools with very high attainment at A Levels, or IB/pre-U equivalent. Every interviewee should be laughing like St Paul's: they are comfortably in the national top 100, twenty-five are in the top forty, fifteen in the top twenty, and eight in the top ten. But laugh, they certainly do not. The consensus position, as stated by most heads, is personified by the St Paul's High Master, Mark Bailey, who mutters darkly in his native Yorkshire tones, 'Those cursed league tables.'

They may be the Premier League of schools, yet being seen as an elite group has strong pejorative connotations, given the social and political context: 'Elitism, in education, is a loaded word in this country. But elitism in the nation's favourite sport, football, is not. Who is going to put a non-elite player into Manchester United or Chelsea's team,' asks Spurr. He points to the start of the coalition government, when Cameron and Clegg shook hands on the steps of 10 Downing Street: the pm went to Eton, his deputy to Westminster, and for good measure, his next door neighbour at number 11, the chancellor, George Osborne, to St Paul's. Spurr's opening chapter critique, 'There were those who were calling out: meritocracy is dead. Well meritocracy is the best-prepared person getting to the top, supposedly,' can be equally applied to the league table positions of independent schools. They are proof positive of elite performance. Meritocracy and elitism may invariably be misused or misappropriated by commentators with an agenda. But in fighting shy of being labelled as elite performers, many heads are defensively dismissive, and sometimes, overtly hostile, towards the very mention of league tables.

One head, who wished his critique to remain anonymous, disagrees: 'They tell you only one thing about the school, they don't necessarily tell you that accurately, and most of all, they tell you about output, not output in relation to input. We all know that. Hamilton (HABS) is openly scathing: 'Waste of time, waste of space, journalists. I've got no time for them, and that's not because we do quite well in them; they are a very narrow indicator of a school's success. They've done more harm than good, and they certainly do a total disservice to those schools which are doing a great job with a different type of pupil.'

The argument that the full value of independent education stretches far beyond a school's collective academic performance from one year group finds a more subtle advocate in Tony Little. 'I am singularly unfussed by league tables', says the Eton head. 'It genuinely doesn't seem to wash with the kind of parents we have here. I've only had three letters of complaint about league tables. All three were in the same week, some years ago, when bizarrely, for some reason, we came top of an A level league table. They were letters on the grounds of: we can't be doing the job properly if we are top of the league tables. There are also certain absurdities which one quite enjoys. For example, when the 'A to C' benchmark was introduced by government, the first time they produced it, Eton, together with Winchester or Westminster, was 0%, because we were early adherents of the IGCSE.'

Blessed by dramatically improved rankings, some heads endorse a more proactive stance, employing their school's enhanced league table performance as a promotional tool. One notable example is the much-acclaimed Brighton College, a mecca for co-ed boarders, and multiple winner of newspaper, *Tatler* and *Good Schools Guide* awards. Brighton has always been progressive: it invented the school magazine, built the first school gymnasium and created the first purpose-built science laboratory. In 2006, it became the first independent school to make learning Mandarin compulsory. Equally progressive in marketing their league table performance, Brighton's website states: '*The Sunday Times* described the College's fifth successive rise in the rankings as "an unparalleled achievement," noting its "staggering climb from 147th position in 2006 based on its ever-improving exam results, which now rival those of much more selective establishments." Most recently, Brighton secured sixteenth place in the A level table.

Ken Baker, now Lord Baker, would be proud to see further tangible evidence of his league table vision at Hampton. Opposite the reception desk at his old school hangs an enlarged page from *the Independent* newspaper, prominently displayed, highlighting the school's A level ranking: eighth place. According to Martin, the head, 'My take is that people look at them, and tend to bracket schools in categories: intensely academic, very academic. Our results improved substantially in my first few years, because when you start from a relatively lowish base, it's easy - improvement stands out. When you get higher up, it's harder to make the marginal improvement. Someone said to me, "You're just trying to turn this place into St Paul's." I said, "No I'm not. I don't want to be a second class St Paul's, I want to be a first class Hampton."'

A year into headship at Harrow, Hawkins pulled out of the league tables, following the example of Winchester, Eton and others: 'We were in a diminishing group of schools of our type within the league tables, looking increasingly isolated; you then find yourselves being compared unfairly with much more selective urban day schools.' This puzzles Gandee, head of the highly ranked St Swithun's: 'The fact that some schools don't enter themselves in the league tables, I think that's slightly odd. I don't know why we don't all do it'. Claughton (KES Birmingham) agrees, 'I had this argument with Manchester Grammar (where he is a governor). I can't understand why they're not in the league tables, they're the best boys' day school north of Oxford. Even if you're thirty-fifth, I'd still be in it.'

At JAGS, which is regularly in the top twenty-five of any league table, Gibbs says, 'We're quite a big school relatively, we might have 112 or 120 something in a year group. I always fantasise: if you chop off and take the top 75 or 90, or whatever they have in some of the schools that beat us in league tables, we'd be doing fine. So, it's quite interesting, we are doing fine.' Cox (RGS Guildford) adds, 'I can't knock them, because every year I can say: we're in a good position in the league tables. What I would like is a league table of ethos in schools. It's impossible, but that is the most important thing, it really is; and again, a league table of how boys and girls enjoy their education, that is equally important.'

Hawkins concedes that in his previous headship, at Norwich School, 'League tables were very useful for us, rather as for Barnaby Lenon (Hawkins' immediate predecessor), in his time, they were very useful for Harrow. If there was a real opportunity for a school to improve its measurable output, you can see: it can be done; why not let the league tables promote that for you? At Norwich, the school was often between 100 and 200, nationally; now, they are 35th or so. Over a ten year period, we were marked about 100 places higher. The same was true for Harrow during Barnaby's time.' He points to the added value of Harrow: 'Our results are in the top two or three in the country, in terms of what's being achieved with boys of this ability, because we've got quite a spread. Large numbers of our boys would not even get close to securing a place at St Paul's.'

Delve into the history of the tables, year-by-year, and you will find the same familiar names consistently appearing at the top level as you would have done twenty years ago: Eton, St Paul's, Winchester and Westminster. Halls, now head of KCS Wimbledon, one of London's Premier League, looks back on his remarkable decade at Magdalen College School with mixed feelings: his trauma is explained earlier. When he started, the school was in 170th position in the A level tables. In 2008, the year he moved to KCS, his former school, MCS made it to number one. But some stellar performers, that were at their peak, have faded over time. 'You think these things are timeless, but schools do go up and down pretty swiftly,' says Haynes at Tonbridge, now comfortably positioned in the upper echelons, far higher than a generation ago.

Of those that have fallen furthest, King Edward's School in Birmingham arguably stands out. In 1991, it was in first place, a fair distance ahead of Eton, Manchester Grammar, Winchester, St Paul's and Westminster. During an animated conversation in his capacious study, the frenetic, plain-speaking Claughton, appointed as KES Chief Master in 2006, outlined the narrative of events. No head could care more obviously about their pupils: his concern is conspicuous, his enthusiasm infectious.

As we talked, he disappeared into an alcove behind me, from where he retrieved a treasured FT cutting, quietly buried away.

Handing over the framed FT league table, hard evidence of former KES glory, he explained what had happened: 'For fifteen years, this school did bugger all, between 1991 and 2006. In 1991, we were the top school in the country, still, when the first league tables were published. It was a big lead. It got colder. It's hard to get bright kids in. The grammar schools have improved. People (in Birmingham) haven't got the money to send their children to independent schools; other schools have caught up. King Edward's had two Chief Masters, who were either inert or lacked ambition, or didn't even know how precious a jewel they had in their possession. When I came here seven years ago, we were very gradually, imperceptibly spiralling downwards, and once you get into a vicious circle - worse results, lower reputation, lower calibre kids, worse results, lower reputation - once you're going down, it's jolly hard to get back up. Heads get really sniffy about league tables, saying they don't tell the whole truth. My problem is: they do tell a truth. One of the main criteria, which affects what my parents think, in whether they want their children to come here and whether we're doing a good job, is what results they get, and therefore, what universities they go to. I'm afraid that *the Daily Telegraph* league table does tell quite a material truth. If six years ago, we were 78th, when once we'd been first, that means we are worse.'

Some heads cull weaker pupils two or three years before GCSEs, or immediately afterwards, to preserve their overall league table performance. Critics point to culling (the removal of under-performing children) as the darker side of independent school management, driven by league tables. No head will openly discuss the details, but Spence at Dulwich College is proud to say that he is not among their number. 'This year, we had a mini-hiccup,' says Spence, who arrived at Dulwich, after headship at Oakham, in 2009. 'I've spent ten years as a head being able to look at a comfortably climbing graph of league table positions. I've been able to say very confidently: I don't look at them because I've moved inexorably up. We are certainly not becoming a culling school. If I believe that a boy, at 16 plus, might not have crossed our GCSE hurdle, can however continue here - his parents having spent as much as they've spent on an education here - for two more good A level years, even if he will get Bs and Cs, he will stay. That costs us in league table terms.'

Beyond the individual stories of schools and their heads, two significant trends have shaped league tables over the last twenty five years: the move towards co-education and the inexorable rise up the tables of the single-sex girls' schools, which now far outnumber the boys' equivalent. Historically, single-sex education was synonymous with independent education. Today, less than 5% of independent schools are boys' only senior schools; in 1986, that figure was 25%. According to *the Times Education Supplement*, 'Boys' schools are in retreat, with numbers falling sharply in recent years. It may be just a matter of time before it is only the likes of Eton and Harrow that are flying the flag for boys' schools.' Radley and Tonbridge might disagree. Townsend, at Winchester, does not. He sees going co-ed as a distinct possibility: to preserve the ethos and academic excellence of his school. But not before 2016.

Co-ed schools begin to dominate numerically, once you go below the Top 50 in any league table. Marlborough paved the way by going co-ed in 1968. Rugby (1995) King's Canterbury (1990) Wellington (2006) and Repton (1992) are just a few of the many boys' schools to follow the fully co-ed route. Co-ed sixth forms are also increasingly common, following examples set at the very top, where Westminster (fully co-ed sixth form 1973), Magdalen College School (2010), and most recently, KCS Wimbledon (2011), stand out. Shrewsbury, which opened its doors to sixth form girls in 2008, will go fully co-ed in 2014. The Perse, which introduced a co-ed sixth form in 1995, went fully co-ed in 2012.

'We're within the M25,' says Hamilton (HABS) 'They often talk about that M25 London south-east bubble where life is still okay, but you're looking around for bodies up in Newcastle.' At Royal Grammar Newcastle, which went co-ed in 2008, the head, Trafford disagrees, pointing to the league tables: 'We're the best school (in England) north of Manchester on any measure of those. That's good for us and it means in a sense we can just park it and leave it there. And there's no pressure on us. We're still trying to get better, we still want to get better A Level results so that even more get A*s because we think they are capable of it if we can get it right. But the nice thing is that's a kind of given and therefore we can ignore it.'

More all boys' schools will inevitably follow. At least three interviewees for this book are reviewing the co-ed option. Parental demand, changing social attitudes, and business pragmatism all play their part. To some extent, so do league tables. Why? Because they achieve more top grades in nearly every A level subject, admitting bright girls - in the sixth form, and lower down - can help a flagging boys' school maintain its position, or move up the tables.

Positive proof comes in cataloguing the triumph of the girls over time. In the first published tables, the top slots went almost entirely to boys' schools. By 2013, girls' schools had been dominant for well over a decade, not just in taking ten of the top twenty places, compared to five boys and five co-ed, but in the top 50 as well. Last year, girls' schools took twenty seven of the top fifty places, against twelve for the boys and eleven for co-ed. Where KES and Manchester Grammar once reigned supreme, Wycombe, St Paul's Girls' and North London Collegiate stand proud. Not far behind come Oxford High, Guildford High, Withington, Haberdashers' Girls, City of London, JAGS, Lady Eleanor Holles, St Swithun's, Manchester High, and an army of similar high-performing girls' schools. Perhaps this explains why some headmistresses are more in favour of league tables than headmasters - the boys don't like being beaten by the girls.

In the neutral camp sits Gandee (St Swithun's): 'In the end, they just record the percentage of A*s, As and Bs at a certain school; it's just a statement of fact, isn't it,' she says. 'They're absolutely fine: you don't even need to treat them with a degree of scepticism'. Retiring Benenden head, Oulton, recalls the impact of her first headship at St Catherine's Bramley, 'The pupil numbers rose very dramatically. I hate to use league tables, but we did go up from about 190th to 17th. We went very rapidly up the league tables, the pupil numbers rose very quickly, the numbers applying just grew.' Success breeding success.

In diametric opposition to most of their male counterparts, there is overt enthusiasm among some of those running girls' schools. During her sixteen years as the dynamic head of North London Collegiate, McCabe has always been very pro-league tables, 'I think they're a fantastic way of opening up the debate about quality', she enthuses, providing perspective in her analysis, 'I've always thought that education suffered in the sixties and seventies from being a bit of a secret garden - schools liked to surround themselves with a mystique about their performance. I've never had a lot of patience with people who say they're much too blunt a measure. Parents are perfectly able to make judgments about schools similar to this one, and schools that are not at all like this one.

It's quite patronising to say that they are too blunt an instrument. It's also an excuse to say they make schools focus just on improving exam results. I just don't believe that.'

Before taking on NLCS, McCabe spent twenty-two years in comprehensive schools, culminating in seven years as head of Chelmsford County High School, from 1990 to 1997. When she started at Chelmsford, the school was 117th; the year she left, it was the highest-ranked state school in the country. She is understandably proud. 'The governors and I, we'd worked so closely together, it was very exciting,' says McCabe. Not all successful female heads share her enthusiasm. 'I'm well known for detesting league tables. I admire very much those schools which have had the self-confidence just to say: "We're not going to put our results in," ' says Marks (Withington), the most consistently successful girls' school outside London and the south-east. 'When I arrived, A stars had just come out at A level. We had the greatest percentage of A stars in the north of England,' adds Marks. 'My question to the staff was: we have 31% A stars and St Paul's Girls', that year, had 54% A stars - are their girls that much more intelligent than our girls? I'm fairly convinced that there isn't much difference between their girls and our girls. Or Wycombe Abbey or North London Collegiate.' Despite her dislike of them, she concedes, 'It would really matter to me if we weren't at the top end of those tables, because it would imply that we weren't bringing the best out of our pupils.'

Educated at North London Collegiate, Hall is, like McCabe, a star in modern headship. Gracious and understated, she is also media-savvy. Before taking over as head of table-topping Wycombe in 2008, Hall was head of St Helen and St Katharine in Abingdon for fifteen years. She speaks modestly of her experience after arriving there, 'I was very lucky because analysing the results, I could see that there was a tail. There wasn't much of a learning support department. By setting up really good learning support, we managed to raise the results quite significantly. Statistically, it can make a lot of difference. We were also helped because the league tables were just coming in: it looked as if the school had shot up the tables. I was interviewed. There was a public statement that I'd turned round the school, which was very awkward for me, because my predecessor was an excellent and highly-regarded head. Because there hadn't been league tables beforehand, she hadn't had the publicity for her work that should have been merited. I came in as a relatively young head, and we did well in the league tables, so it made a story. Because I've been in schools which have been high up in the league tables, I've never really had an issue with them. I see them as free advertising in broadsheets where I wouldn't pay for advertising.'

'When parents come to look at you because they've decided to look at the school's results, the league tables, then you can tell them about all the other things that you do. It makes me sad if people believe that we do things for the league tables, because what we do is, and you will hear this from every head, we try to realise the potential of every girl in the school. We've no idea where that's going to place us in the league tables, year-on-year, and we don't have discussions about the league tables with senior management.' Without doubt, heads such as Hall, Halls and McCabe have, in part, succeeded in their headships because of their schools' improved league table performances. Parents, pupils and governors do take notice.

Once Baker let the genie out of the bottle, there was never any going back on the publication of league tables. Whether heads like it or not, most people still want to know how their school - independent school, state school, old school, new school, potential school, even rival school - has done. Of course, there is so much more to education, and to life, than where your school is ranked. Like most parents, wise heads prefer to look beyond the minutiae of comparative exam results. Ask them about about the relative merits of their school's strong league table showing against their competitors, and they centre their attention instead on the child, who is leaving their care and entering adulthood.

Gibbs (JAGS) concludes: 'The thing that matters to me most is that a girl will leave here, independent, ready for life, ready to roll up her sleeves, understand she's had a privileged education, ready to give back to society, and make a difference for the better. That's the bottom line. But there's also that thing about resilience, that we need to give our girls resilience so they can cope: they need to be ready and resilient. It's a cruel old world out there, very often.' Low, whose school, Lady Eleanor Holles is also a consistent high-flier, presents a wider definition of performance beyond league tables, 'It is that intangible thing of: are they leaving as confident, young women, articulate, with a good set of moral values? Are they ready for the next stage in their lives? That's completely intangible. It's to do with our perceptions. That's really it, isn't it? Yes, they've got great results. Yes, they're going to whatever university, and that's wonderful, but how are they as people? Because in the end, that's what matters. It's not all the bits of paper we've got, it's who we are.'

# CHAPTER FOURTEEN

# GOVERNORS

'I have a fantastic governing board here,' says McPhail at Radley. 'That's something you don't think about before you go into headship - the relationship with your governors, and it's so important.' Hamilton (HABS) adds, 'What really matters is total clarity of expectation and understanding from the governing body. If you've been sent in to sort a mess out you need to know. You don't want to go in and find out that you can't do half the things you thought you would because the finances are in a pickle and that's slowed you down for four years while you fix it.' Another head comments anonymously, 'The governors here used to be grand, remote, rather out of touch with the common room, but not any more.'

According to the DfE website, 'School governors are one of the country's largest voluntary groups with around 300,000 contributing to strategic development and raising standards of achievement at more than 30,000 schools'. Approximately 10,000 of them are in the independent sector, and yet few prospective parents think to consider their background, or even check the list of names, ignoring the fact that the quality of a school can be measured, in part, by its governors. Instead it is taken on trust that governors do a good job. The characteristic that best defines them is altruism: they have the best interests of the school at heart while there is nothing in it for them. In every school, from Ambleside to Amersham, governors are putting something back into their community - unpaid, unselfish and largely unacknowledged. But, and the but is significant, they are also largely unaccountable.

There is no obvious answer to Juvenal's question: Quis cutodiet ipsos custodies - who watches the watchmen - as former Abingdon head, Michael

St John Parker, writing in *Attain* magazine concluded: 'The weakest element in the structure of Britain's independent school sector at the present time is its governance,' adding, 'governing bodies have made critical, and sometimes even fatal, mistakes.' Good schools manifestly need good governance: drawing upon their diverse skills and collective experience, governors have a duty to provide strong support and sound advice to the head. So what are the problems? Parker explains, 'To begin with, many governing bodies exhibit structural weaknesses - of size (too large, or too small, for efficient functioning), of organisation (no committees, or too many), or of composition (too many ex officio figures, or former pupils, or even, sometimes, parents). There are problems of competence - too few governors seek, or receive, training in their responsibilities and functions; some are too busy, but many are not busy enough, in their attendance at school activities.'

As charitable institutions, independent school governors have a legal duty for the conduct of their schools; their legal status is as a trustee, holding the property of the institution in trust. 'In any charity, including any school, it is the governors who have all the power, but they're all non-executive, which, even if they're doing a good job of staying in touch, just creates tension. There's a fine line for governors in independent schools to follow because they are non-executive trustees and they mustn't become executive, they must stand back and try and remain strategic, rather than operational,' explains Smellie (Farrer). Trusteeship responsibilities are primarily supervisory: management is left to the head and the Senior Management Team. Of the governors' specific responsibilities - setting achievement targets, strategic planning, approving finances, complying with legislation (i.e. health and safety, child protection), curriculum supervision and reviewing performance and pay - choosing the head is arguably the most important. It is here that the biggest mistakes can be made.

'There is always an element of risk in appointing the headmaster of a school, and governors are terrified, of course, of getting it wrong. But it's no good appointing a man with an MBA in how to run a school, who might have all the theory but who cannot bring heart, soul, colour, humour, the joy of working with teachers who love their subject and young people,' says Winchester head, Townsend - a steady guiding force, greatly admired for bringing heart, soul, colour and humour to the role since his appointment in 2005. This was much needed after a catalogue of crises experienced by his two immediate predecessors: Edward Tate (2000-2003) and Thomas Cookson (2003-2005). Tate, specifically, did not meet with the governors' approval. 'Governance is terribly important in a school and the relationship between the head and the governors, and particularly the chairman, is crucial,' concludes Townsend.

According to Smellie (Farrer), a governor of four schools, 'Where the head is not performing up to expectation, schools and governors are not going reach for their gun straight away, and in an ideal world, the chairman, and maybe others, can play a really good role in counselling the head, trying to steer the head in the right direction, and hopefully get the right result. Where one has a school that's been through a bit of a ropy period - maybe changed its head quite frequently over a period of time, has got a good and strong head, and the governors really need it to work - in those circumstances, you can see that the head can force it and can get his way, because the governors just cannot afford a falling out and to lose another head. By contrast, where you've got a school which is absolutely sailing along beautifully, in those circumstances, it's much more difficult for a head to take on his or her governors.'

Departing Manchester Grammar head, Ray, adds, 'I was once counselled about even thinking of being head at Winchester: governors are right behind you, until there's any kind of trouble, and then you will not see them for the burning rubber on their Bentleys, as they're going up the drive. In general, governing bodies don't like problems or difficulties. They want to hear everything is fine. A pat on the back if you're lucky.' Ray comments on the relationship between Martin Stephen, his immediate predecessor at MGS (1994-2004) and former High Master of St Paul's (2004-2011) with his respective governors, 'Martin was not overly impressed with the governing body at MGS at that time, the same at St Paul's for different reasons.' In 2010, *the Times* reported an "apparent confrontation" with the St Paul's governors over Stephen's ability to raise £30m needed for the school's redevelopment - a claim swiftly rebutted by the chairman of governors in a Times letter, in which he stated there was "no lack of confidence in his fundraising abilities." Stephen said he left for 'a complex of reasons' - there was 'no shred of truth' in the suggestion that he was quitting after a row with governors. Disagreements between heads and their governing bodies are a prevailing, sometimes painful, fact of life in headship. How they are best handled does not require the ruthless cunning of Machiavelli's Prince, more the determined diplomacy of Eleanor Roosevelt.

Smellie says, 'You see some governing bodies doing a much better job of understanding the issues of the school than others. It's to do with quality of the governors you get and it is also, upward management - a good head will do a good job of upwardly managing his or her governors'.

From a head in the hot seat, Elliott (the Perse) expands upon the theme, 'The bit they never tell you about is upward management, managing your governors, managing your chairman. Before you get thrown into the lion's den, you need to be told that you will have to manage upwards, that you have this group of people who are effectively your bosses, but they are remote bosses, they're not in touch with the institution on an hour-by-hour, day-by-day basis and that you've got to manage, deploy, utilise them in ways that will work well for you, work well for the school, work well for them, maximise their skill set. It's a whole different world talking about school governing bodies. Some are very large, unwieldy, others have wheels within wheels. But if it goes wrong, it can go badly wrong, and that's what normally does for heads. That whole business of how you handle your board of governors, how you use them to maximum effect, but without them micro-managing. You need human understanding, some sort of idea, which the board also share of: what are the expectations, what role are we going to operate here? It's the often-stated difference between governance and management, but within that phrase there are all kinds of multiple confusions.'

Most heads have no developed financial skills when appointed. If their role is that of a CEO, then they lean heavily on their bursar as CFO, where conflict with governors can arise, as Ellis explains, 'If you look at old school photos: the head would be in the middle and the bursar would be down the far end, and he or she's gradually worked their way up and they're standing by the head now in today's photographs. I spend quite some time with governors where they don't have wording in the contract: that the bursar reports to the head on the day-to-day running of the school. Some governors appoint their bursar or finance director, as is becoming more fashionable now, to report directly to them, and it can cause all sorts of problems. If there's going to be a relationships problem, that's where they've been mostly in the past: between bursar and head. I say to governors: it's harder to find a good head than it is a good bursar.

But yes, you could expect them to report to the chairman and the board on finances, but in discussion with the head.

'In terms of finance, previously heads had no experience and it is usually a weak area, and really as CEO, they are responsible for the finance too. A lot of schools have decided to move away from the ex-service bursar, who was marvellous and could stand and give parents a hard time if they hadn't paid their fees, and the next minute they would be clearing a blocked drain. That's what they were like and that's where the services were so good. But now they are looking, and we are being tasked to find, really senior finance people. Schools are having to think more about sweating the assets, and using things in the summer holidays: the head has got to be open to raising funds. It's beginning to happen in schools, but nothing like Oxbridge colleges. Development and fundraising used to be point ten in the list, it's now number one every time.' Gandee (St Swithun's) quips, 'I just want to wave a magic wand at my bursar to sort things out.'

Wright (St Mary's Calne) believes that 'the key skill of governors isn't it always, is in getting the right head' - a task which Ellis regularly fulfils. 'Governors used to focus on marketing and numbers first, finance second and the academic education bit would come further down the line,' says Ellis. 'Because then most governing boards didn't have people with HR experience and recruitment, and there weren't many educationalists, there were financial and legal people and the local Bishop, but not education and recruitment. Which made me think: gosh, there's a need for help with this.

'Governors sometimes don't know their schools very well. There is that group that just go for a meal once a term and don't get involved in the committees and don't get really inside the school. Today, governors and their demands of heads are much higher and it makes the job very difficult because, as I say to them, it's going to be human strengths and weaknesses, and we all have our frailties. Their expectations are terrifically high. I have to give lectures to governors quite regularly - it's a two way process, you've got to make the job of headship attractive too. It's amazing how many of them forget and become quite serious. Many governors will, during the process, suddenly say: gosh, what would the school say if we appointed this candidate, what would the message be to the outside world? So the type of school that they're at, how academic it is, what have they done within it and have they really raised their academic profile and enhanced it and brought the limelight to it so people are all talking about it, are important.'

At RSAcademics, Speirs says that, 'In working with the governing bodies of independent schools in appointing heads, I've been really struck by how varied the quality is. Sometimes you've got some excellent people that just aren't organised very well. In others, you've got people who don't realise just how important it is to give time to the process of appointing a head. That's a common criticism: they don't realise that they do have to invest a certain amount of time themselves, taking time off work, which some are reluctant to do. Worryingly, it's quite rare for governing bodies to have a clear idea of where they want the next head to take the school, and what sort of issues the school might face further down the line and therefore the next head needs to be equipped to tackle. Quite often, it's not until they come to appointing, and they come to think this through within the context of appointment, they actually discuss these things. Many governing bodies are not thinking further down the line, they're not looking beyond their immediate horizon.'

Browse through the board names at independent schools and you will find that the grander the school, the more distinguished and well-connected are the governors. 'Rugby's chairman of governors (Robert Swannell) is the Chairman of Marks and Spencer,' says Ellis. 'They've just got the most fantastic draw there.' Sitting alongside the chairman of Westminster school governors, the Dean of Westminster, Dr John Hall, are several titled folk: the good and the great of academia, commerce, the law, politics and the arts. A similar picture emerges at other top-drawer schools. For parents who do bother to delve a little deeper, these distinguished names are just a list on the school notepaper or website - most never get to meet them.

So what are governors really like? Most heads interviewed for this book are themselves governors at other schools - both maintained and independent. Some, like Little, are governors at several schools. As a journalist, I have engaged with governors from several leading schools. When interviewing some of them, like Dr Alan Borg, Westminster governor and former Director of the V&A, it is hard not be impressed by their specialist knowledge. Possessed of a formidable intellect, Dame Helen Alexander, the governors' deputy chairman at St Paul's Girls' School and former CBI President, is a very effective communicator and multi-talented. When interviewing me at the Economist Group, where she was chief executive, Alexander also struck me as being highly pragmatic.

As an attendee of several Euromoney board meetings, I was equally fortunate to witness Charles Sinclair, a Winchester Fellow (governor) and former chief executive of DMGT (Daily Mail and General Trust), demonstrating one of the sharpest commercial brains in publishing. In writing legal profiles for the Times, I interviewed the formidable Fiona Shackleton, divorce lawyer and Benenden governor, and Laurence Rabinowitz QC, North London Collegiate governor and top-fight commercial silk. His keen forensic mind was very much in evidence. So too was that of international litigation lawyer, Patrick Sherrington, who is proud to relate that both his wife and daughter are former head girls at Wycombe, where he is chair of governors, and Maurice Watkins, chair of the Manchester Grammar governors and principal lawyer to Manchester United, who combines northern nous with strong commercial sensibilities.

Perhaps the most obviously impressive was David Verey, former Cazenove deputy chairman and Lazard CEO, for whom I briefly worked when seconded to Lazard Brothers during my mid-twenties. A grander, more patrician man would be hard to envisage: smooth and urbane, he seemed to know everyone and everything, all the while commanding an air of effortless superiority. No surprise that he was a Fellow (governor) at Eton from 1997 until 2012. Eton head, Little describes how governance operates: 'Because of the governance structure, I spent my first few months at Eton wondering who I was supposed to be talking to about whatever. Who was I offending? It's just not clear. There was nothing ever written down. It's one of those things that's evolved over time. You slightly need eyes in the back of your head. You find a way to deal with that. It's a very high calibre governing body of busy people - you're treated much more like being on the board of a London company. They've read the extensive paperwork in advance, the quality of debate is high, and they go away.

'That's it, except for the fact, uniquely, I have two full time residential governors in the Provost and the Vice-Provost. That's a very different dynamic. This is my house here. I physically live between my chairman of governors and deputy chairman of governors. We live in a tenement block. When I describe the nature of the governing structure here to colleagues who are heads, most of them pale rather, don't quite come out in a rash, but not far short. As an organogram, if you had a blank piece of paper, you wouldn't design it this way. It's fraught with potential difficulties. In living memory, I've been told we've had provost and headmaster who've not been speaking to each other. This is not a great way of doing it. However, I have to say, in my personal experience, I've worked with four: two provosts and two vice-provosts. On all four occasions, in a personal way, it's been a good experience. You make it work. If you're talking about the kind of skill people need in headship, I don't know if skill's the right word, needs to have a disposition to come alongside people. That is hugely important'. Ellis (Odgers) adds, 'That whole business at Eton of having your chairman in the next door office and living next to you, it's very difficult.'

When some heads take up their post - as Gandee did at St Swithun's in 2011 - things are not always as they expect 'I don't think the governors knew what was going on in the school. I don't think they understood the extent of the problem. The previous head had said, 'Oh, when there's a new head, you'll dip in numbers.' Now, that doesn't have to be true at all. We have had a dip in numbers and part of it's because of the previous head. So I had to explain all that to the governors.' One head speaks of his experience, ''The previous chairman of governors here, dreadful chairman, though did many things for the school, he ran companies, he thinks the two things to look for in a school are league table position, which he takes as an absolute, and level of surplus, the bigger the surplus, the better the school. Bollocks.'

Another head comments anonymously, 'The big issue for me here which I'm now dealing with is sorting out the governance. We're in the middle of a very radical review about how governance is going to work here. I'm pushing on that because it's key: we've got to get the right committees, the right governors, people who are ambitious for change, but also understand about human nature and education and how it all works, and marketing. I have had to get my governors into the mode of change pretty quickly. The thing about governors is that they appoint somebody who they know is up for change, but then they get a bit twitchy about it. So I just need to keep them very much on thinking about what is the best for the foundation, where are we going and yes there are hard decisions to make and you guys have got to make these decisions and then let us get on with it.'

As a matter of good politics, heads generally praise their bosses, 'I've got high calibre governors, it's a real privilege to work with them and my chair of governors I see on a very regular basis,' says Hewitt at Manchester

High. 'Every two or three days we will be emailing. She is a real hands-on chair, comes in at the slightest drop of a hat and really has her finger on the pulse. Just as I listen to stake holders, I know that she listens constantly and therefore she knows what's going on'. She points to the flowers in her office with a card from the chair: "For the anniversary of you being here, of you joining the school." '

Wright, at Merchant Taylors, is equally effusive, 'I've been blessed with brilliant governing bodies. They were not as competent in my last school, but when the chips were down they were on my side. This lot are outstanding quality and challenging, but in the right way. They ask questions, they don't sit aside. All our governors visit once every two years for half a day: they watch lessons, they talk to stakeholders, they do exit interviews. We have a number of subcommittees who are very much involved in what's going on in the school - we have to fight them off occasionally and say: you're not executives. They know what is going on, they ask the right questions.' Wright has been single minded in his focus, 'We're now getting towards being completely disabled access. That has been my biggest achievement, having ambushed governors with expenses that they weren't anticipating and shaming them into agreeing to it. I felt I'd done the right thing. The former chairman came in recently and said, "I was very much against what you ambushed us with, but I now know it was the right thing to do," which was very decent of him.'

At Wycombe, Hall describes her relationship with governors, 'It's been very good. I've always enjoyed the support of all governors. I have been very lucky because I've heard stories of heads being made to sit on narrow benches, waiting to be invited in by august bodies, to say their piece. In both my schools, I've enjoyed a relaxed, entirely supportive relationship with my governors. It doesn't mean they always agree with me. I will tell them their role is to put me on the spot, ask me questions: they need to satisfy themselves about why certain decisions have been made in the school and I expect to be answerable to them. In a way, that means that they're helping me to do a reliable job. I expect to be held accountable.' Alleyn's head Savage concurs, 'Well, I'm lucky, in that the board here do understand, because not all boards do, the differences between governance and management, and I am allowed to manage. The governors, of course, hold me to account in terms of budgets, results and the strategic direction of the school, but they never intervene in managerial issues at all. The chairman's always been very clear to me that whilst I am running it, it is my school; they are governing. They give me that responsibility. I can go off and do it.'

Before Eton, Little recalls his previous headship at Chigwell, 'The chairman of governors I had for seven years, the chap who appointed me, was a bluff, cricketing, non-intellectual, almost anti-cultural, accountant. Big fish. He'd run a big company in the City. He said to me right at the beginning, as I started: 'I'll back you up in everything you do until you cock it up, and then I'll sack you.' That was very much his kind of style. I used to speak to him about once a month on the telephone before governors' meetings. That was about it. He was very hands off. That was absolutely fine. And here's the thing, whilst one might feel that it would make one feel the more exposed, actually, I felt it didn't. It gave me freedom and also a quiet voice of confidence. On the occasions when I did need help, he delivered. We got on very well. I once had a rather irksome local vicar who kept interfering. My chairman of governors told him quite literally to bugger off.'

Ray (MGS) says, 'It may be that a governing body is aware that there are problems in a school, and that they are hiring a particular head to deal with those problems. What they don't expect is to be drawn into them. They don't want the aggravation if it spills out into some kind of open conflict. The relationship between the head and the chairman is critical. First of all, no head wins a battle against his governing body. You will not win. As soon as you know there's a problem, you look for an exit. You don't wage the war. As soon as you know there's a battle, you look for an exit. The one thing you can't do is go to war with the governors because you will lose.'

In response, McCabe (NLCS) says, 'I don't agree with that. Governance was by far the most challenging thing I had to deal with when I first came here. I have a fantastic governing body now - it was bloody difficult to start with, for six years. The main problem, as with a lot of independent schools, and you don't get this in the state sector, the division between the bursar and the head, and the bursar reporting directly to the chairman of finance and there being two strategic plans: the head being in charge of the curriculum, instead of being chief executive, which wasn't at all my style.

'Everything I'd learnt on my MBA suggested it was a disaster and I couldn't imagine operating anything where I wasn't the chief executive.

I do delegate. I've got strong views inevitably about what I think should happen, the direction of the school, and money is part of that. I would always want to give people their own world to work in without interfering too much, one has to a bit. That complete division, with the chairman of finance saying: that she thought her job was to clip the head's wings, that very old fashioned view of the head being the professional leader and that's all, and the governors really running the school. I'm summarising it now in a very black and white way. It wasn't always that difficult, but if I can put it like this, getting the governors - obviously I don't appoint the governors, but there are ways aren't there? - getting the governors that the school and I needed was the most challenging thing.'

Did McCabe bide her time? 'I wouldn't say I bided my time, I fought tooth and nail,' is her combative reply. 'It is true that the relationship with the governors, particularly in the independent sector, is very sensitive. Because in the state sector, they're up for election all the time, they're representatives, they don't have the power that independent school governors do. I still think that a good head will be able to influence the constitution of a governing body. I'm conscious that I'm being a little too directional about some things probably, particularly about governors, it's a very subtle business isn't it, working with governors. Being plain, when you need governors to move on as well, if a governor is at odds with a head, in the end, when things were particularly difficult, I did have in my mind: well if I can't get this sorted out I would go somewhere else. But it didn't get to that. Usually people step down if they feel that they're not supporting the head, they've appointed the head, they've got to support the head. But I do think you have to make your own luck with governors too. Running girls' schools, sometimes some governors are a little bit patronising and slightly dismissive - male governors in particular, of a certain generation - it is a girls' school run by a female head.'

However much the upward management of governing bodies can be achieved by a successful head, it is the governors who have the whip hand in appointment and dismissal. So what should they look for in a new head? Townsend offers the following advice, 'Governing bodies look for whole school experience, which is why the funnel of deputy headship has become almost de rigueur these days. It would be difficult for someone to have my career now (before becoming a head). I had run a department of sixteen people, admittedly at a famous school, but my management experience was limited. It didn't seem to matter so much then. Yet what mattered then, is still what should matter most: the person and the personality.'

When applying for his first headship in Scotland, McPhail (Radley) recalls, 'In my interview at Strathalan, I was given a series of scenarios. In one of them, I was asked to explain what I was going to do if a group of old boys go on a rampage after some old boy function. And it's in the national press and so on. I went through this, "bang bang bang - I'm going to do this, I'm going to do that." And then, when I'd finished someone said, "Is that it?" I said, "yes." Which is always a slightly worrying comment. And from the end of the table, this wonderful Northern Irish Judge said, "Well it would have been nice if you'd informed the chairman of governors!" At which point, all you can do is agree. You just have to retain a sense of humour.' One head who always adds humour to illustrate his point is Claughton at KES, 'I'm always saying to the chairman of governors here, you should have just got on with appointing me, why did you need all those interviews, you should have just appointed me, it was bleeding obvious. He said the problem was your CV was so short. And it's true, I can get my CV on a page: Eton seventeen years, Master of Cricket, House Master... I kind of ran out.'

When it comes to final responsibility where there are problems, Gibbs (JAGS) makes it clear that the head must shoulder the burden, 'When something really awful happens, and we've had a few things that have, the buck stops here. There is a point when you are the one, you lift up your broad shoulders, and you deal with it. You take the hit, you report to the governors, and you deal with things. You have to be prepared to support, and be the person who takes the ultimate decision, writes the letter, reports to the governors, attends the tribunal, all those things. There isn't anyone else who can do it.'

# CHAPTER FIFTEEN

# MISTAKES

We all make mistakes. No matter how distinguished or important the individual, making mistakes is part of the human condition. What matters is how we respond and what we learn from them. Watch David Dimbleby on *Question Time*, pointing to someone in the audience, 'The woman there, no, the person in the white shirt there, in the second row…the man there.' Or 'You sir, up there, the man with the spectacles…er, lady.' Both of these gender identity faux pas are on YouTube. Yet Dimbleby's blunders do not diminish him, nor is his authority undermined: the audience laughs along as he dismisses each slip with characteristic aplomb. 'Once a programme,' he quips, offering a self-deprecating smile.

Automaton-like, most politicians dedicate themselves assiduously to the avoidance of error; hence the humour in their mistakes - real or imaginary - forms the satirical fabric of *Have I Got News for You*. Human error is also a cornerstone of YouTube's success. Think of George Bush's genuine gaffes, or Boris Johnson's carefully-crafted clangers, the buffoonery only adding to his appeal. But what happens at school and what do children learn about getting things wrong? Not so very long ago distinctive red biro markings - tortured circles or heavily engrained underlining - would signify the obvious displeasure of teachers when presented with flawed work. No longer. Youngsters are positively encouraged to make their own mistakes and to learn from them. It is part of education. As Gandee (St Swithun's) writes on her welcome page, 'They will not do everything perfectly straight away and they will make mistakes, but that is often when the best learning takes place. In the words of Samuel Beckett: "Ever tried. Ever failed. No matter. Try again. Fail again. Fail better." '

Inevitably, if pupils make bad mistakes through serious breaches of school rules, there can be consequences, as Hamilton (HABS) explains, 'The bottom line is that you may forfeit your right to be part of this community. The "may" is simply because you could just happen to have been in a group of boys in the wrong place, wrong time and not done anything but still target the same. Or you could be the lead instigator. It is always very interesting when people want hard and fast on rules on "what you will to do somebody if" because it's never cut and dried. And one would want to give second chances. If you can't make mistakes, reasonable mistakes, at school where the hell can you make mistakes? But on the other hand, some mistakes are beyond the pale.'

For heads to admit their mistakes and make light of them requires both courage and confidence. As authority figures, representing omniscience and omnipotence, public confession of personal frailty does not always come naturally. When asked to give an example of mistakes he had made and what he learned from them, one distinguished head, who had been a paragon of fluent, well-constructed prose and insightful argument up to that point, sat silently opposite me for twenty seconds or so, before responding, 'I might have to think about that and drop you a line.' Needless to say, he did not. Wright (St Mary's Calne) reacts as many of us would when recalling our mistakes, 'I probably try and consign most of those things to a deep, dark pocket in the back of my brain.' But Wright (Merchant Taylors) was less coy in response to the same question, 'Crikey, how long have you got? I'm making mistakes all the time and I deal with people wrongly all the time and it's easier not to make definite promises.'

Halls (KCS) says, 'The worst mistakes I've made are the ones you can't revisit. You've done or said something you can't call back so you just have to think, "Oh God, I must never do that again." I can think of several. Where a mistake is repairable through eating humble pie, you've got to do that, definitely.' Evans (KEHS) is philosophical, 'I haven't really got any separation from my professional life and my personal life. That's a mistake. Because that doesn't really help me open myself up enough to new ideas and things. I've singularly failed to do that enough, somehow.'

Wise heads learn from their mistakes, as Hawkins (Harrow) explains, 'In one of my early speech days at Norwich (where he was head from 2002 until 2011) I made a flippant, I thought quite amusing comment about university degrees and it was just to get a laugh really. I said, "I've found the most exotic combined honours courses that you could do, like Theology and Waste Management, and Politics and Aromatherapy." It was just a gag, but some very humourless, earnest reporter for the local newspaper wrote this up as "Independent school head (so many thousand a year) berates…" Then they had interviews with left wing MPs saying: this is typical, disparaging these hard working students. You just don't want to pull your punches, and stop trying to make your speeches funny, but it just illustrated to me the care that one must take.'

Some mistakes, although small, are never forgotten, as Lusk (Abingdon) explains, 'The mistake that I made which taught me a very important lesson very early on, was on my first teaching practice, at the age of twenty, when I made the mistake of sitting in the chair that was reserved for the headmistress at morning coffee. Now that sounds very inconsequential, but I can tell you when I did it, there was complete silence. There was then a gasp as the headmistress swanned into the staff room, and I hadn't realised it was her chair. But I learnt very quickly about hierarchy, earning your stripes and just keeping an eye out for who the people are that matter on the way up, equally keeping an eye out when you've gone past people, keeping an eye out on people who you've left behind a bit.'

Marks (Withington) learned the hard way that good intentions don't always work in practice when she became head of Tormead (2001-2010) after only six years in teaching, 'We had a drive which was shared for both cars going down and up and also girls walking down and up. It was dangerous, particularly in the evening. When staff were trying to get out, parents were trying to come in to pick up their daughters who they didn't want to walk for various reasons, and some of the girls were trying to walk to buses. The SMT had a discussion about this and it was suggested that what we could do was put up rising bumps so that traffic could only flow in one direction at particular times of the day. It seemed a terrific idea. I gave the go ahead and the bumps were duly installed. We put notices in the letters that went home - it was a salutary lesson to me in how few of those are read. We also had big notices up outside saying: 'No Entry.' On the first day, four individual parents drove the wrong way over those bumps and shredded their tyres - you can imagine how thrilled they were. Two days later, we had a netball fixture and the parent of a girl from the opposing team did the same thing, and when the signs were pointed out to her, she said, "I've always come to watch matches at

Tormead by driving down here." It was shown there have always been signs saying 'No Entry', and she said, "Well I've always taken no notice." I realised at the end of the first week that sometimes having the moral high ground doesn't necessarily work. It just didn't pay to antagonise the parent body by shredding their tyres. So we took the bumps out. That's one I wouldn't do again.'

Some mistakes are more serious, as Spence, who took over as Dulwich head in 2009, explains, 'I gave the benefit of the doubt to a bad apple. Everyone else told me he was a bad apple. And six months later, I had to admit: My God, it would have been better had that person not come back. It was one of those cases of allowing a boy to stay in the sixth form. It wasn't just academic weakness, there was something in the very demeanour, and in the whole set up, that it would have been cleaner to have said goodbye to that family. I could have done so, but I did give the benefit of the doubt. That, writ large, is where I've reached at this stage in life as a head. The listening to your staff and learning who to trust, and against what you see as a head, of a very convincing lad who can come in here, and seem to be fine. If there's a build up of people telling you something, listen to that. Don't try to be the saviour in that sort of situation. That, in spite of lots of good examples of - yes, that person proved better than they did - of being a little more sensitive, and therefore, a bit more hard-edged at the beginning for the sake of the school as a whole. It's your responsibility to an individual versus one's duty of care to the whole. It's always there in every decision you make.'

Most mistakes stem from something that is said, on purpose, in error or sometimes with good intent, as Vernon (CLGS) recalls, 'They'll see me get things wrong or misread things in assembly, and I just say: Oh dear, I've misread that, haven't I? Again I think that's fine. That's life. People will do things wrong. I'm more likely to do that with the staff because I see them on a day-to-day basis, so they will be probably more critical on a day-to-day basis than parents. Yes, there are times when of course I have to say I'm sorry to a parent - we don't appear to have handled that as well as we might have done - and again, that's important. And the girls. Gosh, dare I admit to this? When Bin Laden was killed and McCain was saying fantastic, wonderful, I'm so glad he's dead, glorying in slaughter. I suddenly thought well I'm proud to be British. I talked about being proud to be British in morning assembly, and relating that to all the values that I felt were important for all of us. I was talking in the context of the three critical events that had happened at the same time, one of which was Osama Bin Laden's death. William Hague had given a much more measured response than McCain. I compared that and said, at that moment, I was very glad not to have been American because of the way that McCain was behaving. I took my hat off to a girl in year 7. She's American. She came to see me the next day and said, "Miss Vernon, you really upset me yesterday in assembly." I said, "I'm very sorry why was that?" She said: "Because you said you were glad not to be American." It must have taken quite a lot of courage on her part to come in and say: you've upset me. So obviously, I said, "Well I'm very sorry, I didn't meant to upset you and let's just think about what I said and the context in which I said it. But yes of course, I'll say sorry." I think that's important.'

Marks (Withington) speaks of her assembly experience, 'On a bad day, I think about mistakes I have made that have caused distress. It can be silly things, something I've said in assembly without taking on board that somebody was going to be very affected by it. I did an assembly where I was talking about New Year's resolutions and I said one of mine is to be a more considerate driver: I make it every year and try very hard. I was talking about us setting realistic expectations for ourselves. I made a couple of light-hearted comments about my own driving without realising, which I didn't until later, that my head girl and another sixth form girl had been involved in a bump that morning. I couldn't have known because they hadn't told me at that point, but nonetheless I beat myself up about it afterwards and thought: I should really have considered more carefully whether that might have happened to anybody. It's those sort of things though, off the cuff remarks, that can have a real impact on people; you have to be very careful in this job to weigh things up.'

Undue stress inevitably leads to mistakes as Haynes (Tonbridge) recalls, 'When I was at St Paul's, there was a summer term when Peter Pilkington (High Master 1986-1992) announced he was going to leave to become chairman of the Broadcasting Complaints Commission. Peter was a historian, who taught a special subject, in the upper sixth. He was virtually never there anyway, so they were largely self-taught - luckily they were extremely clever boys. But it did strike me that it was outrageous, really. Ever since I became a head, I said I will never teach an exam class. In March, the governors appointed the then Surmaster, Stephen Baldock, to be High Master from September onwards, but told him he had to go on sabbatical for the summer term. During the Easter holidays, Stephen asked me if I'd be his Surmaster, which was fantastic. I was called Under Master, a sort of head of the Middle School. I was already head of the sixth form as well. I was already doing two middling jobs when I became acting Surmaster during the Summer term as well. There was no director of studies and Peter Pilkington wasn't a terribly hands on head, so I was effectively running St Paul's single handedly at the age of about thirty-five. With a hefty timetable, and with little notice.

'It was the most stressful, unbelievable…mad, absolutely mad. There were two boarding houses. The head of one of them did some silly prank, part way through the summer term. The housemaster was apoplectic with fury, and wanted me to suspend him, because Peter wasn't there. I duly did. The boy and his parents got terribly upset. When I stood back, I realised I had overreacted. I was under a lot of pressure, I was inexperienced, Peter wasn't around to ask, and I gave into the housemaster. I learnt from that: take your time, don't be rushed into things. I also learnt, because Peter picked up the pieces behind me, I had done it in good faith. Peter never ticked me off about it. He supported me, he smoothed the waters with the parents, and it was all alright. Had he blasted me out, I would have gone back into my shell and I would have shrunk.'

The real value in owning up to mistakes sometimes lies in admitting to being foolish or looking foolish. Although they may not see it that way, being a headmaster of disaster or headmistress in distress can be admirable. Townsend (Winchester) is able to laugh at himself in recalling his experience when he was recruited from being head of English at Eton to become head of Sydney Grammar. 'I went out to Sydney and I was taken down to the playing fields. It was a Saturday. You can imagine, all the games and the intensity of metropolitan Sydney: thousands of people go to these games. It's one of the great reliefs of running an English school. Here, you get about three people. It's marvellous. So there I was, being shown round Sydney Grammar School by the Head of Sport. We were looking at a game, and I said, 'There's much more intensity about the rugby here than there is at Eton.' He turned to me, and said, 'This isn't rugby, old chap, it's football, or soccer.' It was soccer. That's how ignorant I was. That story still abides, probably, in Sydney: that I just had no idea what I was looking at.'

Gibbs (JAGS) makes a positive virtue of deliberate mistake, casting herself as Mrs Malaprop, 'I have a wonderful persona that I use occasionally in assemblies, when I get things slightly wrong to show the children that I'm just an unreconstructed, old-fashioned, old bat. I did a brilliant thing, where I was talking about something like skirt length, and I said something about 'The Only Way Is Chelsea', and they laughed like drains, which proved how out of touch I was that I didn't even know the name. Sometimes, I'm a bit naughty like that.' For those unfamiliar with popular culture rivalry, The Only Way is Chelsea purposefully confuses two competing programmes: *The Only Way is Essex* and *Made in Chelsea*.

There are mistakes we all make, like Little (Eton), when consciously trying not to say something, 'Having promised my wife when head of department at Brentwood, that wherever we went, it would be out of Essex, I then took the job at Chigwell, which is just up the road. They are both soccer playing schools. The first time I spoke at the big soccer dinner at Chigwell, I was telling myself: I must not say the word, Brentwood. I must not. Of course, I did. You learn lessons from that too.'

There is also making a suggestion in jest, like Martin (Hampton), which has unintended consequences, 'One thing I learnt fairly early on, but I still cocked it up here, was: you can say something to a colleague as a joke, but it's not a joke to them,' says Martin. 'Because you hold the office you do, therefore your pronouncement must be serious. Somebody suggested that we should have a prize for the highest achieving academic boy, who doesn't hold an academic scholarship. I said in jest: "Well we could go down the same route as Eton. They have a Scholars' House and a Captain of Scholars. And they have something called Oppidans, i.e. the town dwellers. So the highest achieving non scholar is called the Head of Oppidans. Then I looked at the next Senior Prize giving draft list, and there it was: Oppidans' prize! This is not Eton. I thought, okay I've set something off here. I'll let it run. It was a joke! I said, "Let's stick with Oppidans."' Hampton's Oppidans' prize has been awarded ever since.

Then there are things which are said which others were not intended to hear like McCabe (NLCS), 'It makes me sound like Mrs Thatcher sometimes, but I don't really do humour although I did do something very embarrassing last term. I sit on a National Curriculum Advisory Committee - civil servants were always ringing me up about the consultation over the different subjects. I had a phone call - my deputy was in the room too - from a woman civil servant, who was asking me about modern languages. I was doing my usual elitist thing, saying that: everybody should be entitled to learn about literature, I think it's a crying shame that we don't teach literature at A level any more, it must be there. She was saying: well, do you think children in inner cities are capable of that? I was fulminating about: of course they are, why would you think they shouldn't, why is it there should be one set of standards for one group of people.

'We were going on like that. She was asking lots of questions, which had a political agenda to them, which annoyed me, because I was talking to a civil servant. My phone had been on a conference call with my deputy there, talking and answering too. I put the phone down and as he was going out of the door, he said to me something like, "Why was she so prejudiced?" I said something like, "These bloody people in the Department of Education, she's probably come straight from university, she's got a very left wing bias, she knows nothing about schools, blah, blah, blah." Two minutes into this diatribe, this little voice came out of the phone saying, "I'm still here and I've been a teacher myself, etc, etc." I was just so mortified. I wrote a card just apologising, saying: I believe you may have heard a private conversation between me… That was mortifying.' When I suggested it could have been worse, McCabe responded, 'Could it? I don't know. That was terrible.'

Most obviously humiliating is when a head makes a complete fool of him/herself in front of a class, or indeed, the whole school. Trafford (RGS Newcastle) recalls, 'I have a strong sense of the absurd. I can tell when I'm being absurd so I will laugh at myself. You've got to be fairly confident to do that, some won't. There are stupid times when you fall over the step going up to assembly. You might as well make a joke because they are going to laugh at you anyway. My finest hour was storming into a Chemistry class to tell off the form, I don't know what they had been doing wrong but I had to go in and give them a real rocket. I turned on my heel and marched out. Instead of going out the door, I went into the chemical cupboard. It was a great moment. Unfortunately it couldn't be sustained,. I thought the teacher was going to wet herself trying not to laugh. And there's nothing you can do.'

There can be benign schadenfreude in the mistakes of others on an even grander scale, as Cox (RGS Guildford) explains, 'It wasn't me, it was a friend of mine, Mark Bishop of Trinity, but it was great. He'd just taken on the role of head, he'd done his speech and it all went very well. He'd had good vibes in the first assembly, and he thought, a great speech from the throne which had gone very well. At the end of it, he walked out through the door which was a cleaner's cupboard - everyone else in the assembly hall knew it was a cleaner's cupboard that he'd just gone into. He was in there thinking: now, I can either stay here, or I can come back out. In the end, he came back out again, to much applause.'

Claughton (KES) confesses to a catalogue of cock ups, worthy of a comic sketch, 'One of my problems, as I am getting older, is whether I can continue to live with what might be described as a high energy way of dealing with things may get harder as, and I hesitate to say this, but I am now 56, and I think I'm still 32. I get really cross with it and I can't believe when I look at these old people around me and they're my age, it really upsets me. I live by adrenaline. I'm always living on the edge and I can't write my speech day speech until the Saturday morning when it's speech day. It does produce a better speech, but it means that those hours before that are bloody stressful and bloody difficult. Because I'm on the edge, things go wrong. Three years ago, at speech day, I managed to say 'penis' when I meant 'pianist'. The whole thing collapsed, and then I got so confused. We had Lee Child, the author and an old boy, as our speaker, and I started leading Lee Child off the stage in the middle of singing *Jerusalem* because I thought it was the end. Last year, I forgot the school song completely. In a funny kind of way, part of this persona is this sort of, almost Mr Bean failure, capacity to make a complete Horlicks of things. I must admit I don't protect myself much in that way and I suppose - what you see is what you get.'

On the penis/pianist malapropism, Bailey (St Paul's) comments, 'I can't even begin to go anywhere close to that, only Claughton would do that! I believe it instantly, that definitely wasn't made up. I can think of thousands of mistakes I've made; I'm not sure how many of them had amusing consequences. At Leeds Grammar, there was the most brilliant inspirational deputy head, much loved and a fantastic man to learn from, as my first headship parachuted into schools. He just had an ability to fill a room, and if there was just slight petty misbehaviour - cheering for example, when kids drop a plate - how do you deal with that? It's not appropriate, but how do you deal with it? He would stand on a table, and have this great booming voice, and say, "We do not laugh!" And the whole place would fall silent - it's a huge dining hall! Everybody could hear him. "We do not laugh at the misfortunes of others, unless the misfortune is mine!" Staff as well were laughing, and he could just do this - this voice came from somewhere, and it boomed.

'I saw half a dozen lads from my office, running around the back of the bike sheds or something.' It is worth mentioning at this stage that Bailey is a physically imposing man - a former England rugby winger, who stands at six foot five. 'I thought: right. So I dashed down and went after them and there was a whole group of boys behind the bike sheds and I dug deep for this voice, because I had seen it done, and it was just a croaky, little whimper. Somehow I lacerated my voice, because I could hardly speak for two days afterwards. So not only couldn't I do it, but I damaged my normal voice. I did, metaphorically, limp back to my office after firmly chastising them with nothing like the presence and the booming voice that the great man could achieve. I never tried it again.'

# CHAPTER SIXTEEN

# ADVICE TO FUTURE HEADS

A thousand years of teaching and three hundred years of headship - that is the collective experience of the heads interviewed. In more than sixty schools, they have recruited and developed several thousand staff, and shaped the academic performance and life chances of countless children. A head's relationship with children and staff may only be an inch deep, but it is a mile wide. Good heads spread themselves right across their schools.

So what advice would they give to heads of the future? Assorted suggestions outlined below are drawn from their own experience and passed down to them by their predecessors, as the craft of headship is re-evaluated and reshaped by successive generations. The wisdom of retired and former heads was often cited by those reflecting upon their role with a sense of history, just as the legacy of today's heads is being passed on to those who will follow. Added to them, I offer a few of my own observations, derived from what I have learned in the course of writing this book: no accumulated wisdom here, merely an outsider's perspective, looking in.

'It amuses me that they say that you can do a qualification or go on a training course to be a head,' says Hamilton (HABS). 'There is no course that can teach you. Much of it is to do with what you gain by osmosis through the schools you have gone to and the people you have worked with. You've seen good people doing great things and making a real hash of things. Nothing prepares you for it like the first day in the job. When you first get appointed, you are going in to a place which hasn't necessarily chosen you: the staff, the kids, the parents haven't had a say in it. The governors have, and you're walking into a whole bunch of inherited teams. You very quickly need to gain their confidence.'

McCabe (NLCS) develops the confidence theme, 'There's nothing that prepares you for the unremitting rigour and challenge of headship - all day, every day. You need to have done all the jobs, so you don't need to think about them, you don't need to worry about how to do things. You've got the confidence to know how they should be done and the confidence to delegate to other people. From my own experience, that comes from working in as many different sorts of schools as possible to get that real sense of balance and different dimensions. The great challenge of headship? It's a bit like the difference between being a passenger in the car and driving, you don't see it until you're there. You absolutely can't take your eye off the road when you're driving, you just don't see that before you've learnt to drive.'

To decide if the job is for you, Hawkins (Harrow) advises, 'One of the key things is to establish whether or not whole school management is for you, by getting a taste of whole school responsibility, both in terms of having the big picture, but also dealing with the challenge of managing people with all sorts of different interests. Practically, one must have stamina and resilience, and certainly with this job, if you don't relish being on your feet, being public and being under scrutiny the whole time, if that's overly stressful, it probably isn't the job for you because life will be pretty hellish. When the pressures on the cracks will open, rather like Gordon Brown from chancellor to prime minister.'

McPhail (Radley) highlights other skills, 'The ability to read people, and to read the situation in terms of the way you're going to respond to it. Even if you're looking at tone in a letter or a note, some people just simply can't see that at all. And the damage you can do by getting that wrong is really major. That's quite hard to learn. You can learn it if you have someone overseeing you, and saying, "Well hold on, don't you think it might be better if…what about doing…" But of course, as a head, you don't tend to have someone doing that. You don't want to be going to your chairman of governors and saying, "Would you mind redrafting this letter?" Those skills are probably things you need to have.'

To equip themselves with the necessary skill set to impress governors and get the job, heads advise in various ways. 'Being involved, being enthusiastic, being competent, those are the things that really help. Get your hands dirty, take risks and just get on with it, not moan about it,' says Lusk (Abingdon). 'There's an element of bean counting. Governing bodies now like to see Masters Degrees, MBA's, Masters of Education. They like to see some business acumen. There is a need to acquire that,' says Ray (MGS). 'No heads are now being appointed who have not previously been deputies. You need to have some solid understanding of how at least one institution works. Then, go to a different kind of institution and bide your time, whatever the governors say to you. Not least because you're going to have to make up your mind, if significant change is required, whether the governors will be supportive, or otherwise.'

Vernon (CLGS) would 'encourage volunteering for different things to expand your experience as much as possible. I would also counsel (would-be heads) in terms of: what sort of school do you think you want to run, what's important for you, is rugby important, are academics important, is the whole child, do you want to be in the country, town? You have to be sure that you're not compromising yourself in terms of whatever school you're running. If it's a question of seeing a particular job, go and have a look at it and give it a go because you can only know by going down there and going through the whole interview experience. I would always say: give it a go. In life, you've got to.'

To develop yourself, 'Don't rush it and do experience a lot,' advises Halls (KCS Wimbledon), 'because when you see a head who is just too naïve or single minded, they're not pleasant to work with and tend to make mistakes and they sometimes crash and burn. Run a department, enjoy running a department. I ran mine for seven years, I wouldn't wish it a day less, I loved running that department, sometimes I'm surprised with the speed that people want to digest a job and move on.' Marks (Withington) suggests, 'The first thing is don't let go of an aspiration to be the best teacher you can possibly be. That's important because when you're leading a group of staff it's important that they see you can still do it and you still understand what it's like. It really helps if you have a passion for teaching and you can demonstrate it, so don't let go of that. The second thing is to develop an interest in all the other issues, particularly in the art of leadership, in what's now called HR management, particularly in finance and marketing, because it's a generalist role.'

Claughton (KES) believes, 'The best preparation for headship is school mastering, not administration. I'm really woeful at administration, organisation, structure, strategy, plans, but I believe that headmastering, like school teaching, is character acting, not method acting. In the end, you're going to get a good head's job because governors like you as a character, think you have that richness of experience as a character, not particularly because you've been on a lot of courses. So the richness of experience as a school master, all that encompasses, beyond teaching and being involved with school, is the best preparation.' At MCS Oxford, Hands' advice is threefold, 'One, you must be a good teacher. Two, you're very unlikely to become a good head unless you've got extra-curricular expertise of some kind. Three, you must have proven that you're good with pupils who find life tough.' Gibbs (JAGS) adds, 'You don't have to experience something personally to empathise. However, if you have a very limited management or life experience, that can make it harder.'

Elliott (the Perse) argues, 'You need a broad range of experience. It helps if you've been a frontline class teacher, that you've perhaps done the head of department role, that you've had a pastoral role so that you understand all of the different components of the school engine. One thing everyone who becomes a head should do, but very few of them actually do, is timetabling. Time consuming, difficult, but boy, do you then understand your cost base, your resources, the deployment of your staff. That's how you really understand the school engine.' Cox (RGS Guildford) believes it is more about personality than skills, 'You've got to be the right fit for the right school and different schools have different requirements, so I wouldn't worry about acquiring a skill set particularly, because different places will need different skills. The one thing that I would advise any prospective head to get experience of and to think carefully of, is this issue of empathy and communication and support and having a persona that people would like to chat to.'

Evans (KEHS) takes another angle, 'Women believe in a meritocracy. They think that if you work hard, and do your job well, you will get on and you'll move up the career ladder. I don't think that's true in schools or anywhere else - the people who get to the top, by are large, have done other things and they have learnt a lot from outside of their school. They're very good at networking, they have built up powerful and useful contacts outside the school as well. They are very good at communicating their own strengths, which is a particular difficulty for women.'

Westminster head, Spurr, suggests vision is key, 'In terms of leaders of the future, you do want to talk up the whole idea of vision, taking young people's education forward and career progression. You will want to gain experience of school-wide issues to help develop and propagate that vision, and in doing so, you will discover in yourself what most people never think about, that they can think strategically, they can develop, they can learn the arts of management, while also developing the vision.'

To his future Eton successor, Little offers a broad panorama. 'I'm going to argue two different things in two different directions. I've thought about this quite a bit. It's exciting that I suspect in the next ten years, the classroom is going to look rather different. There is a voice of opinion that within twenty years, schools as we know them, will largely be redundant because the nature of technological advance, the ability to have online courses: you see HarvardX which is a major brand, globally. You could impart knowledge in a cheaper, more effective way, a virtual way. So, in theory, you don't need schools at all. I think that schools are profoundly important because of community and development. In squaring off those two things, my successor of the future will need to be someone who has enough breadth of vision and understanding of what's happening in the world of education and technology, as it affects pedagogy, to be able to tune into all that, but then to reconcile it with what is the traditional profound need and value of a school. That's going to be the trick.'

As someone who has never even taught a lesson, there is no advice worth mentioning that I can give any head. But after listening to their collective critiques, I can perhaps fly a few kites. Listed below are ten things which occur to me, not ten commandments so much as ten personal observations, designed to be thought-provoking, rather than proscriptive. Think of them as an exam paper with ten questions, where only four of ten need to be attempted - or even considered - by any one candidate. Then ignore the rest as you wish.

1. At first blush, headship requires the intellectual breadth of Aristotle, the financial acumen of Warren Buffett, the leadership of Wellington, the passion of Boadicea, the patience of Job, the philosophical wisdom of Plato, the empathy of Florence Nightingale and the management ability of Sir Alex Ferguson. In ridiculous overstatement, there is a serious point: heads need many talents, and should not be damned because of one or more deficiencies. They can learn. Or delegate. True wisdom may come from experience, but the best heads - as advocates for their schools and their communities - are human. They sell themselves well as people, allowing their weaknesses to be forgiven.

2. Children respond to humour, warmth and enthusiasm. The best teachers know this. Buried in their problems, heads sometimes forget that the impression they give to others matters too. The best heads talked to me in interview as if I were an old friend: candid, genial, thoughtful and interested in my questions. We had a conversation - this was particularly true at Winchester, where Townsend was thoroughly engaging and charming. A few were guarded, distant, remote, aloof, or by far the worst, self-obsessed. In each case, I put myself in the shoes of a child thinking: would I like this man or woman to be my head? For future heads and for some existing heads: tape a conversation or speech, listen to what you say and how you sound, and maybe think again.

3. There can be a mismatch between governors, who expect management by numbers and results, and staff, who want to be led by a philosophy, vision and structure that they endorse. Creating or maintaining a culture that bridges the divide is immensely challenging. Some heads seem to shoulder too much of the burden. They may talk of delegation and sharing tasks with their senior management team, but in some cases, the pressure of always assuming too much responsibility manifests itself as benign autocracy, poor management or simply, an overworked, stressed individual. The happiest schools appear to be those where the head is admired, not feared or avoided.

4. Heads tend not to clock in and out at set times; some never seem to clock off. The EU Working Time Directive, which limits working hours to 48 per week, does not feature uppermost in their minds. Overwork and very long hours causes stress, depression and illness - no head admitted to this, but some are no doubt affected. Having a life outside school matters too. Switching off, having other interests, getting away. The hugely increased demands of the job require very long hours. In some cases, governors could do more to limit how much heads work and to consider more carefully their health and well-being. The same applies to heads themselves.

5. Because they live in a bubble, most heads have only a modest understanding of the commercial world outside. Given that independent headship requires strong business and personnel management skills, it is surprising that these are not further developed much earlier by independent schools among a cadre of young teachers from their mid-twenties onwards. Beyond external qualifications and courses, little seems to be done within schools by existing heads to identify and prepare these heads

of the future with practical headship training. Mentoring is only the gift of the few, it should be for the many.

6. The man or woman who strides enthusiastically to meet you, shakes your hand firmly and smiles, makes a good impression. Beneath their confidence lies tangible energy: a key trademark of the best heads, sometimes reflected in the persona of their secretaries, whose importance is much underrated. Most evident when absent, energy and its twin, enthusiasm, make a big difference. In their place, lethargy hits you like a damp rag. Only two heads made this impact: one I suspect through age, the other through natural demeanour. A good head should have as much energy as the teenagers running around them: they may not run as fast, but they should aim to think, inspire, lead and communicate with the same energy as Usain Bolt.

7. As a parent of three teenage children, I am constantly reminded of my technological deficiencies. Many heads suffer the same problem. They do not need to know the respective merits of the latest mobile phone or computer game, but they should monitor the social networking sites most-favoured by their pupils and have some idea of what they are saying, as well as knowing the educational resources available on the internet. This is not to advocate a spying charter, but heads do need to understand how the Facebook generation thinks, feels and communicates. Future heads will have to keep up as fast as they can to develop a keen awareness of what goes on virtually, what children say and how they say it. In this area of technology, heads really do need to be at the cutting edge.

8. Shortly after he left one of the schools which I had visited, a talented, personable boy whom I have known since his infancy, delivered a damning indictment on the current head, 'He sat next to me at lunch in my final week and talked to me for the first time in seven years. He knew nothing about me and wasn't really interested.' All heads profess to show an interest in their pupils. Most do. But it is hard to see why someone would become a head in the first place without having a genuine interest in their pupils' activities and achievements. For some teachers, headship may be the pinnacle of their career; ideally, it should be a calling. Their mission should not be self-aggrandisement, but delighting in and having a genuine interest in their pupils.

9. Heads are well-paid; they have status; they are kings and queens of their own domain. But the ever-increasing demands of the role, as

evidenced in previous chapters, deter many potential future heads. State sector headship is in near-crisis: many schools cannot find heads, and some appointees are of insufficient calibre. Some in the independent sector periodically face similar problems. Among the most impressive heads interviewed were those who had entered the profession after a career elsewhere: they bring with them a valuable added dimension. In this century, when few careers will be for life, it would be good to see more future heads with a strong background outside education and more being done to attract people of proven talent from elsewhere.

10. Teaching is one of very few careers where only a small minority enters the profession with ambitions to do one of the top jobs. Given the number of available headships and deputy headships, this is surprising. The stated ambitions of many young lawyers, doctors, bankers, accountants or management trainees are more frequently transparent in wanting to reach the top, even if their chances of doing so are more remote. How many young teachers are asked in interview if they would like to be a head one day? How many ever say that is their goal? If naked ambition is not part of the culture, and the process more evolutionary, should this change? Perhaps more young, highly ambitious teachers could be identified earlier, and if they have the ability, they should be developed in a fast track programme. Perhaps it already happens, but in that very English way - unstated and understated.

Teachers who aspire to be heads share a desire to lead, a love of children and a love of teaching. The management requirements of headship do much to remove them from teaching and children. It is in many ways a lonely job, however strong the support they receive from those around them. The man or woman in charge does their best for the children they serve - whether a state or independent school, the job and its essential purpose are the same. Those who happen to do it in independent schools should not be derided because their salaries are paid by parents rather than by the state. They are remarkable men and women, deserving of respect and admiration for a difficult job well done: first class managers of first class institutions. That should be acknowledged by more people, more often. Without prejudice.

And yet the massed ranks of detractors will continue to assault the bastions of privilege, which is all they choose to see when they think of independent schools. There are many things in our history for which we rightly feel embarrassed and ashamed. Independent education, alive and kicking in the twenty-first century, is not one of them. Instead, we should be proud of what is achieved. Are independent schools and their heads 'basically fair game,' as Elliott (the Perse) suggests? How will Gove and Cameron, who promises 'not to defend privilege but to spread it,' really deliver? There are no immediate answers. For now, the army of armchair critics might consider that if state education were uniformly excellent, like many of the state grammars and top-performing academies already are, they would have no reason to exist.

Logic would suggest that bad schools do not exist because there are good ones, no more than bad people exist because of the good: the good cannot be blamed for the bad being bad. Only if all state schools achieve standards of genuine excellence over the next generation will the hostility finally subside. Perhaps it is not so much the polarised opposites of failure and success that provokes genuine anger, but a culture of tolerating or even encouraging mediocrity. Overcoming that is the responsibility of future politicians and teachers working together. Parents meanwhile should be free to choose their children's school, and not be pilloried for doing so.

On my first day at Manchester Grammar, the boy sitting next to me said that his father was a gardener in the local parks. I felt embarrassed telling him about my family, but it did not matter then or thereafter. The social mix of MGS in the 1970s, so integral to its philosophy, was a huge bonus - more diverse and categorically meritocratic than any school I visited in writing this book. No-one cared that half the boys who got in were on grant-assisted places: we all deserved to be there and our background was of no importance in the classroom or outside. If independent schools need structural reform as academies evolve, some might revisit the philosophy once applied at MGS as part of that reform.

Heads are not responsible for education policy, nor can their schools be true engines of social mobility without the resources and systems to achieve it. The role of heads is to run their schools to the best of their ability. That is not to say that much more cannot be done to help beyond the school gate. Yes, every independent secondary school should sponsor or co-sponsor an academy, and every independent head needs to do whatever they can to ensure wider access to their own schools while supporting, assisting and developing state schools in their local community and beyond. But the primary duty of independent heads, as with heads everywhere, is to their own school community: children, parents, staff and governors. In doing that, they too need the support and help of everyone involved.

The final words must go to an experienced head. Co-director of the Southwark Schools' Learning Partnership and head of JAGS, Marion Gibbs. Her words reflect the manifestations of good headship everywhere, 'One hopes that a young head has the wisdom to seek advice or counsel, and to listen before jumping to conclusions. It's not about wisdom, so much in the wise, or intelligent sense. It's human understanding. Some people never get it, however old they are, whatever their experiences are. The key is not assuming that you know things, not jumping to conclusions. Always listening. If you've had a meeting in your room, and you've done all the talking, it's not a meeting is it. What do I want written on my tombstone? Two words: she cared. End of. I really do care. That is what matters most.'

# ACKNOWLEDGEMENTS

Writing may be a solitary task, but no book is possible without the assistance of others. Accordingly, I am very grateful to Andrew Lownie and David Haviland for seeing this volume into print: it has been a pleasure and a privilege to work with them. Andrew's unwavering support for the project proved invaluable, as did his measured advice and wise counsel. *Heads Up* was written without research or editorial support. Mistakes are my own, and readers will hopefully forgive any errors or omissions that have crept through my sub-editing. Sources are wide-ranging: information compiled by the BBC, the Department for Business, the Department for Education (DfE), LSE, NSPCC, the Office for National Statistics (ONS), Opinium, Oxford University, the Sutton Trust, UCAS, YouGov and various media groups is incorporated.

I am especially grateful to my wife, Rachel, for helping to produce verbatim transcripts from dozens of lengthy taped interviews, and for showing inexhaustible patience with me throughout the research, writing, editing and proofing. Thanks are also due to my sons, Charlie and Tristan, for their help in transcribing and in making suggestions about different topics for consideration, and to my daughter, Isobel, who showed remarkable insight for a thirteen year-old as to what readers might want to know about individual heads. A variety of parents and teachers also provided background on many of those interviewed; their anonymity is preserved, given that comments were mostly made off the record.

There were others that helped along the way to whom thanks are also due: David Smellie, Head of the Employment Team and the Schools Group at Farrer & Co, who provides legal advice to nearly half of the heads interviewed; Diana Ellis, Head of the Education Practice at Odgers Berndtson, who finds many leading heads on behalf of governors; Russell

Speirs at RSAcademics for his constructive analysis; Lord Baker, former Conservative education secretary, who encouraged the idea in the belief that more needs to be written about leading heads and what they do; Sophie Stutter for her incisive judgment on the manuscript; Luke Mann, who provided useful insight into London schools; and George Marsh - retired head of Dulwich Prep, who unwittingly sowed the seeds of this book through various informal discussions over the years - a man of wisdom and integrity, and a model for everything good headship should be.

Above all, my thanks go to the heads listed below for giving up their time to be interviewed, and for their courtesy and candour in response to my questions. Most of their recorded observations are attributable; in a few cases, heads asked that specific remarks be included without attribution. Their wishes have been respected. An impressive, powerful group, the headmasters and headmistresses of England's leading independent senior schools were interviewed face-to-face in their studies, except for two, who were interviewed by phone. All heads were in position as of June 2013 with the exception of Dr Helen Wright, who left for a new headship in Australia at the beginning of the year. My best wishes go to those just retired, and to others who have moved on to new positions of responsibility elsewhere.

Ingram Content Group UK Ltd.
Milton Keynes UK
UKHW010807270323
419227UK00004B/342